INTERNATIONAL MONETARY FUND

GLOBAL FINANCIAL STABILITY REPORT

Bridge to Recovery

2020
OCT

©2020 International Monetary Fund

IMF CSF Creative Solutions Division
Composition: AGS, An RR Donnelley Company; and The Grauel Group

Cataloging-in-Publication Data

IMF Library

Names: International Monetary Fund.
Title: Global financial stability report.
Other titles: GFSR | World economic and financial surveys, 0258-7440
Description: Washington, DC : International Monetary Fund, 2002- | Semiannual | Some issues also have thematic
    titles. | Began with issue for March 2002.
Subjects: LCSH: Capital market—Statistics—Periodicals. | International finance—Forecasting—Periodicals. |
    Economic stabilization—Periodicals.
Classification: LCC HG4523.G557

ISBN 978-1-51355-422-8 (Paper)
    978-1-51355-851-6 (ePub)
    978-1-51355-855-4 (PDF)

Disclaimer: The *Global Financial Stability Report* (GFSR) is a survey by the IMF staff published twice a year, in the spring and fall. The report draws out the financial ramifications of economic issues highlighted in the IMF's *World Economic Outlook* (WEO). The report was prepared by IMF staff and has benefited from comments and suggestions from Executive Directors following their discussion of the report on September 30, 2020. The views expressed in this publication are those of the IMF staff and do not necessarily represent the views of the IMF's Executive Directors or their national authorities.

Recommended citation: International Monetary Fund. 2020. *Global Financial Stability Report: Bridge to Recovery.* Washington, DC, October.

Please send orders to:
International Monetary Fund, Publications Services
P.O. Box 92780, Washington, DC 20090, U.S.A.
Tel.: (202) 623-7430 Fax: (202) 623-7201
E-mail: publications@imf.org
www.bookstore.imf.org
www.elibrary.imf.org

CONTENTS

Tables

Figures

ASSUMPTIONS AND CONVENTIONS

The following conventions are used throughout the *Global Financial Stability Report* (GFSR):

. . . to indicate that data are not available or not applicable;

— to indicate that the figure is zero or less than half the final digit shown or that the item does not exist;

– between years or months (for example, 2019–20 or January–June) to indicate the years or months covered, including the beginning and ending years or months;

/ between years or months (for example, 2019/20) to indicate a fiscal or financial year.

"Billion" means a thousand million.

"Trillion" means a thousand billion.

"Basis points" refers to hundredths of 1 percentage point (for example, 25 basis points are equivalent to ¼ of 1 percentage point).

If no source is listed on tables and figures, data are based on IMF staff estimates or calculations.

Minor discrepancies between sums of constituent figures and totals shown reflect rounding.

As used in this report, the terms "country" and "economy" do not in all cases refer to a territorial entity that is a state as understood by international law and practice. As used here, the term also covers some territorial entities that are not states but for which statistical data are maintained on a separate and independent basis.

The boundaries, colors, denominations, and any other information shown on the maps do not imply, on the part of the International Monetary Fund, any judgment on the legal status of any territory or any endorsement or acceptance of such boundaries.

FURTHER INFORMATION

Corrections and Revisions

The data and analysis appearing in the *Global Financial Stability Report* are compiled by the IMF staff at the time of publication. Every effort is made to ensure their timeliness, accuracy, and completeness. When errors are discovered, corrections and revisions are incorporated into the digital editions available from the IMF website and on the IMF eLibrary (see below). All substantive changes are listed in the online table of contents.

Print and Digital Editions

Print

Print copies of this *Global Financial Stability Report* can be ordered from the IMF bookstore at imfbk.st/29273.

Digital

Multiple digital editions of the *Global Financial Stability Report*, including ePub, enhanced PDF, and HTML, are available on the IMF eLibrary at www.elibrary.imf.org/OCT20GFSR.

Download a free PDF of the report and data sets for each of the charts therein from the IMF website at www.imf.org/publications/gfsr or scan the QR code below to access the *Global Financial Stability Report* web page directly:

Copyright and Reuse

Information on the terms and conditions for reusing the contents of this publication are at www.imf.org/external/terms.htm.

PREFACE

The *Global Financial Stability Report* (GFSR) assesses key vulnerabilities the global financial system is exposed to. In normal times, the report seeks to play a role in preventing crises by highlighting policies that may mitigate systemic risks, thereby contributing to global financial stability and the sustained economic growth of the IMF's member countries.

The analysis in this report was coordinated by the Monetary and Capital Markets (MCM) Department under the general direction of Tobias Adrian, Director. The project was directed by Fabio Natalucci, Deputy Director, as well as by Claudio Raddatz, former Advisor, Anna Ilyina, Division Chief, Evan Papageorgiou, Deputy Division Chief, Mahvash Qureshi, Division Chief, and Jérôme Vandenbussche, Deputy Division Chief. It benefited from comments and suggestions from the senior staff in the MCM Department.

Individual contributors to the report were Sergei Antoshin, Romain Bouis, John Caparusso, Yingyuan Chen, Dan Cheng, Fabio Cortes, Reinout De Bock, Andrea Deghi, Xioadan Ding, Dimitris Drakopoulos, Kelly Eckhold, Ibrahim Ergen, Salih Fendoglu, Ken (Zhi) Gan, Deepali Gautam, Rohit Goel, Pierpaolo Grippa, Marco Gross, Pierre Guérin, Sanjay Hazarika, Frank Hespeler, Henry Hoyle, Mohamed Jaber, Phakawa Jeasakul, Oksana Khadarina, Piyusha Khot, Annamaria Kokenyne, Ivo Krznar, Dimitrios Laliotis, Fabian Lipinsky, Pavel Lukyantsau, Elizabeth Mahoney, Sheheryar Malik, Samuel Mann, Manuel Perez, Dmitri Petrov, Nicola Pierri, Thomas Piontek, Umang Rawat, Jochen Markus Schmittmann, Patrick Schneider, Dulani Seneviratne, Can Sever, Juan Solé, Felix Suntheim, Thierry Tressel, Tomohiro Tsuruga, Germán Villegas Bauer, Jeffrey Williams, Yizhi Xu, Dmitry Yakovlev, Akihiko Yokoyama, and Xingmi Zheng. Input was provided by Hee Kyong Chon, Alan Feng, Caio Ferreira, Alejandro Lopez, Luc Riedweg, and Julia Xueliang Wang. Magally Bernal, Monica Devi, Leroy Perumal, and Andre Vasquez were responsible for word processing.

Gemma Diaz from the Communications Department led the editorial team and managed the report's production with editorial assistance from Christine Ebrahimzadeh, David Einhorn, Lucy Scott Morales, Katy Whipple/ The Grauel Group, AGS, and Vector Talent Resources.

This issue of the GFSR draws in part on a series of discussions with banks, securities firms, asset management companies, hedge funds, standard setters, financial consultants, pension funds, central banks, national treasuries, and academic researchers.

This GFSR reflects information available as of September 29, 2020. The report benefited from comments and suggestions from staff in other IMF departments, as well as from Executive Directors following their discussions of the GFSR on September 30, 2020. However, the analysis and policy considerations are those of the contributing staff and should not be attributed to the IMF, its Executive Directors, or their national authorities.

FOREWORD

The COVID-19 pandemic has triggered a global economic crisis of unprecedented magnitude. The *World Economic Outlook* forecasts a sharp global economic contraction for 2020. Despite the expected rebound in growth in 2021, the level of global output is anticipated to remain below precrisis levels for several years. The swift, aggressive, and broad economic policy response has contained the immediate damage, providing a bridge to recovery. Central banks have eased monetary policy across the globe, with a nearly $7.5 trillion balance sheet expansion to date in G10 countries, and with about 20 emerging market central banks deploying asset purchases for the first time. The post-2008 regulatory framework has been put to the test for the first time, and has been proven largely successful, as the global banking system entered the crisis with relatively high capital and liquidity buffers. In addition, a fiscal policy response of $12 trillion globally has provided substantial support to households and firms.

As a result of these policy actions, the adverse macro-financial feedback loops that were so prevalent and pernicious in the 2008 crisis have largely been contained. Financial conditions have eased significantly and rapidly since late March, allowing countries and firms to benefit from continued access to capital market and bank funding, and preventing liquidity pressures from turning into broad-based insolvencies. Capital flows to emerging markets have started to rebound, with many economies regaining market access. While insolvency risks still loom large, widespread corporate and banking distress has, to date, been contained. In fact, the global banking system remains fairly well capitalized against additional adverse shocks.

But financial vulnerabilities are rising, putting medium-term macro-financial stability and growth at risk. Stretched valuations in risk asset markets persist, despite the September repricing in equity markets, giving rise to a disconnect between the evolution of the economy and the assessment of risk in financial markets, reflecting in part investor expectations of continued policy support. Corporate debt is rising, and it is estimated to be at record levels relative to gross domestic product in most countries. Despite the resilience exhibited so far, there is a weak tail of fragile banks in some countries. Fragilities in the nonbank financial sector became clearly evident during the financial market strains in March, with market volatility jumping, margin calls rising, and liquidity in even the most liquid and deep bond markets drying up. Furthermore, sovereign debt is at historically high levels. This is a critical issue for many low-income countries and some emerging market economies, where a debt crisis might be inevitable without prompt and decisive policy action—a theme that is explored at length in the *Fiscal Monitor*.

Policymakers face stark trade-offs between short-term support and medium-term macro-financial stability risks, and they need to closely monitor any potential unintended consequences of their unprecedented support. In the corporate sector, massive liquidity may lead to significantly higher debt and medium-term resource misallocation, potentially allowing insolvent firms to survive for years. For banks, the usage of buffers may lead to too little capital being available in the future to cushion shocks. In capital markets, the easing of financial conditions may fuel future vulnerabilities. For emerging markets, limited policy space can prevent optimal policies in the short and the medium term. For many frontier economies and low-income countries—many of which continue to be shut out of international markets—further pandemic pressure and the challenging global economic environment are formidable headwinds for their macro-financial stability.

In this *Global Financial Stability Report*, we take stock of key recent market developments and present a forward-looking analysis of banks, nonbank financial institutions, nonfinancial firms, and emerging market capital flows that can help policymakers navigate difficult policy trade-offs in the next phases of the pandemic and recovery. We also attempt to quantify the impact of policies in our asset valuation assessments, which can help policymakers better assess risks to financial conditions. In addition, we assess the pandemic's impact on firms' environmental performance to gauge the extent to which the crisis may result in a reversal of the gains posted in recent years. The analysis underscores the importance of climate policies and green investment packages to support a green recovery and the transition to a low-carbon economy.

Tobias Adrian
Financial Counsellor

Bridge to Recovery: October 2020 *Global Financial Stability Report* at a Glance

- Near-term global financial stability risks have been contained for now. Unprecedented and timely policy response has helped maintain the flow of credit to the economy and avoid adverse macro-financial feedback loops, creating a bridge to recovery.
- However, vulnerabilities are rising, intensifying financial stability concerns in some countries. Vulnerabilities have increased in the nonfinancial corporate sector, as firms have taken on more debt to cope with cash shortages, and in the sovereign sector, as fiscal deficits have widened to support the economy.
- As the crisis unfolds, corporate liquidity pressures may morph into insolvencies, especially if the recovery is delayed. Small and medium-sized enterprises are more vulnerable than large firms with access to capital markets. The future path of defaults will ultimately be shaped by the extent of continued policy support and the pace of the recovery, which is expected to be uneven across sectors and countries.

- While the global banking system is well capitalized, there is a weak tail of banks, and some banking systems may experience capital shortfalls in the October 2020 *World Economic Outlook* adverse scenario even with the currently deployed policy measures.
- Some emerging and frontier market economies face financing challenges, which may tip some of them into debt distress or lead to financial instability and may require official support.
- As economies reopen, accommodative policies will be essential to ensure that the recovery takes hold and becomes sustainable—see the following Policy Road Map. The post-pandemic financial reform agenda should focus on strengthening the regulatory framework for the nonbank financial sector and stepping up prudential supervision to contain excessive risk taking in a lower-for-longer interest-rate environment.

Monetary and Financial Policy Road Map after the Great Lockdown

Gradual Reopening under Uncertainty

Monetary policy—Maintain accommodation to support the recovery

Liquidity support—Maintain support but adjust pricing to incentivize a gradual exit

Credit provision—Encourage banks to use capital and liquidity buffers to continue lending

Nonfinancial private sector—Extend moratoria on debt service only if necessary to prevent widespread insolvencies, support viable firms through restructuring and efficient out-of-court workouts to reduce the debt burden, as well as by providing solvency support (as appropriate)

Multilateral support—Provide support to emerging and frontier market economies facing financing difficulties

Pandemic under Control

Monetary policy—Maintain accommodation until monetary policy objectives are achieved

Liquidity support—Gradually withdraw

Credit provision—Require banks to gradually rebuild capital and liquidity buffers, develop credible plans to reduce problem assets, and create markets for problem assets

Nonfinancial private sector—Recapitalize, restructure, or resolve nonviable firms

Green recovery—Encourage more proactive management of climate-related risks and green investments

Digitalization—Encourage greater digital investment to enhance financial sector efficiency and inclusion

Post-pandemic Financial Reform Agenda

Nonbank financial sector—Strengthen the regulatory framework to address vulnerabilities exposed during the coronavirus disease (COVID-19) crisis

Lower for longer—Implement prudential measures to contain risk-taking in the lower-for-longer interest-rate environment

Figure 1. Proportion of Systemically Important Countries with Elevated Vulnerabilities, by Sector
(Percent of countries with high and medium-high vulnerabilities, by GDP or assets; number of vulnerable countries in parentheses)

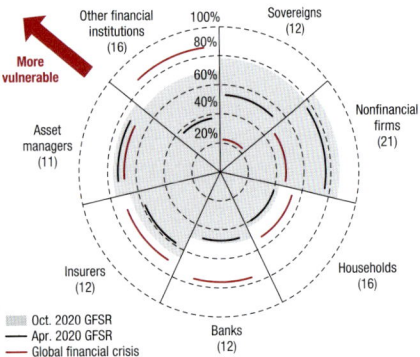

Sources: Bank for International Settlements; Haver Analytics; national authorities; Standard & Poor's; WIND Information Co.; and IMF staff calculations.
Note: Based on 29 jurisdictions with systemically important financial sectors (see Chapter 1 for details). "Global financial crisis" reflects the maximum 2007–08 vulnerability value. GFSR = *Global Financial Stability Report*.

Figure 2. Key Drivers of Global Financial Conditions Indices
(Standard deviations from mean)

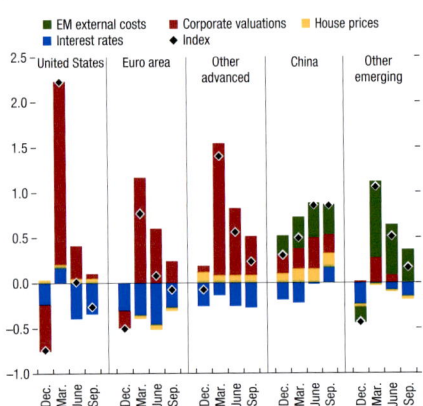

Sources: Bank for International Settlements; Bloomberg Finance L.P.; Haver Analytics; IMF, International Financial Statistics database; and IMF staff calculations.
Note: Higher number indicates a tightening of financial conditions. See Chapter 1 for details. EM = emerging market.

Figure 3. Near-Term Global Growth Forecast Densities
(Probability densities)

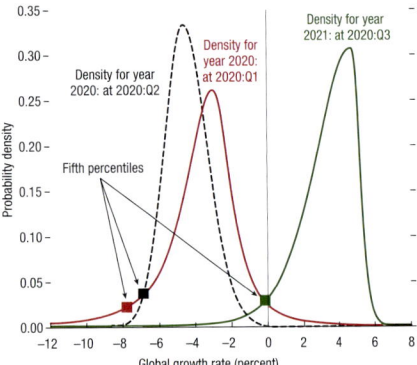

Sources: Bank for International Settlements; Bloomberg Finance L.P.; Haver Analytics; IMF, International Financial Statistics database; and IMF staff calculations.
Note: Forecast density estimates are centered around the respective *World Economic Outlook* forecasts for 2020 and 2021. Given the unprecedented nature of the current crisis, model-based growth-at-risk estimates are inevitably subject to larger-than-usual uncertainty bounds.

Confronted with a global health and economic crisis, policymakers have taken extraordinary measures to protect people, the economy, and the financial system. However, prospects for recovery remain highly uncertain and will depend on the availability of reliable COVID-19 treatments and vaccines. In addition, many countries have entered the crisis with elevated preexisting vulnerabilities in some sectors—asset management, nonfinancial firms, and sovereigns—and vulnerabilities are rising, representing potential headwinds for the recovery (Figure 1).

Since the June 2020 *Global Financial Stability Update*, global financial conditions have remained accommodative on the back of continued policy support. In advanced economies, low interest rates and a recovery in risk asset markets have continued to support further easing in financial conditions (Figure 2). Financial conditions have generally eased also in emerging markets (excluding China) over the same period, although external costs for many countries are still above pre–COVID-19 levels (Figure 2). In China, financial conditions have remained broadly stable, as authorities have scaled back expectations for further interest rate reductions amid improving economic activity and rising financial sector risks.

Although the sharp easing of financial conditions since late March has helped prevent a financial crisis and cushion the impact of COVID-19 on the economy, the deterioration of the economic outlook has shifted the expected distribution of global growth in 2020 deeply into negative territory (Figure 3). Looking ahead, the global economy is expected to grow by 5.2 percent in 2021, according to the October 2020 *World Economic Outlook* (WEO). This expected rebound and easy financial conditions imply that the odds of negative growth next year are low, though the balance of risks is tilted to the downside (Figure 3).

Unprecedented policy actions taken in response to the pandemic have been successful in boosting investor sentiment and maintaining the flow of credit to the economy. To cope with cash flow pressures, firms have stepped up bond issuance, tapped bank credit lines (most notably in the United States), and taken advantage of government-guaranteed loans (see Chapter 3).

Hard currency bond issuance in emerging markets has been strong as well. Aggregate portfolio flows have recovered from their March lows, though about half of emerging market economies have continued to experience outflows over the past three months. Easy financial conditions have improved the outlook for portfolio flows to emerging markets, with the probability of outflows over the next three quarters falling from about 60 percent at the peak of market turmoil to 25 percent in September (Figure 4), though still above its pre–COVID-19 level.

Global equity markets have rebounded strongly from pandemic lows, with notable differentiation across countries depending on the spread of the virus, the scope of policy support, and sectoral composition. Equity markets in China and the United States have outperformed other markets, driven by technology stocks (dark and light green bars, Figure 5), notwithstanding the market correction in September. More contact-intensive sectors (hotels, restaurants, leisure) have been hurt by lockdowns and social distancing. The underperformance of the energy and financial sectors (red and yellow bars, Figure 5) reflects investors' assessments of weaker growth prospects.

The disconnect between rising market valuations and the evolution of the economy, discussed in the June 2020 *Global Financial Stability Update*, persists. For example, analysis of year-to-date US stock market performance shows that a sharp decline in the corporate earnings outlook has been more than offset by lower risk-free rates and a compression of the equity risk premium, reflecting central banks' policy rate cuts and other measures that have boosted investor sentiment despite higher economic uncertainty (see Chapter 1). Similarly, the decline in corporate bond yields has been driven by the fall in risk-free rates and the compression in credit spreads—in many cases below values estimated to be consistent with economic fundamentals (Figure 6). The spread compression can be partly attributed to policy support and, in the case of emerging markets, it can also be traced to policy easing by central banks in advanced economies. If markets believe that policy support will be maintained or scaled up in response to deterioration in the economic outlook, current risk asset valuations could be sustained for some time. However, if investors reassess the scope for policy support or if the recovery is delayed, the odds of a sharp adjustment may rise.

Nonfinancial firms have come under significant liquidity strains following the COVID-19 outbreak. More vulnerable firms—with weaker solvency and liquidity positions, as well as smaller firms—have experienced greater financial stress than their peers in the early stages of the crisis (see Chapter 3). To cope with cash shortages, many firms—notably those whose earnings fell short of their interest expenses—have increased their borrowing (Figure 7), adding to the already high corporate debt levels in several economies (Figure 8). Default rates have been on the rise as well. As the crisis continues to unfold,

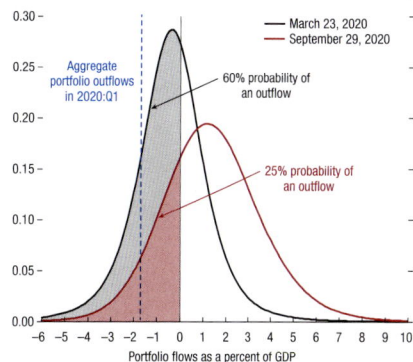

Figure 4. Capital Flows at Risk: Near-term Forecasts of Portfolio Flows
(Probability density function)

Sources: Bloomberg Finance L.P.; Haver Analytics; IMF, World Economic Outlook database; JP Morgan estimates; national sources; and IMF staff estimates.
Note: Based on debt and equity portfolio flows for 19 largest emerging markets; near term = next 3 quarters. See Chapter 1 for details.

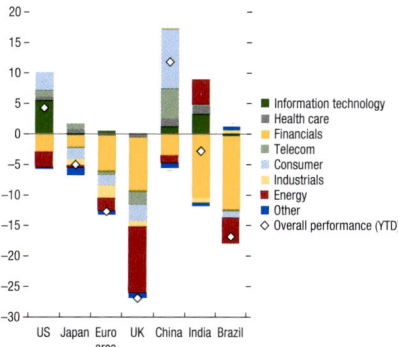

Figure 5. Stock Market Performance in 2020: Sectoral Contributions
(Percent, year to date)

Sources: Bloomberg Finance L.P.; MSCI; and IMF staff calculations.
Note: All country indices are local currency MSCI sub-indices. Overall performance is based on aggregation of sectoral indices. "Consumer" is the sum of the consumer discretionary and consumer staples sectors and "other" is the sum of the utilities, materials, and real estate sectors. UK = United Kingdom; US = United States; YTD = year to date.

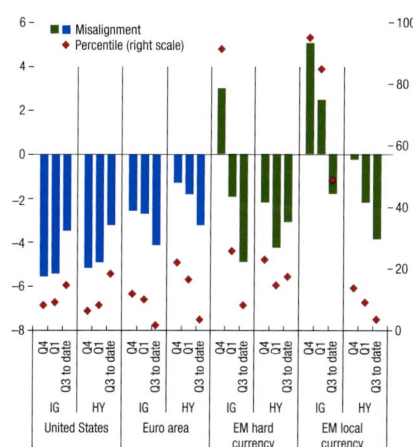

Figure 6. Bond Spread Misalignment
(Deviation from fair value per unit of risk, left scale; percentile based on 1995–2020, right scale)

Sources: Bloomberg Finance L.P.; Consensus Economics; Haver Analytics; Refinitiv I/B/E/S; and IMF staff calculations.
Note: Misalignment is the difference between market- and model-based values scaled by the standard deviation of monthly changes in spreads; negative values on the left scale indicate overvaluation. See Chapter 1 for details. EM = emerging market; HY = high yield; IG = investment grade.

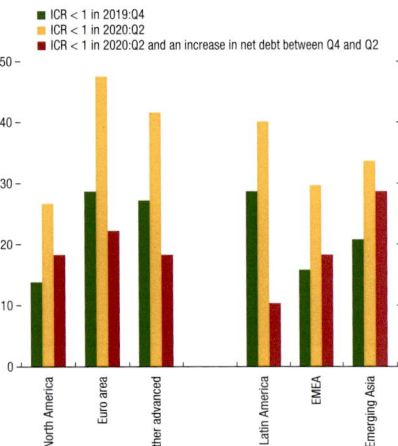

Figure 7. Publicly Listed Firms: Debt at Risk
(Percent of debt of sample firms)

Sources: Bank for International Settlements; Bloomberg L.P.; Haver Analytics; Institute of International Finance; S&P Global Ratings; S&P Leveraged Commentary and Data; and IMF staff calculations.
Note: The sample includes firms with quarterly statements. The bars show the share of debt at firms with ICR < 1 and with an increase in net debt as a share of total debt in the sample. EMEA = Europe, Middle East, and Africa; ICR = interest coverage ratio.

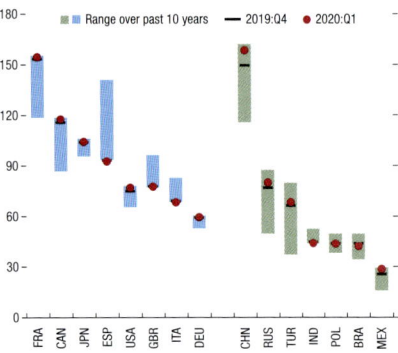

Figure 8. Aggregate Nonfinancial Corporate Debt
(Percent of GDP)

Sources: Bank for International Settlements; Haver Analytics; and IMF staff calculations.
Note: For France, corporate debt is reported on an unconsolidated basis. Data labels use International Organization for Standardization (ISO) country codes.

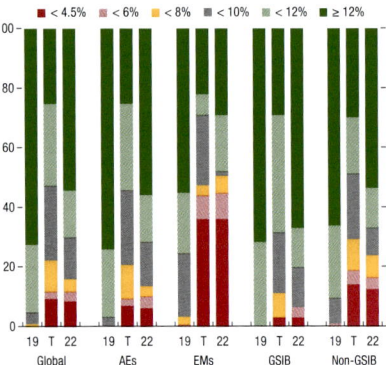

Figure 9. Distribution of Bank Assets by Capital Ratio under the October 2020 WEO Adverse Scenario, with Policy Mitigation
(CET1 ratio, percent)

Sources: Bloomberg Finance L.P.; Fitch; IMF, World Economic Outlook database; and IMF staff estimates.
Note: The scenario takes into account mitigation policies (see Chapter 4 for details). AEs = advanced economies; CET1 = common equity Tier 1; EMs = emerging markets; GSIB = global systemically important bank; T = trough year.

and especially if a sustainable recovery is delayed, liquidity pressures may morph into insolvencies.

Barring a significant tightening in funding conditions, large firms with access to capital markets are likely to avoid significant solvency pressures. Firms in sectors most affected by the pandemic, however, are facing weaker growth prospects and greater liquidity strains, and hence a higher risk of default and insolvency. Small and medium-sized enterprises, which are generally more vulnerable, could be a significant channel for transmission of the economic shock. Furthermore, small and medium-sized enterprises tend to dominate some of the most contact-intensive sectors (hotels, restaurants, entertainment), which have taken a beating from COVID-19.

Banks entered the COVID-19 crisis with significantly stronger capital and liquidity buffers than they had in 2008–09. This has allowed them to continue to provide credit to the economy. Policies aimed at supporting borrowers and encouraging banks to use the flexibility built into the regulatory framework have likely supported banks' willingness and ability to lend. However, some banks are already starting to tighten their lending standards, which could have adverse implications for the recovery. A forward-looking analysis of bank solvency in 29 countries (not including China) shows that in the October 2020 WEO *baseline scenario* most banks will be able to absorb losses and maintain capital buffers above the minimum capital requirements (see Chapter 4). In the WEO *adverse scenario* characterized by a deeper recession and a weaker recovery, a sizable weak tail of banks could see their capital buffers depleted to the levels that could constrain their lending capacity (Figure 9). These weak banks' capital shortfall relative to broad regulatory requirements—which include the counter-cyclical capital buffer, capital conservation buffer, and systemic buffers—could reach $220 billion, even after accounting for borrower- and bank-oriented mitigation policies (see Chapter 4).

Nonbank financial institutions (NBFIs) have entered the crisis with elevated vulnerabilities (Figure 10). They have managed to cope with the pandemic-induced market turmoil thanks to policy support, but fragilities remain high. Asset managers, for example, could be forced into fire sales if portfolio losses are larger and redemptions last longer than during the March sell-off. NBFIs play a growing role in credit markets, including riskier segments, and the increased links between NBFIs and banks imply that fragilities could spread through the financial system.

Sovereign vulnerabilities have increased because countries have expanded fiscal support, and sovereigns may face a sharp rise in contingent liabilities. Vulnerabilities have increased across multiple sectors, with 6 out of 29 jurisdictions with systemically important financial sectors now showing elevated vulnerabilities in the corporate, banking, and sovereign sectors (Figure 11).

Because of the pandemic, the financing needs of emerging markets have risen sharply. Concerns about new debt supply and weak domestic fundamentals may have curtailed demand for local currency bonds from foreign investors (Figure 12), especially where they hold large shares of debt and where the domestic investor base may not be sufficiently deep. Some emerging market central banks purchased a substantial share of bonds in the secondary market to stabilize market conditions (see Chapter 2). Frontier market economies face even greater financing challenges, as the COVID-19 shock pushed borrowing costs for many to prohibitive levels—calling for official support.

As policymakers build a bridge to recovery, policies will have to adjust, depending on the evolution of the pandemic and the pace of the economic rebound (see Policy Road Map in the at-a-glance box at the beginning of this Executive Summary). At each step, policymakers should be mindful of intertemporal trade-offs and of unintended consequences—the benefits of using available buffers today should be carefully balanced against the possible need for further support in the future, as well as the risk of exacerbating future vulnerabilities.

As economies reopen, continued monetary policy accommodation and targeted liquidity support will be essential for sustaining the recovery. A robust framework for debt restructuring will be critical for reducing debt overhangs and resolving nonviable firms. Low-income countries with financing difficulties may require multilateral support. Despite its adverse effect on firms' environmental performance, the COVID-19 crisis also presents an opportunity to engineer a transition to a greener economy (see Chapter 5).

After the pandemic is fully under control, policy support can be gradually withdrawn and policy priorities should focus on rebuilding bank buffers, strengthening regulation of nonbank financial institutions and stepping up prudential supervision to contain excessive risk taking in a lower-for-longer interest-rate environment.

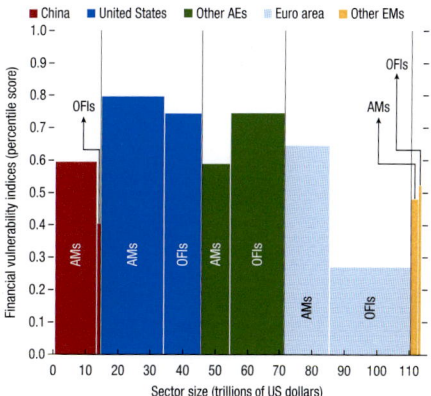

Figure 10. Nonbank Financial Institutions: Financial Vulnerability Indices and Sector Size

Sources: Banco de Mexico; European Central Bank; Haver Analytics; Reserve Bank of India; Securities and Exchange Commission of Brazil; WIND Information Co.; and IMF staff calculations.
Note: See Chapter 1 for details. AEs = advanced economies; AMs = asset managers; EMs = emerging markets; OFIs = other financial institutions.

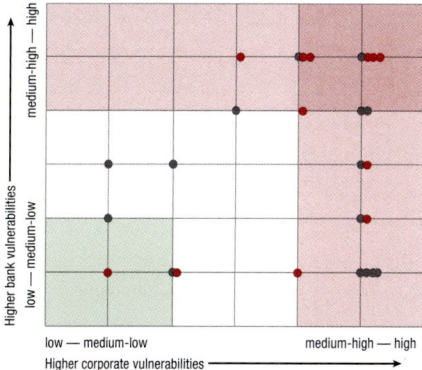

Figure 11. Corporate, Bank, and Sovereign Vulnerabilities in 29 Jurisdictions with Systemically Important Financial Sectors

Sources: Bank for International Settlements; Haver Analytics; Institute of International Finance; IMF, October 2020 *World Economic Outlook*; and IMF staff estimates.
Note: Based on the data underlying Figure 1; red dots denote countries with medium-high or high sovereign vulnerabilities.

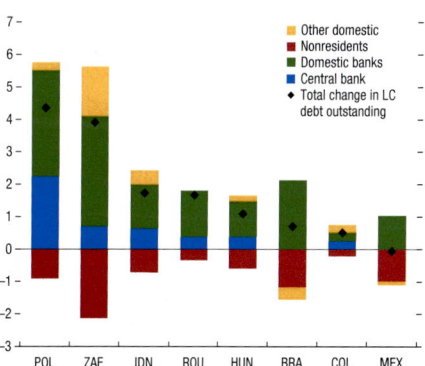

Figure 12. Change in Local Currency Government Bonds Outstanding by Holder, end-February–June 2020
(Percent of GDP)

Sources: Bloomberg Finance L.P.; Haver Analytics; IMF, World Economic Outlook database; national sources; and IMF staff estimates.
Note: Data are not adjusted for inflation-linked debt. South Africa total differs slightly from aggregated component changes. Indonesia central bank holdings of government securities reported as net of monetary operations by source. Data labels use International Organization for Standardization (ISO) country codes. LC = local currency.

IMF EXECUTIVE BOARD DISCUSSION OF THE OUTLOOK, OCTOBER 2020

The following remarks were made by the Chair at the conclusion of the Executive Board's discussion of the Fiscal Monitor, Global Financial Stability Report, *and* World Economic Outlook *on September 30, 2020.*

Executive Directors broadly concurred with the assessment of the global economic outlook, risks, and policy priorities. While noticing the stronger-than-expected economic activity in the second quarter, especially in advanced economies, they agreed that the path to prepandemic activity will be long and precarious with persistent scarring effects on output and employment. They noted that the projections assume that social distancing will continue into 2021 and then fade over time as therapies improve and vaccines become more broadly available. Directors noted with concern that the pandemic is having dramatic effects on vulnerable people, leading to higher inequality, and a sharp increase in the number of people living in extreme poverty.

Directors agreed that the uncertainty surrounding the baseline projections remains exceptionally large as the economic recovery will be shaped primarily by the path of the pandemic, the efficacy of containment measures, and pharmaceutical innovations. More rapid development of new therapeutics and wide distribution of effective vaccines could accelerate the economic recovery, while medical setbacks and new waves of infections could require new lockdowns. Other important sources of uncertainty include the extent of global spillovers, the damage to the supply potential, the efficacy and duration of policy support, and potential shifts in financial market sentiment. Directors also noted prepandemic risks stemming from trade and technology tensions, geopolitical challenges, and climate change.

Directors agreed that effective and decisive policy support is needed to ensure stronger, more equitable, and resilient growth. Key near-term priorities include supporting the economic recovery, protecting vulnerable people, and strengthening health care systems. They stressed the need to reduce the scarring effects of the crisis on potential output and employment and to reverse the development toward greater inequality and setbacks to human capital accumulation. Most Directors also saw the crisis as an opportunity to stimulate innovation, develop the digital infrastructure, and to transition to lower carbon emissions using different climate tools, such as green investment and a gradual increase of the carbon price, with due consideration to offsetting negative social impact.

Directors welcomed the unprecedented fiscal actions in response to the pandemic. Directors emphasized that, as economies tentatively reopen, governments should ensure that lifelines are not withdrawn prematurely. Support should gradually shift from protecting jobs to helping displaced workers find new jobs through retraining and reskilling. Directors noted that when the pandemic is under control, governments will need to address the legacies of the crisis, including record deficits and public debt levels, elevated unemployment, and increased poverty. Directors agreed that public investment should play a crucial role in supporting the postpandemic recovery, noted its sizable job creation potential, and underlined that good governance, budget execution, and communication, remain crucial to reap the full benefits of fiscal support and maintain public trust.

Directors emphasized that governments will need to do more with less and prepare credible and equitable measures to reduce fiscal deficits and debts over the medium term. Countries with limited fiscal space should protect public investment and support lower-income households that have been disproportionately hit by the pandemic. Governments could consider increasing progressive taxation as well as reforms to modernize business taxation, including multilateral cooperation on the design of international corporate taxation to respond to the challenges of the digital economy. LICs in particular are faced with significant financing constraints, and many countries will require external support, including in the form of debt relief, grants, and concessional financing.

Directors agreed that bold policy actions taken by central banks to ease monetary policy, provide ample liquidity, and maintain the flow of credit have helped contain the near-term risks to global financial stability. They noted, however, that vulnerabilities are rising, most notably in the nonfinancial corporate sector as liquidity pressures may morph into insolvencies, especially for small and medium-sized enterprises. The credit outlook will ultimately be shaped by the extent of continued policy support and the pace of the recovery, which is expected to be uneven across sectors and countries. Rising defaults could lead to significant losses at banks and nonbank financial institutions. While the global banking system is overall well capitalized, some banks and banking systems may experience aggregate capital shortfalls in the WEO adverse scenario. Directors also highlighted the importance of improving access of emerging markets and frontier economies to capital markets.

Directors emphasized that as economies reopen, accommodative policies and the continued flow of credit to borrowers will be essential to sustaining the recovery. Once the pandemic is under control, policy support can be gradually withdrawn. The postpandemic financial reform agenda should focus on strengthening the regulatory framework to address vulnerabilities in the nonbank financial sector exposed by the crisis and stepping up prudential supervision to contain excessive risk taking in the lower-for-longer interest rate environment.

Directors underscored the importance of international cooperation in the fight against the global health and economic crisis. A key priority is to scale up production capacity and develop distribution channels to ensure that all countries have access to an effective, affordable, and safe vaccine. Directors noted that several emerging market and developing countries require international assistance through debt relief, grants, and concessional financing. They pointed out that the IMF has rapidly scaled up its lending facilities since the onset of the pandemic, providing swift financial assistance to more than 80 countries. Directors discussed opportunities for multilateral cooperation to alleviate trade and technology tensions between countries and to collectively implement climate change mitigation policies.

BRIDGE TO RECOVERY

Chapter 1 at a Glance

- **Near-term global financial stability risks have been contained** for now. Unprecedented and timely policy response has helped maintain the flow of credit to the economy and avoid adverse macro-financial feedback loops, creating a bridge to recovery.
- However, **vulnerabilities are rising**, intensifying financial stability concerns in some countries. Vulnerabilities have increased in the nonfinancial corporate sector as firms have taken on more debt to cope with cash shortages and in the sovereign sector as fiscal deficits have widened to support the economy.
- As the crisis unfolds, **corporate liquidity pressures may morph into insolvencies**, especially if the recovery is delayed. Small and medium-sized enterprises (SMEs) are more vulnerable than large firms with access to capital markets. The future path of defaults will be shaped by the extent of continued policy support and the pace of the recovery, which may be uneven across sectors and countries.
- While the **global banking system is well capitalized**, there is a weak tail of banks, and some banking systems may experience capital shortfalls in the October 2020 *World Economic Outlook* adverse scenario even with the currently deployed policy measures.
- **Some emerging and frontier market economies face financing challenges**, which may tip some of them into debt distress or lead to financial instability, and may require official support.
- As **economies reopen, continued policy support remains critical**. Accommodative monetary and financial conditions, credit availability, and targeted solvency support will be essential to sustaining the recovery, facilitating the necessary structural transformation and transition to a greener economy.
- The **post-pandemic financial reform agenda should focus on addressing fragilities unmasked by the coronavirus disease (COVID-19) crisis**, strengthening the regulatory framework for the nonbank financial sector and stepping up prudential supervision to contain excessive risk taking in a lower-for-longer interest-rate environment.

The COVID-19 Pandemic Has Led to a Deep Recession

The COVID-19 pandemic has led to an unprecedented contraction in economic activity globally, with global growth projected at –4.4 percent this year, according to the October 2020 *World Economic*

Prepared by staff from the Monetary and Capital Markets Department (in consultation with other departments): The authors of this chapter are Anna Ilyina (Division Chief), Evan Papageorgiou (Deputy Division Chief), Sergei Antoshin, Yingyuan Chen, Fabio Cortes, Rohit Goel, Phakawa Jeasakul, Sanjay Hazarika, Kelly Eckhold, Frank Hespeler, Henry Hoyle, Piyusha Khot, Sheheryar Malik, Thomas Piontek, Akihiko Yokoyama, and Xingmi Zheng, under the guidance of Fabio Natalucci (Deputy Director). Magally Bernal and Andre Vasquez were responsible for word processing and the production of this report.

Outlook (WEO). Both advanced and emerging market economies will suffer deep and broad-based declines, with more than 85 percent of countries around the world expected to see subzero growth this year (red shaded area in Figure 1.1). Confronted with a global health and economic crisis, policymakers have taken extraordinary measures to protect people, the economy, and the financial system. Despite forceful policy action, however, the prospects for recovery remain highly uncertain.

The October 2020 WEO baseline global growth forecast of +5.2 percent for 2021 assumes that continued unprecedented monetary policy accommodation and large fiscal lifelines will keep financial conditions easy and help offset COVID-19–related cash flow pressures on firms and households, thus

Figure 1.1. GDP Growth: The COVID-19 Crisis versus the Global Financial Crisis

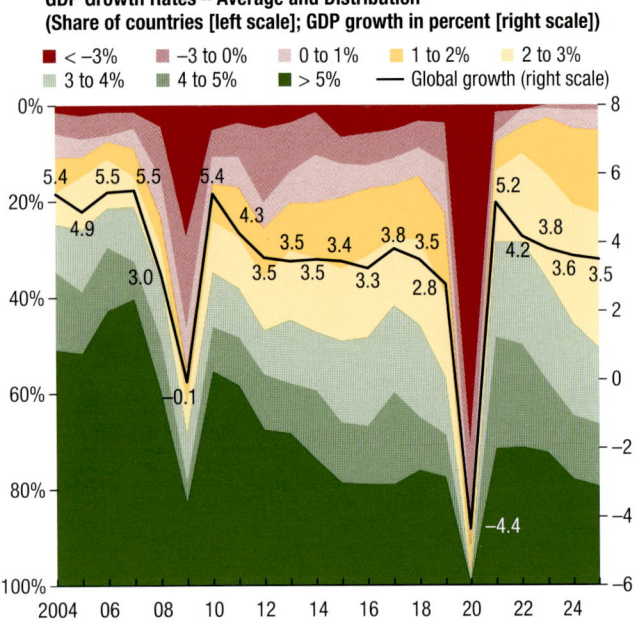

Sources: IMF, October 2020 *World Economic Outlook*; and IMF staff calculations.

keeping insolvencies at bay. Nevertheless, some vulnerable firms (such as SMEs) and sectors (notably the contact-intensive sectors) will experience greater distress. Furthermore, if the recovery were delayed, liquidity pressures could reemerge and insolvencies could rise sharply and become more widespread. Such an adverse scenario would entail repricing of risk in credit markets and a tightening of financial conditions—ultimately testing the resilience of the financial system, as well as the capacity of country authorities to provide additional policy support.

The deterioration of the global economic outlook early in the year shifted the expected distribution of global growth in 2020 deeply into negative territory (Figure 1.2, panel 1). Besides changes in the WEO baseline global growth forecast, around which these distributions are centered, these shifts reflect changes in financial conditions, and hence are heavily influenced by investor perceptions and assessment of future growth outcomes. The massive easing of financial conditions (discussed in the June 2020 *Global Financial Stability Report* [GFSR] *Update*) has helped contain downside risks to growth and financial stability despite

the worsening in the WEO baseline forecast between April and June.[1]

Looking ahead, current economic and financial conditions, combined with the expected rebound of 5.2 percent in global GDP growth next year, imply that the 2021 growth forecast distribution will shift back into positive territory (shown in green in Figure 1.2, panel 1). Nonetheless, the shape of the 2021 growth distribution suggests that there are still significant downside risks. For example, the probability of global growth falling below zero in 2021 is close to 5 percent, indicating that risks are elevated by historical standards (Figure 1.2, panel 2).

Several possible developments could delay the recovery and lead to worse-than-expected growth outcomes, putting financial stability at risk. A resurgence of the virus in some countries may require partial lockdowns and more prolonged social distancing, leading to job losses and renewed pressures on corporate and financial sector balance sheets (see the WEO Scenario Box). Policy missteps, such as a premature withdrawal of policy support (as discussed in the October 2020 WEO), could trigger investor reassessment of risks, market turbulence, and tightening of financial conditions. For example, market participants have been increasingly attuned to the progress on Brexit negotiations given the looming deadline, a development that could lead to increased market volatility.

Unprecedented Policy Support Has Helped Buy Time

Unprecedented policy actions taken in response to the pandemic have been successful in boosting investor sentiment and maintaining the flow of credit to the economy. Central banks' interventions have stabilized key markets by lifting investor risk appetite through both anticipated and actual central bank demand for safe and risk assets (Figure 1.3).

[1]The growth-at-risk framework assesses the downside risks to financial stability by gauging how the range of severely adverse growth outcomes (5th percentile of the growth distribution) shifts in response to changes in financial conditions and vulnerabilities (see Chapter 3 of the October 2017 GFSR for details). Assumptions pertaining to policy responses or macroeconomic shocks are captured in the growth-at-risk framework to the extent that they affect the current economic and financial conditions, or the baseline growth forecast. Given the unprecedented nature of the current crisis, model-based growth-at-risk estimates are inevitably subject to larger-than-usual uncertainty bounds.

Figure 1.2. Global Growth at Risk

The unprecedented policy support helped reduce the downside risks to growth and financial stability, but even with growth projected to rebound next year ...

... risks are expected to remain tilted to the downside and within the danger zone.

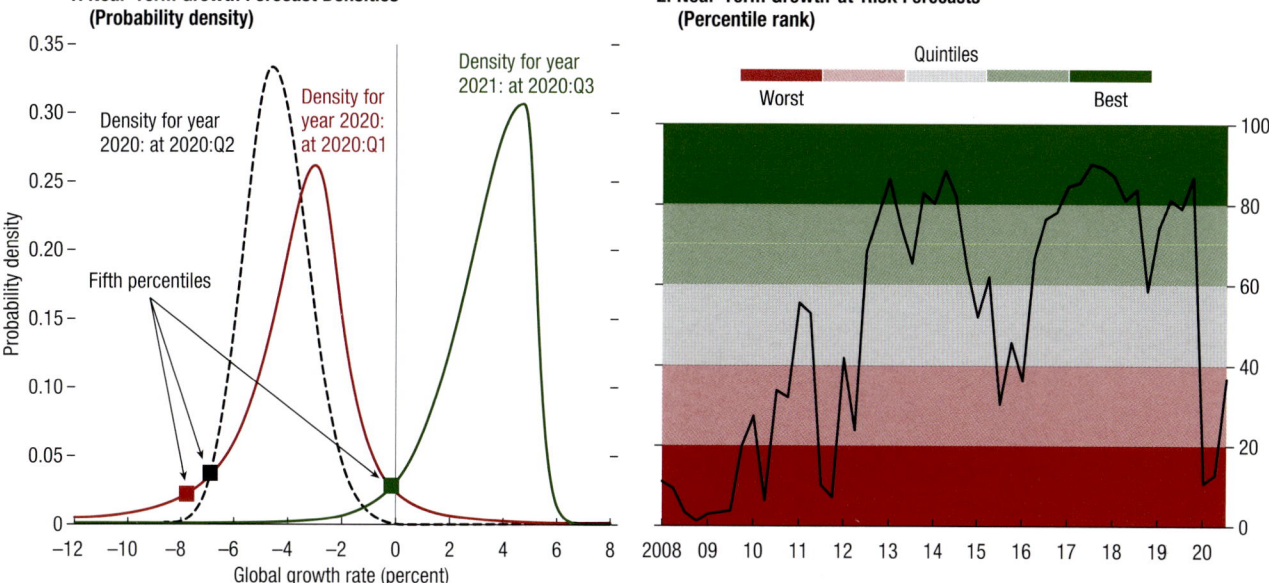

Sources: Bank for International Settlements; Bloomberg Finance L.P.; Haver Analytics; IMF, International Financial Statistics database; and IMF staff calculations.
Note: Forecast density estimates are centered around the respective *World Economic Outlook* forecasts for 2020 and 2021. In panel 2, the black line traces the evolution of the 5th percentile threshold (growth-at-risk) of near-term growth forecast densities. The color of the shading depicts the percentile rank for the growth-at-risk metric, from 1991 onwards. See the April 2018 *Global Financial Stability Report* for details.

Many emerging market central banks have, for the first time, engaged in asset purchases to stabilize their local currency bond markets or to ease domestic financial conditions (see Chapter 2). Unprecedented policy support has been a game changer—it has lessened risks to financial stability and bought time for country authorities to take steps to address the health crisis and contain its economic fallout. However, these policy measures may have unintended consequences, for example, by contributing to stretched asset valuations or fueling financial vulnerabilities (see subsequent sections), especially if these policies remain in place for an extended period of time and investors become used to them. These considerations should be taken into account as central banks plan for the eventual withdrawal of support (see the policy section).

Since the June 2020 GFSR *Update*, global financial conditions have remained accommodative on the back of continued policy support (Figure 1.4, panel 1). In *advanced economies*, low interest rates and a recovery in risk asset markets have continued to support further

easing in financial conditions (Figure 1.4, panel 2). With nominal yields already at low levels, central bank measures have driven real yields down to historic lows. Market-implied inflation expectations for the near to medium term have recovered since the March sell-off but remain slightly below pre–COVID-19 levels (see Online Annex 1.1).[2] In other *emerging markets* (excluding China), financial conditions have generally eased since June (Figure 1.4, panels 3 and 4), more so in emerging market economies in Asia and Latin America than in those in Europe, the Middle East, and Africa. External spreads for many emerging markets remain above the pre–COVID-19 levels, reflecting a deterioration in domestic economic activity.[3]

---

[2]While the decline in real yields has mechanically pushed up inflation breakevens (given stable nominal yields), this appears to have been driven in part by liquidity and technical factors.

[3]IMF staff analysis, using the fundamentals-based JP Morgan Emerging Market Bond Index Global model, shows that the key driver of widening of spreads in 2020 has been the deterioration in domestic factors, following the deep and sudden recession in most economies.

Figure 1.3. Central Bank Measures in Major Advanced Economies—Game Changer
(Index, left scale; number of policy announcements, right scale)

Central bank actions were forceful and swift, and targeted a range of key markets using an array of policy tools.

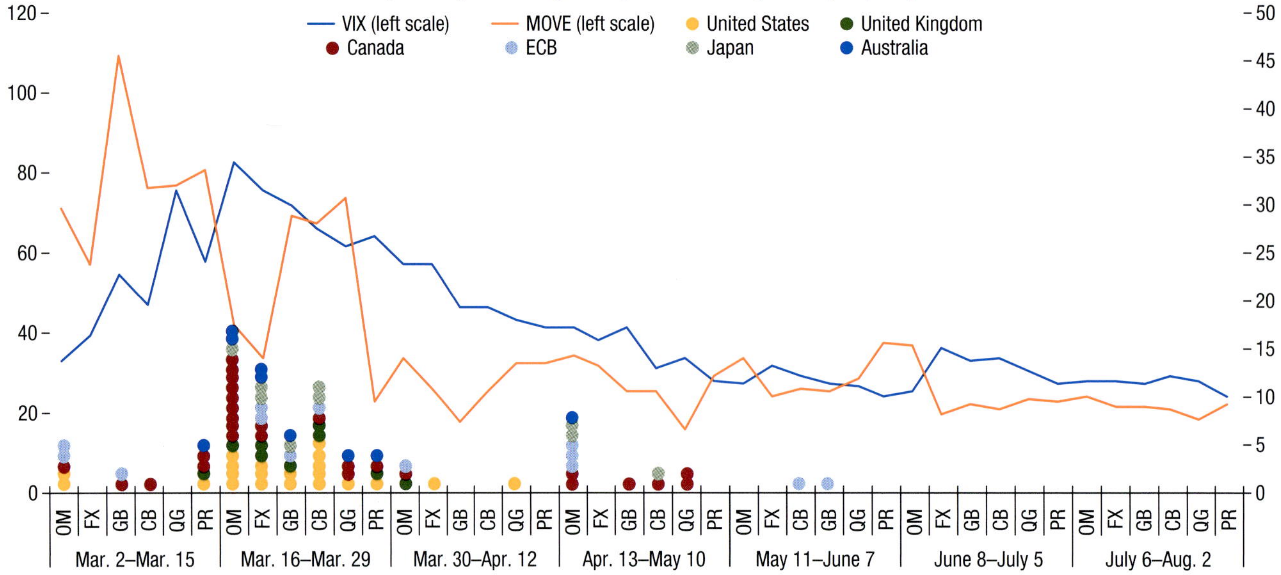

Sources: Bloomberg Finance L.P.; central bank websites; Haver Analytics; and IMF staff calculations.
Note: Intervention types refer to expansion/enhancement of OMs, FX, GBs, CBs, QGs, and PRs. Each dot refers to an announced enhancement or new operation or facility. The policy intervention types correspond to the economic nature of the interventions undertaken, even though in some cases the technical mechanism varies. CB = commercial paper, asset-backed securities, and corporate bond purchases; ECB = European Central Bank; FX = foreign exchange swap lines and foreign exchange lending operations; GB = government securities purchase; MOVE = Merrill Lynch Option Volatility Estimate; OM = open market operation, collateral framework, and standing liquidity facility; PR = reduced policy rate; QG = purchase of quasi government or government-guaranteed/-supported securities; VIX = Chicago Board Options Exchange Volatility Index.

In *China*, financial conditions have remained broadly stable over the summer (Figure 1.4, panels 1 and 2). After initially cutting policy rates and deploying measures to directly increase bank credit, authorities in May scaled back expectations for further interest rate reductions, leading to a rebound in bond and money market yields (Figure 1.4, panels 1 and 2). The policy shift came amid improving economic activity but also concerns about rising financial sector risks. Rapid increases in risky asset management product borrowing contributed to large swings in interest rates, whereas most banks saw limited pass-through from policy rates to funding costs, posing risks to bank profitability (see Online Annex Box 2.1). Other People's Bank of China measures have helped direct credit to vulnerable borrowers and support the economy, but these may be adding to nonfinancial sector vulnerabilities (Figure 1.9, panel 2).

The Pandemic Has Hit Some Economic Sectors Harder than Others

Behind the broad rebound in risk asset prices there are clear signs of *differentiation* across sectors. Some sectors (such as airlines, hotels, energy, and financials) have been more affected by the lockdown and social distancing, whereas those that are less contact-intensive (information technology, communications) have been faring better. Equity market indices with a larger share of sectors less affected by COVID-19 have seen a stronger rebound (Figure 1.5, panel 1).

Market analysts' earnings forecasts may provide an indication of the likely pace of recovery from the pandemic across sectors and countries. Certain sectors—notably consumer services (hotels, restaurants, leisure), industrials (capital goods), and financials (banks)—have seen large swing in their 2020–21 earnings per share forecasts, the large dispersion of forecasts across analysts, and significant downgrades

Figure 1.4. Global Financial Conditions

Global financial conditions have eased further since the June 2020 GFSR *Update* ...

1. Global Financial Conditions Indices
(Standard deviations from mean)

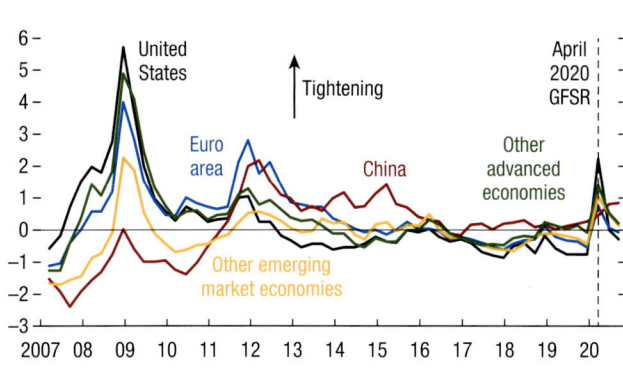

... on the back of a continued decline in interest rates and recovery in risk asset markets.

2. Key Drivers of Global Financial Conditions Indices
(Standard deviations from mean)

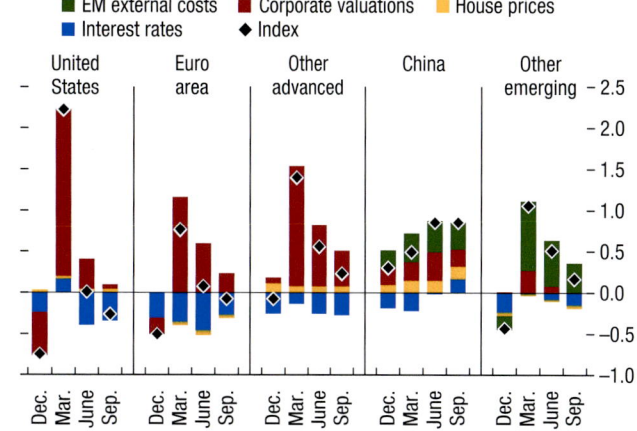

In emerging market economies, financial conditions have eased as well.

3. Financial Conditions Indices for Emerging Market Regions
(Standard deviations from mean)

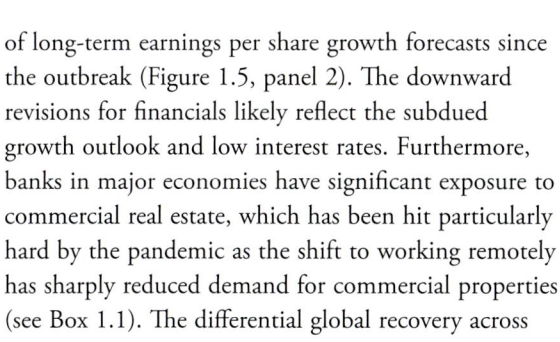

External funding costs have declined but remain elevated relative to pre-COVID-19 levels.

4. Key Drivers of Emerging Market Financial Conditions Indices
(Standard deviations from mean)

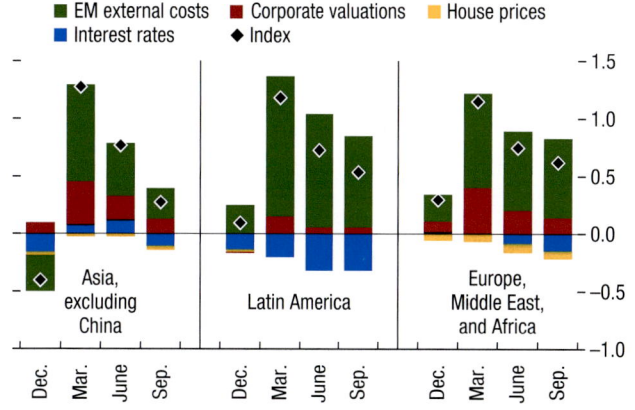

Sources: Bank for International Settlements; Bloomberg Finance L.P.; Haver Analytics; IMF, International Financial Statistics database; and IMF staff calculations.
Note: Panels 1 and 3 show quarterly averages for 2007–2019 and monthly averages for 2020; panels 2 and 4 show monthly averages. In panels 2 and 4, the interest rate component contains real short-term interest rates, term spreads or medium-term interest rates, and interbank spreads. See the April 2018 *Global Financial Stability Report* (GFSR) for details. EM = emerging market.

of long-term earnings per share growth forecasts since the outbreak (Figure 1.5, panel 2). The downward revisions for financials likely reflect the subdued growth outlook and low interest rates. Furthermore, banks in major economies have significant exposure to commercial real estate, which has been hit particularly hard by the pandemic as the shift to working remotely has sharply reduced demand for commercial properties (see Box 1.1). The differential global recovery across

sectors means that some countries may recover faster than others.

Risk Assets Have Rebounded despite High Economic Uncertainty

The disconnect between rising market valuations and weak economic activity, discussed in the June 2020 GFSR *Update*, has persisted notwithstanding

Figure 1.5. Global Equity Markets: Impact of COVID-19 on Countries and Sectors

Countries and regions with a higher share of less contact-intensive sectors (such as information technology and telecommunications) have done better, whereas energy and financial stocks have been a drag on stock market performance.

Some sectors (such as consumer services, industrials, and financials) have seen large fluctuations in their near-term forecasts as well as notable downward revisions of the long-term earnings per share forecasts.

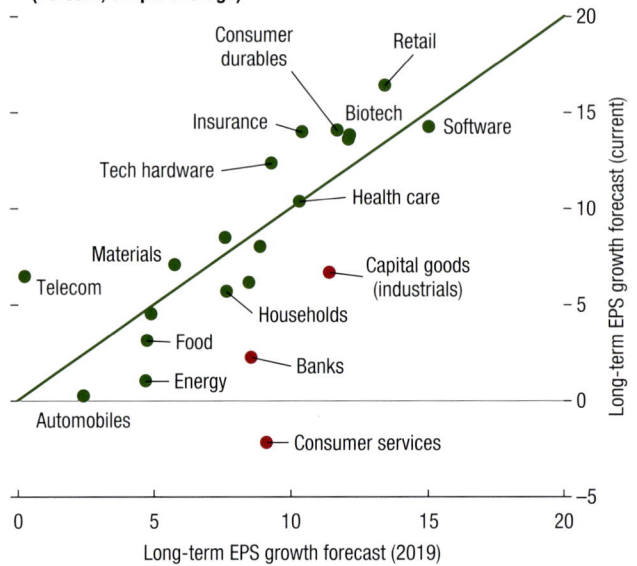

1. Stock Market Performance in 2020: Sectoral Contributions (Percent, year to date)

2. Long-term EPS Growth Forecasts: United States, Euro Area, and Japan (Percent, simple average)

Sources: Bloomberg Finance L.P.; MSCI; Refinitiv I/B/E/S; and IMF staff calculations.
Note: In panel 1, all country indices are local currency MSCI sub-indices. Overall performance is based on aggregation of sectoral indices. "Consumer" is the sum of the consumer discretionary and consumer staples sectors and "other" is the sum of the utilities, materials, and real estate sectors. In panel 2, red dots denote the largest downward forecast revisions. Long-term forecasts cover three- to five-year horizon. All indices are national benchmark indices by sector. UK = United Kingdom; US = United States; YTD = year to date.

the September correction in equity markets. Despite subdued activity and a highly uncertain outlook, global *equity markets* have rebounded from the March lows, though with notable differentiation across countries, depending on the spread of the virus, the scope of policy support, and sectoral composition (see Figure 1.6, panels 1 and 2).

The stock market recovery has been largely driven by *policy support*. A simple decomposition of the S&P 500 year-to-date performance into the contributions of three factors—earnings (current and projected), the risk-free rate, and the equity risk premium—shows that a sharp deterioration in the corporate earnings outlook has contributed negatively to stock market performance (Figure 1.6, panel 3). But such a negative contribution has been more than offset by a lower risk-free rate (green bars) and a compression of the equity risk premium (shown as a positive contribution in gray), reflecting the Federal Reserve's policy rate cuts and other policy measures that have boosted risk sentiment.

Factors such as the *sectoral composition, investor base, and other technical factors* have also played a role in driving equity valuations.[4] For example, US stock market performance has been boosted by a large share of tech firms in the S&P 500 index, as the pandemic has had pronounced implications for work and consumption behavior that are expected to encourage spending on new technologies (Figure 1.6, panel 4). Despite the September sell-off, five tech giants have significantly outperformed the rest of the index since June 2020, benefiting from their business models and diversified business revenues (Figure 1.6, panel 5).[5] In addition, in some countries, retail investors, who tend to chase growth and technology stocks, have

[4]For example, the US stock market is dominated by sectors and large firms that have been less affected by the pandemic than the broader economy. SMEs, which are not publicly listed but play an important role in the economy, could also account for some of this disconnect between stock market and the broader economy.
[5]The top five S&P stocks by market cap (AAPL, AMZN, GOOG, FB, MSFT) account for about 25 percent of total market capitalization.

Figure 1.6. Equity Market Valuations

Markets rebounded on strong policy support, but with clear differentiation across countries and sectors.

1. Global Equity Markets: Countries and Regions
  (Percent)

2. Global Equity Markets: Economic Sectors
  (Percent)

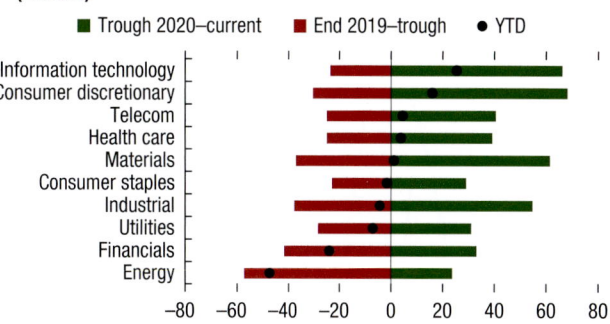

Falling risk-free rates and equity premium compression have supported equity market performance, despite the drag from a weaker earnings outlook.

3. S&P 500: Decomposition of Equity Market Performance
  (Percent contribution to cumulative returns)

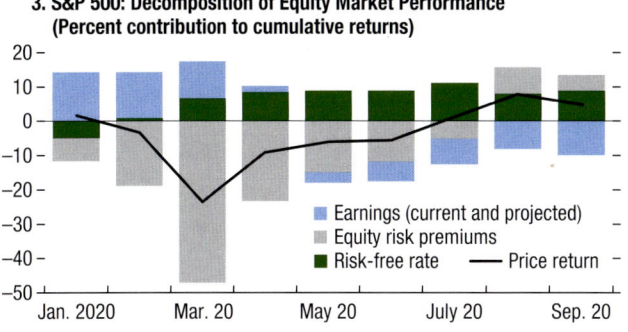

In the United States, a few large firms have significantly outperformed the rest of the stock market since the COVID-19 outbreak.

4. US Stock Market Performance
  (Indices; February 19, 2020 = 100)

These top five firms tend to dominate certain sectors (information technology, telecommunications, consumer discretionary) and have large international exposures.

5. Stock Market Performance and Shares of Foreign Revenues and of Top Five Tech Firms by Sector
  (Price changes in percent since February 19, 2020, shares in percent)

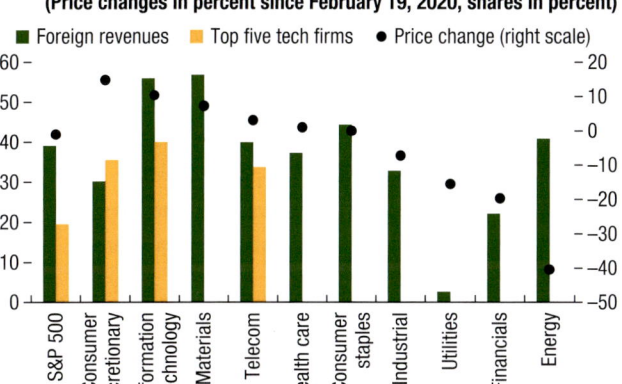

Valuations in major equity markets have become increasingly stretched by historical standards.

6. Equity Market Misalignments
  (Deviation from fair value per unit of risk, left scale; percentile based on 1995–2020 period, right scale)

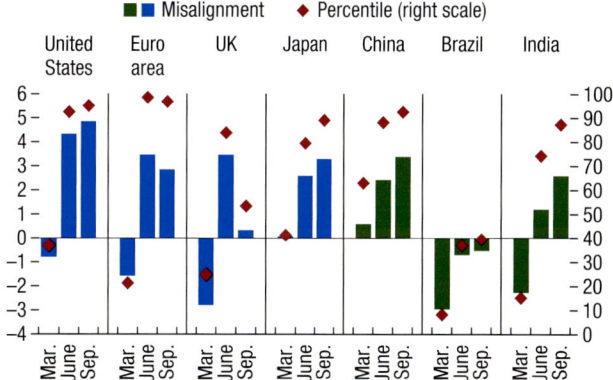

Sources: Bloomberg Finance L.P.; Consensus Economics; Haver Analytics; Refinitiv I/B/E/S; and IMF staff calculations.
Note: In panel 3, the decomposition is based on a standard three-stage dividend discount model. See Panigirtzoglou (2002). In panel 4 and 5, the top five firms are Alphabet (Google), Amazon, Apple, Facebook, and Microsoft. In panel 6, misalignment is the difference between market- and model-based values scaled by the standard deviation of weekly returns; positive values indicate overvaluation. Intuitively, this measure indicates how many standard deviations of weekly returns (or "units of risk") it would take to get back to fair value. Misalignment in the euro area, Japan, and the United States is measured at the sector level and aggregated to the index level by market capitalization. For other countries, misalignment is measured at the index level, due to data limitations. EM = emerging market; EMEA = Europe, Middle East, and Africa; ex. = excluding; Latam = Latin America; UK = United Kingdom; US = United States.

Figure 1.7. Market Volatility and Economic Uncertainty

Despite an uncertain earnings outlook, the VIX and realized market volatility have declined ...

... as central banks' actions have stabilized market conditions.

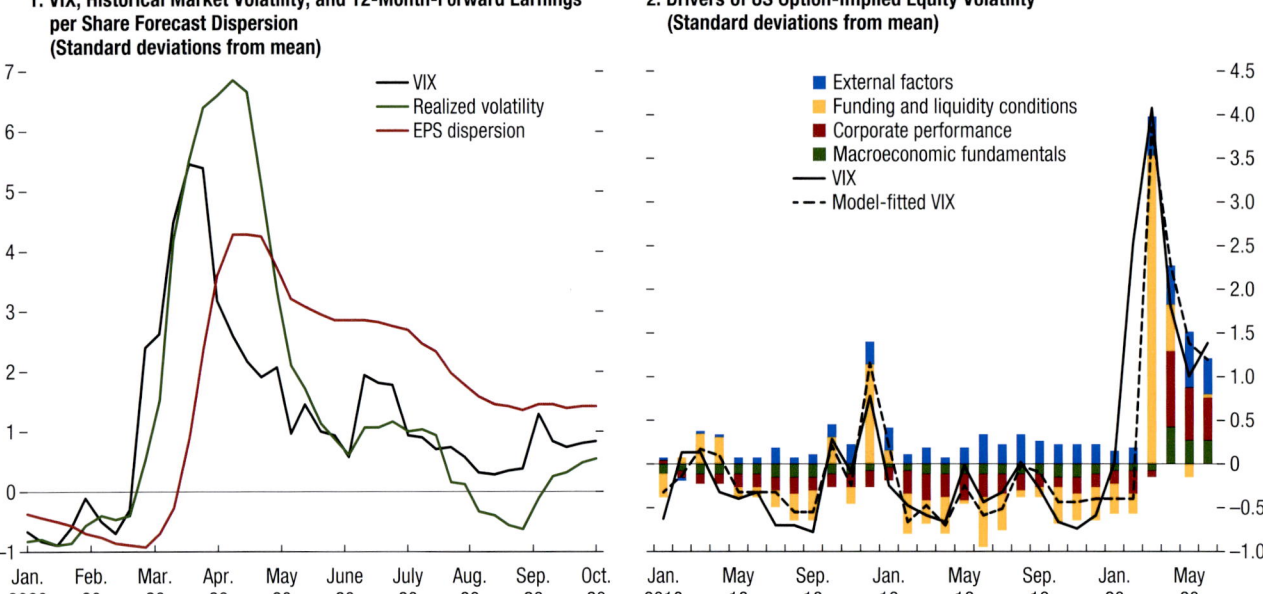

1. VIX, Historical Market Volatility, and 12-Month-Forward Earnings per Share Forecast Dispersion
(Standard deviations from mean)

2. Drivers of US Option-Implied Equity Volatility
(Standard deviations from mean)

Sources: Bloomberg Finance L.P.; Consensus Economics; Refinitiv I/B/E/S; and IMF staff calculations.
Note: In panel 1, EPS dispersion is the standard deviation of EPS forecasts across analysts. Panel 2 is based on the VIX model presented in the October 2019 *Global Financial Stability Report* (see Figure 1.2). EPS = earnings per share; VIX = Chicago Board Options Exchange Volatility Index.

significantly increased their participation in the stock market in recent months, likely providing further support to equity prices.[6] According to market analysts, the unwind of retail positions, including in derivatives markets, may have contributed to the correction in the tech sector.

Has the stock market rebound gone too far? The IMF staff's equity valuation models suggest that overvaluations are at historically high levels in some countries (see Figure 1.6, panel 6).[7] This disconnect has also been evident in a notable divergence between elevated

economic uncertainty and compressed equity market volatility, though this gap has narrowed during the September sell-off. For example, both option-implied volatility (Chicago Board Options Exchange Volatility Index [VIX]) and realized market volatility have declined sharply in late March-April, reflecting improvement in funding and liquidity conditions following policy interventions, even though uncertainty about earnings outlook has remained elevated for some time (Figure 1.7). Although these misalignments could be partially an unintended outcome of policy measures aimed at supporting investor sentiment and keeping markets open, it is difficult to separate intended from unintended effects quantitatively.

Yields in credit markets have declined since the start of the pandemic, reflecting both the decline in risk-free rates and the compression in credit spreads on the back of continued policy support. For example, the IMF staff's valuation model for US investment-grade corporate bonds suggests that central bank policy rate cuts and "other policy support" (including asset purchases and other facilities) have partly offset the impact of the deterioration in economic fundamentals that has occurred since the outbreak and that would have otherwise pushed bond

---

[6]For example, in China, margin trading outstanding, which is often cited as an indicator of retail investors' activities, has increased sharply since last year. In the United States, E*TRADE, Fidelity, Schwab, Robinhood, and Interactive Brokers all reported increased activity, new account sign-ups, or both. Trading on Robinhood tripled in March 2020 compared with March 2019.

[7]The extent of equity price misalignments—the difference between the actual price and the model-based value—can be interpreted as the portion of the equity risk premium that cannot be explained by the explanatory variables included in the model: expected corporate earnings (the mean earnings per share forecasts), uncertainty about future earnings (the dispersion of earnings per share forecasts), term spreads, and interest rates (see the October 2019 GFSR Online Annex 1.1 for details). The model relies on 12-month- and 18-month-ahead earnings forecasts and does not capture the impact of the longer-term earning growth expectations on equity valuations.

Figure 1.8. Credit Market Valuations

Much of the decline in the US investment-grade corporate bond yield since March has been driven by policy support.

Most bond spreads appear to be too compressed relative to fundamentals across both advanced and emerging markets.

1. Decomposition of Changes in US Investment-Grade Corporate Bond Yields
(Basis points, left scale; percentage points, right scale)

2. Bond Spread Misalignments
(Deviation from fair value per unit of risk, left scale; percentile based on 1995–2020, right scale)

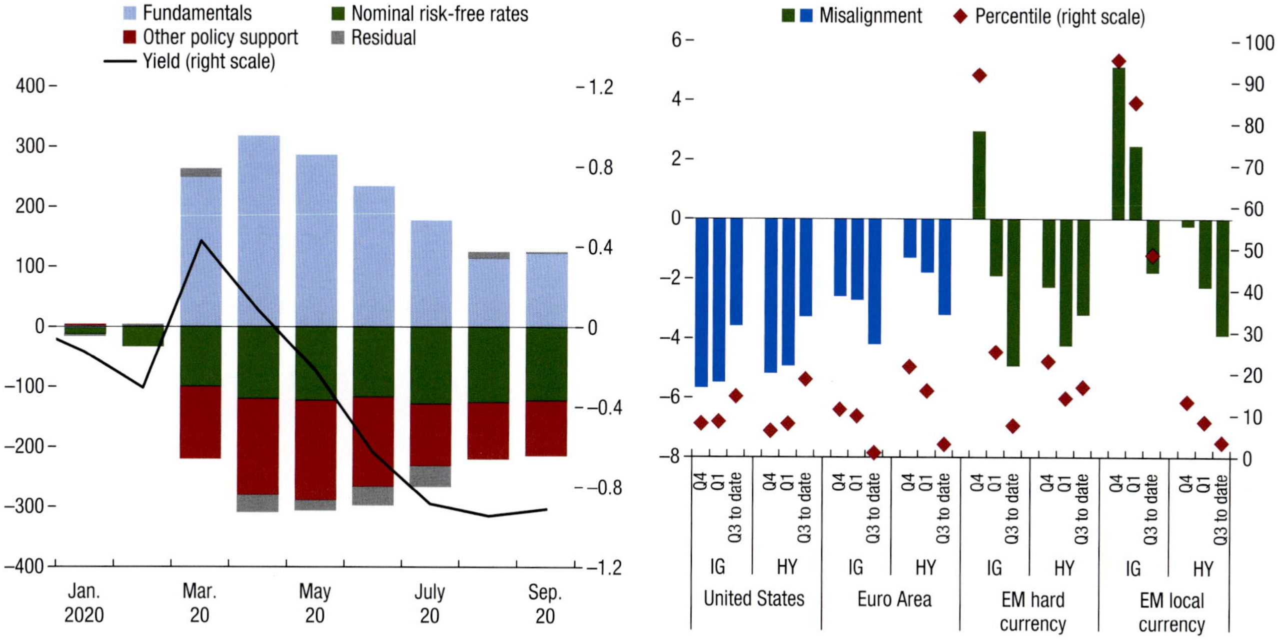

Sources: Bloomberg Finance L.P.; Consensus Economics; Haver Analytics; Refinitiv I/B/E/S; and IMF staff calculations.
Note: The corporate bond valuation model in panel 1 is based on four groups of explanatory variables: economic (firm value) factors, uncertainty measures, leverage metrics, and policy support factors. The group of policy support factors includes five variables: the size of the Federal Reserve's balance sheet, the number of announced policy measures, a dummy (0 before March 2020 and 1 thereafter), the amount of the Federal Reserve US dollar swap lines used (flow), and the outstanding amount of the Federal Reserve US dollar swap lines (stock). The estimates are based on extreme bound analysis (see Durham 2002), which entails running a large number of regressions covering all possible linear combinations of the explanatory variables in each of the four groups. The final model-implied bond spread corresponds to the weighted average fitted value estimated across the various model combinations, in which the weights correspond to the R-squared obtained from the respective regression. In panel 2, misalignment is the difference between market- and model-based values scaled by the standard deviation of monthly changes in spreads; negative values on the left scale indicate overvaluation. Historical data go back to 1995 or earliest available. Latest data are through September 29, 2020. The valuation model for the United States and the euro area is based on three groups of explanatory variables: economic factors, uncertainty measures, and leverage metrics. For details, see October 2019 *Global Financial Stability Report* Online Annex 1.1. EM = emerging market; HY = high yield; IG = investment grade.

yields higher (Figure 1.8, panel 1).[8] More broadly, credit *spreads* appear to be too compressed relative to economic fundamentals across both advanced and emerging markets (Figure 1.8, panel 2).[9] In emerging markets, the decline in hard currency bond spreads and in local currency bond

[8]The corporate bond valuation model in Figure 1.8, panel 1, is based on four groups of explanatory variables: economic (firm value) factors, uncertainty measures, leverage metrics, and policy support factors.

[9]The measures of misalignment shown in Figure 1.8, panel 2, for advanced economy corporate bond spreads and emerging market sovereign bond spreads/yields may partly reflect the unprecedented policy support. Adding the policy support proxies to the corporate bond valuation model (as shown in Figure 1.8, panel 1) can help explain some, but not all, of the misalignments shown in Figure 1.8, panel 2.

yields since March can also be traced to policy support, including the spillovers from policy easing in advanced economies. Rough estimates of the pass-through of US policy actions to emerging market yields suggest that US policy actions since the COVID-19 sell-off account for about one-quarter to one-half of the decline in emerging markets' long-term interest rates (see Online Annex 1.1). In local currency bond markets, both conventional and unconventional policies, such as asset purchases by emerging market central banks, have helped push short rates and long-term yields lower (see Chapter 2).

The sharp rebound in asset valuations, even if it is partially the intended outcome of policies aimed at creating a bridge to recovery, does raise concerns about the possibility of a market correction—as witnessed, for example, with respect to tech stocks in September. Current market valuations may be sustained for some time, as long as there is a perception in markets that policy support will be maintained or scaled up in response to deterioration in economic conditions. Valuations may also continue to rise if pandemic- and policy-related uncertainties decline. However, the risk of a sharp adjustment in asset prices or periodic bouts of volatility remains and may rise should investors reassess the extent or duration of policy support or if the recovery is delayed.

Global Financial Vulnerabilities Have Increased since the COVID-19 Outbreak

The COVID-19 pandemic could be a major resilience test for the global financial system. Before the outbreak, financial vulnerabilities were already elevated in several sectors—including asset management companies, nonfinancial firms, and sovereigns—across 29 jurisdictions with systemically important financial sectors (henceforth, S29) (see Figure 1.9) and likely contributed to stress in financial markets during the March sell-off (see the April 2020 GFSR).[10]

Since the COVID-19 outbreak, vulnerabilities have continued to rise. Triggers such as new virus outbreaks, policy missteps, or other shocks could interact with preexisting vulnerabilities and tip the economy into a more adverse scenario (see the October 2020 WEO). In such a scenario, more widespread bankruptcies could lead to a repricing of credit risk, tightening of bank lending standards, and a renewed sharp tightening of financial conditions (see Chapter 3 for an analysis of this dynamic in March).

As the crisis continues to unfold, rising vulnerabilities may create headwinds to recovery:

- *Widespread bankruptcies* have been avoided so far thanks to large and frontloaded policy support. However, as firms have borrowed more to cope with cash shortages, some solvency risks have shifted into the future. SMEs, especially in contact-intensive

industries, are much more vulnerable than large firms with access to capital markets.
- *Credit losses* could deplete banks' capital buffers, affecting their ability and willingness to provide credit to households and firms. Although the global banking system is well capitalized, there is a weak tail of banks, and some banking systems may experience capital shortfalls in the adverse WEO scenario even with the currently deployed policy measures.
- *Fragilities in the nonbank financial sector* have aggravated market dislocations during the March sell-off. Central bank support has limited the fallout from these fragilities but has not eliminated them. Market expectation that central banks will extend policy support in response to adverse shocks may encourage risk taking over and above desired levels.
- As *policy space shrinks*, the public-sector capacity to continue to provide a backstop to the private sector may come into question, especially where vulnerabilities are high and rising across several sectors of the economy.
- *External financing challenges* facing emerging and frontier markets may tip some of them into debt distress or lead to financial instability.

The rest of this section will focus on each of these areas. The rise in financial vulnerabilities increases the likelihood of adverse macro-financial feedback loops in response to negative shocks, potentially requiring further liquidity and solvency policy measures.

Solvency Risks in the Nonfinancial Sector Have Been Mitigated by Policy Support So Far

Nonfinancial firms in many systemically important economies entered the COVID-19 recession with elevated vulnerabilities, with the share of S29 economies with high or medium-high corporate sector vulnerabilities already close to 80 percent (by GDP) before the pandemic (Figure 1.9).[11] After the outbreak, cash flows took a hit as economic activity declined sharply. More vulnerable firms—those with

---

[10]The S29 include the euro area economies (Austria, Belgium, France, Germany, Ireland, Italy, Luxembourg, The Netherlands, Finland, Spain), other systemically important advanced economies (Australia, Canada, Denmark, Hong Kong SAR, Japan, Korea, Norway, Singapore, Sweden, Switzerland, the United Kingdom, the United States), and systemically important emerging market economies (Brazil, China, India, Mexico, Poland, Russia, Turkey).

[11]For example, the increased share of BBB-rated companies among investment-grade borrowers in global credit markets and the rapid expansion of risky credit markets raise the risk that credit rating downgrades and corporate defaults in the current downturn will surpass levels observed during previous recessions. For details, see the April 2019, October 2019, and April 2020 GFSR issues.

Figure 1.9. Global Financial Vulnerabilities: High and Rising

Vulnerabilities have increased across more regions in the corporate and sovereign sectors as corporate borrowing surged amid the COVID-19 pandemic, whereas vulnerabilities in the nonbank financial sectors remain elevated.

1. Proportion of Systemically Important Countries with Elevated Vulnerabilities, by Sector
(Percent of countries with high and medium-high vulnerabilities, by GDP [assets of banks, asset managers, other financial institutions, and insurers]; number of vulnerable countries in parentheses)

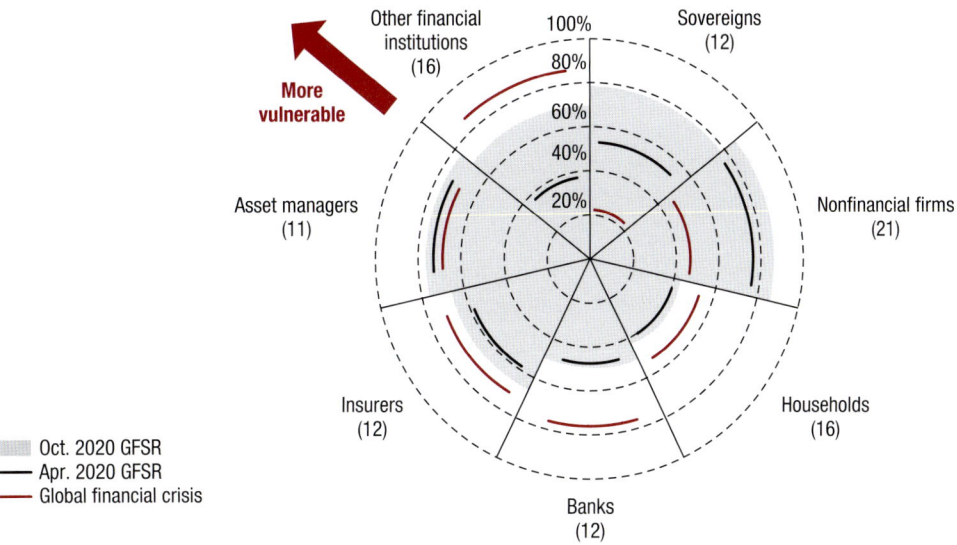

2. Financial Vulnerabilities by Sector and Region

Quintiles

Worst   Best

	Sovereigns		Nonfinancial Firms		Households		Banks		Insurers		Asset Managers		Other Financial Institutions	
	Apr. 2020	Oct. 2020	Apr. 2020	Oct. 2020	Apr. 2020	Oct. 2020	Apr. 2020	Oct. 2020	Apr. 2020	Oct. 2020	Apr. 2020	Oct. 2020	Apr. 2020	Oct. 2020

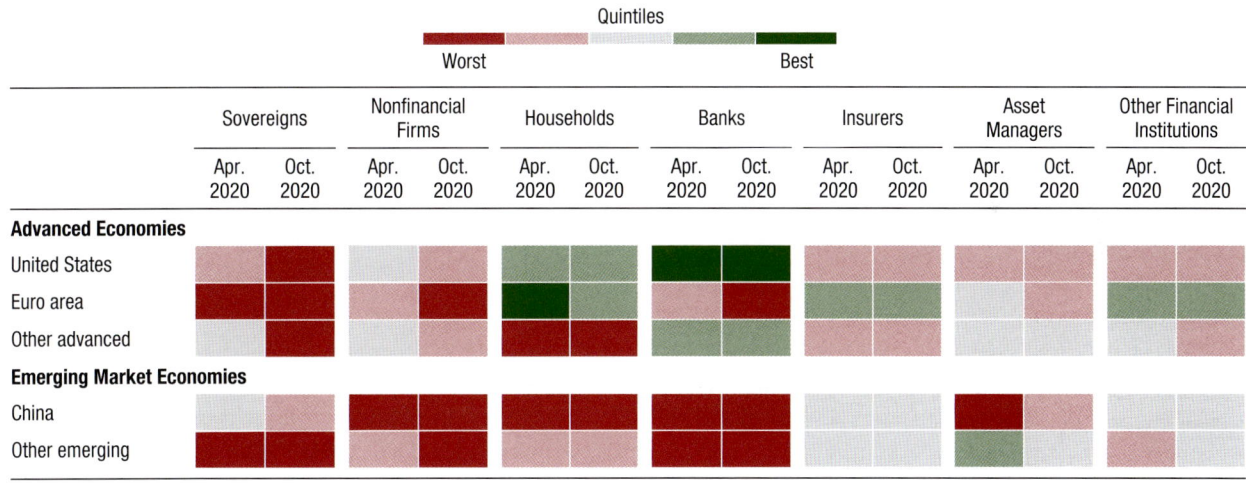

Advanced Economies
United States
Euro area
Other advanced

Emerging Market Economies
China
Other emerging

Sources: Banco de Mexico; Bank for International Settlements; Bank of Japan; Bloomberg Finance L.P.; China Insurance Regulatory Commission; European Central Bank; Haver Analytics; IMF, Financial Soundness Indicators database; Reserve Bank of India; S&P Global Market Intelligence; S&P Leveraged Commentary and Data; Securities and Exchange Commission of Brazil; WIND Information Co.; and IMF staff calculations.
Note: In panel 1, "global financial crisis" reflects the maximum vulnerability value during 2007–08. In panel 2, dark red shading indicates a value in the top 20 percent of pooled samples (advanced and emerging market economies pooled separately) for each sector during 2000–20 (or longest sample available), and dark green shading indicates values in the bottom 20 percent. In panels 1 and 2, for households, the debt service ratio for emerging market economies is based on all private nonfinancial corporations and households. Other systemically important advanced economies comprise Australia, Canada, Denmark, Hong Kong Special Administrative Region, Japan, Korea, Norway, Singapore, Sweden, Switzerland, and the United Kingdom. Other systemically important emerging market economies are Brazil, India, Mexico, Poland, Russia, and Turkey. Even though the latest readings for the insurance sectors in the United States and Japan and asset managers in China—based on the available data—put them slightly below the threshold for the "medium-high vulnerability category" as of 2020:Q1, given the exceptionally high uncertainty these sectors are categorized as "medium-high" in this assessment. The assessment for the insurance sector in the April 2020 GFSR was also revised as a result of a change in Japan's reading to "medium-high," based on an update of the data available at the time. GFSR = *Global Financial Stability Report.*

weaker solvency and liquidity positions as well as of smaller size—experienced greater financial stress than their peers in the early stages of the crisis (see Chapter 3). Taking advantage of the massive easing in financial conditions, firms in advanced and emerging market economies stepped up their bond issuance (Figure 1.10, panels 1–3), and also increased their borrowing from banks (Figure 1.10, panel 4) to cope with cash shortages, refinance their debt, or build precautionary cash buffers. The rapid expansion of bank credit in the first half of this year partly reflects sizable credit line drawdowns, especially in the United States, as well as government guaranteed loans and lending under government-supported programs (Figure 1.10, panel 5). The share of firms that had to raise new debt because they could not generate enough cash to cover their debt service costs rose sharply (Figure 1.10, panel 6). In all likelihood, without the policy support that facilitated such borrowing, nonfinancial firms would have seen a sharp rise in bankruptcies. However, this further expansion of corporate debt has added to already high debt levels in several economies (Figure 1.10, panel 7).

As the crisis continues to unfold, liquidity pressures may morph into insolvencies. Increased net borrowing has helped reduce liquidity pressures and mitigated an otherwise larger increase in defaults for now. However, rising debt may lead to a deterioration in repayment capacity over the medium term, putting solvency at risk. Corporate credit quality has already shown signs of deterioration—credit rating downgrades initially spiked and year-to-date speculative-grade defaults have risen quickly, particularly in the United States (Figure 1.11, panel 1). Missed debt payments were reported as the leading cause of defaults in 2020 to date. Firms in sectors most affected by the pandemic—air travel, retail, hospitality, and energy—have seen higher default rates (Figure 1.11, panel 2). Looking across the credit spectrum, the largest increase has been among high-yield bond issuers, followed by leveraged loans and middle-market loans, even though defaults are still significantly lower than in 2008–09 (Figure 1.11, panel 3). The pace of defaults has recently slowed in the United States and has remained relatively subdued in Europe. Looking ahead, the range of speculative-grade default forecasts for 2021 by credit rating agencies is fairly wide (Figure 1.11, panel 4), which reflects significant

uncertainty about the evolution of the pandemic and corporate credit quality. At the same time, credit market pricing suggests a notably more sanguine picture, likely reflecting expectations of continued policy support.

The future path of defaults and bankruptcies will critically depend on the evolution of the pandemic and on policymakers' capacity to maintain accommodative funding conditions and continue to provide fiscal support to viable firms (see the October 2020 *Fiscal Monitor*). *Large firms* with access to capital markets can likely avoid a significant erosion of their equity positions unless there is a significant tightening in funding conditions. However, *SMEs* are much more vulnerable (as discussed in Chapter 2 of the October 2019 GFSR), as they tend to have thin equity cushions, low liquidity buffers (lack of precautionary credit lines and liquid and noncore assets), limited financing options, and nondiversified revenues. Furthermore, the COVID-19 shock was particularly damaging for SMEs because they tend to dominate some of the most contact-intensive sectors (hotels, restaurants, entertainment). Widespread insolvencies among SMEs could have a significant direct macroeconomic impact as well as adverse implications for the health of the banking sector. Notably in Europe, SMEs account for more than half of total output and about two-thirds of employment and thus can affect financial stability through macro-financial linkages. Because SMEs rely almost entirely on bank financing, they could be a source of vulnerability, especially for regional and small banks.

In the *household sector*, the COVID-19 pandemic has resulted in unprecedented job losses, especially in the United States, as well as in some emerging market economies, where unemployment support has been more limited (see the October 2020 *Fiscal Monitor*).[12] With sharply reduced personal income of the affected households, their indebtedness has risen to cover lost income, further weakening their debt servicing capacity in the future. The new buildup of debt is taking place on top of already elevated household leverage in a number of major economies (Figure 1.12, panel 1). Historically, higher unemployment portends more

---

[12]A number of jurisdictions, notably in the euro area, have implemented job retention schemes aimed at sustaining employment levels and mitigating financial vulnerabilities potentially arising from households.

Figure 1.10. Easier Funding Conditions and Rising Debt

Bond markets have reopened for a broad range of issuers, with lower-rated issuers paying spreads higher than those before COVID-19.

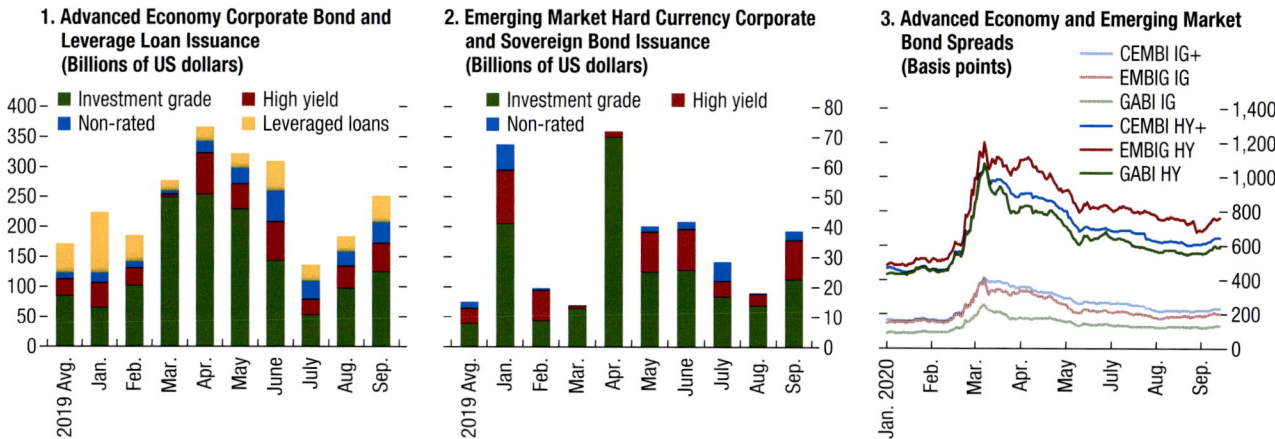

1. Advanced Economy Corporate Bond and Leverage Loan Issuance (Billions of US dollars)

2. Emerging Market Hard Currency Corporate and Sovereign Bond Issuance (Billions of US dollars)

3. Advanced Economy and Emerging Market Bond Spreads (Basis points)

Bank lending to nonfinancial firms was strong in the first half of the year ...

... in part driven by credit line drawdowns and government guarantees.

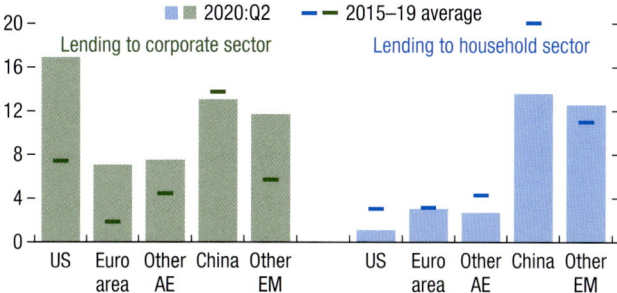

4. Bank Credit Growth in Advanced and Emerging Market Economies, 2020:Q2 (Percent)

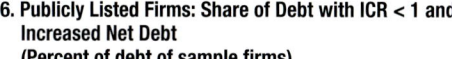

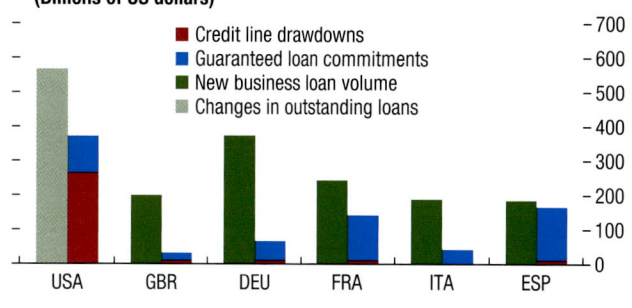

5. New Loans, Credit Lines, and Government Guarantees in Major Advanced Economies, since March 2020 (Billions of US dollars)

Increased borrowing helped firms cope with liquidity pressures as earnings collapsed following the outbreak ...

... and has pushed aggregate corporate debt levels to new highs in several countries.

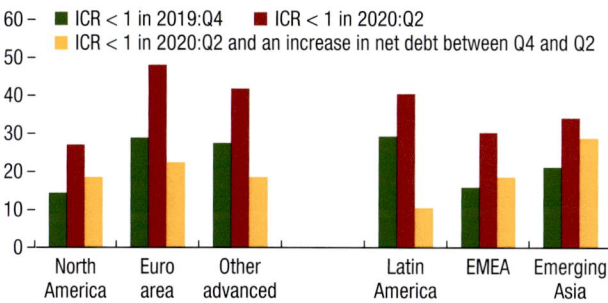

6. Publicly Listed Firms: Share of Debt with ICR < 1 and Increased Net Debt (Percent of debt of sample firms)

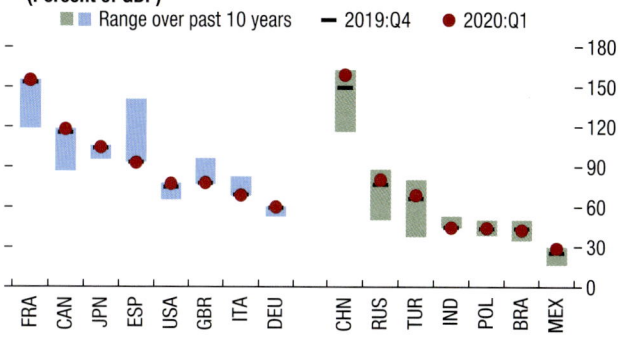

7. Aggregate Nonfinancial Corporate Debt (Percent of GDP)

Sources: Banca D'Italia; Bank aus Verantwortung (KfW); Bank for International Settlements; Bank of England; Bank of Japan; Bloomberg Finance L.P.; BondRadar; Dealogic; Emerging Portfolio Fund Research Global; Federal Reserve; French Ministry of the Economy and Finance; Haver Analytics; JPMorgan Chase & Co.; S&P Global Market Intelligence; S&P Leveraged Commentary and Data; Spanish Instituto de Credito Oficial (ICO); and IMF staff calculations.
Note: In panel 5, the credit line draw downs are cumulative since 2019:Q4. New business loan volume and changes in outstanding loans are as of 2020:Q2. The guaranteed loan commitment is as of July for United Kingdom and Italy, and as of August for the other countries. In panel 6, the sample includes firms with quarterly statements. The bars show the share of debt at firms with ICR < 1 and with an increase in net debt as a share of total debt in the sample. In panel 7, for France, corporate debt is reported on an unconsolidated basis. Data labels in panels 5 and 7 use International Organization for Standardization (ISO) country codes.
AE = advanced economy; CEMBI = JP Morgan Corporate Emerging Market Bond Index; EM = emerging market; EMBIG = JP Morgan Emerging Markets Bond Index Global; EMEA = Europe, Middle East, and Africa; GABI = JP Morgan Global Aggregate Bond Index; HY = high yield; ICR = interest coverage ratio; IG = investment grade; US = United States.

Figure 1.11. Solvency Risks in the Corporate Sector

Liquidity pressures and weaker credit quality have led to a rapid rise in corporate defaults.

Global consumer services and energy sector default rates have been more pronounced.

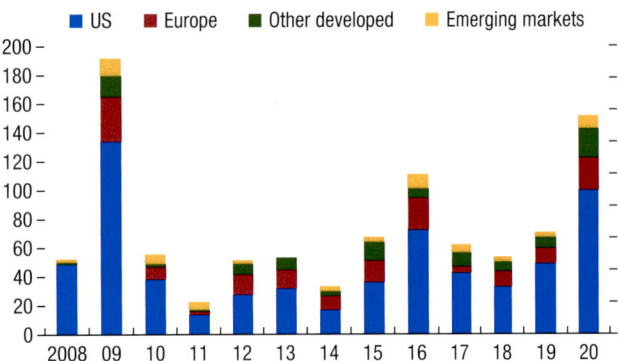

1. **Global Speculative-Grade Corporate Defaults**
   (Year-to-date number of defaults)

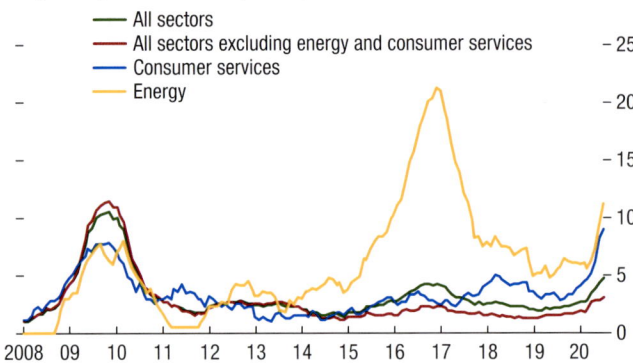

2. **Global Speculative-Grade Corporate Default Rates**
   (Trailing 12-month rate, percent)

Defaults have risen across risky markets, with the largest increase among high-yield bond issuers, followed by leveraged loans and middle-market loans ...

... and rating agencies have revised their default forecasts up, though the range of forecasts is fairly wide.

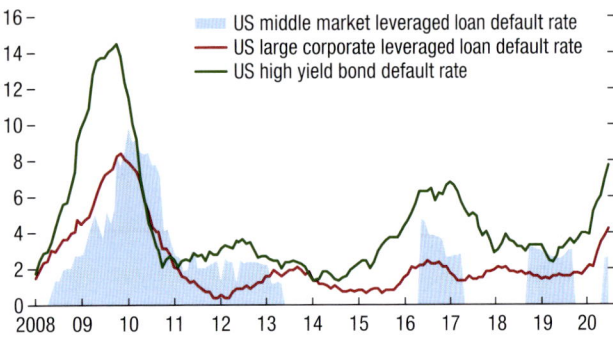

3. **US Speculative-Grade Corporate Default Rates by Market**
   (Percent)

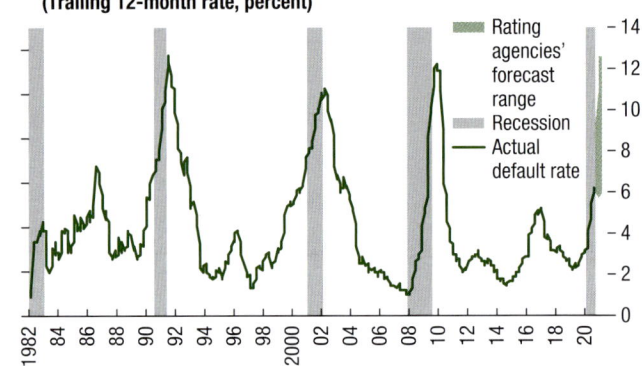

4. **US Speculative-Grade Default Rate: Actual and Forecasts by Credit Rating Agencies**
   (Trailing 12-month rate, percent)

Sources: Fitch; Haver Analytics; International Institute of Finance; Moody's; S&P Global Ratings; S&P Leveraged Commentary and Data; and IMF staff calculations.
Note: In panel 4, the range in the projection period corresponds to the forecasts from Fitch, Moody's, and Standard & Poor's.

delinquencies and larger bank losses on unsecured consumer credit. For example, delinquencies on US credit cards already started to accelerate in the first quarter of this year, whereas delinquencies on mortgages remain low (Figure 1.12, panel 2). In the housing markets, real house price growth was positive in most advanced economies in the first quarter, boosted by broad policy support, particularly lower mortgage rates and moratoriums on interest payments, foreclosures, and evictions. In emerging market economies, year-over-year real house prices declined in China and India—following notable appreciation in previous years—but continued to rise in other major economies.

Most Banks Will Be Able to Absorb Losses, but There Is a Weak Tail

Banks entered the COVID-19 crisis with significantly stronger capital and liquidity buffers than they had at the time of the global financial crisis thanks to regulatory reforms (see Figure 1.9). Policies aimed at supporting borrowers and at encouraging banks to use the flexibility built into the regulatory framework have likely further supported their willingness to continue to provide credit to the economy. However, banks in some countries have started tightening their lending standards in response to deterioration in economic conditions and borrowers' financial positions (see Chapter 4).

Figure 1.12. Solvency Risks in the Household Sector

Household debt is elevated relative to the size of the economy in several advanced economies and in China ...

... and rising unemployment may portend higher delinquencies on loans to households.

1. Aggregate Household Debt
(Percent of GDP)

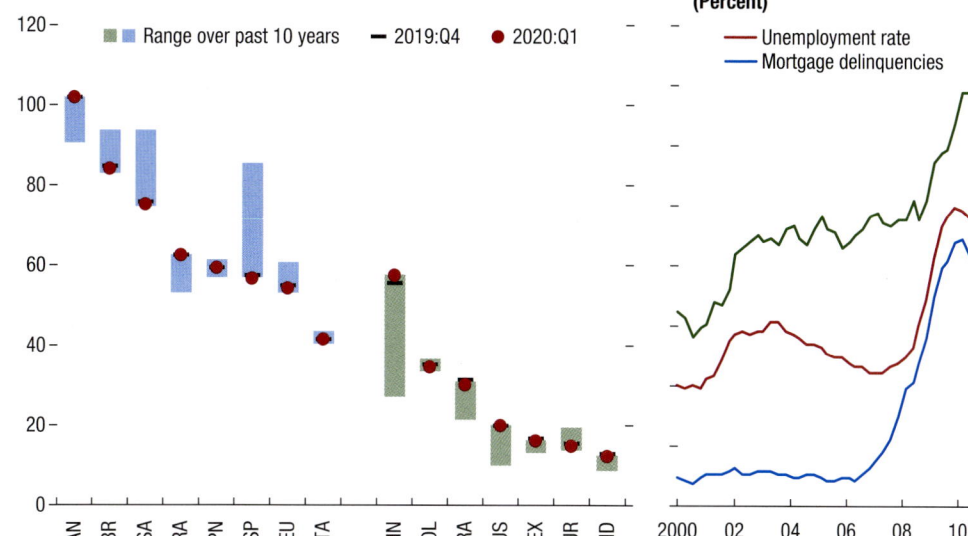

2. US Unemployment Rate and Delinquency Rates on Credit Card and Mortgage Loans
(Percent)

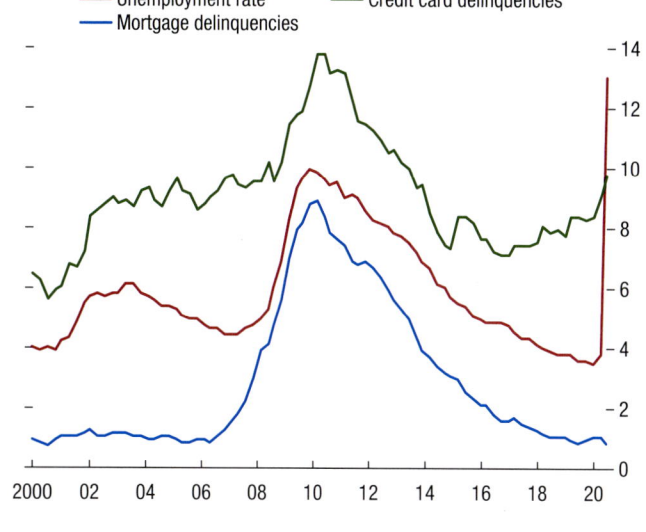

Sources: Bank for International Settlements; Federal Reserve; US Bureau of Labor Statistics; and IMF staff calculations.
Note: Data labels in panel 1 use International Organization for Standardization (ISO) country codes.

Looking ahead, the resilience of banks will depend on the depth and duration of the COVID-19 recession, governments' ability to continue to support the private sector, and the pace of loss recognition. Chapter 4 presents a forward-looking bank solvency analysis based on the October 2020 WEO baseline and adverse scenarios, taking into account announced policies to mitigate borrower distress and support bank capital levels.[13] In the *baseline scenario*, most banks are able to absorb losses and maintain capital buffers above the minimum regulatory capital requirements. In the *adverse scenario*, characterized by a deeper recession and a weaker recovery, there is a sizable weak tail of banks whose

capital falls below regulatory minimum (Figure 1.13, panel 1).[14] Global systemically important banks tend to fare better, while banks in emerging markets appear to be less resilient than their peers in advanced economies (Figure 1.13, panel 1).

In the October 2020 WEO *adverse scenario*, the capital shortfall relative to minimum capital requirements is about $110 billion, whereas the overall capital shortfall relative to broad capital requirements—which include the countercyclical capital buffer, the capital conservation buffer, and systemic risk buffers—could reach $220 billion, after accounting for policy support (Figure 1.12, panel 2, and Chapter 4). This implies that the average capital shortfall in the adverse scenario is close to 1 percent of GDP. For comparison, the median government bank recapitalization during the global financial crisis was about 3.6 percent of GDP. That said, the full fiscal cost of ensuring that banks are adequately capitalized must also include the direct fiscal support to firms and

---

[13]The analysis is carried out for about 350 banks accounting for about 75 percent of global banking assets. The exercise covers 29 jurisdictions, comprising Australia, Austria, Belgium, Brazil, Canada, Denmark, Finland, France, Germany, Greece, Hong Kong SAR, India, Indonesia, Ireland, Italy, Japan, Korea, Luxembourg, Mexico, The Netherlands, Norway, Portugal, Singapore, South Africa, Spain, Sweden, Switzerland, the United Kingdom, and the United States. In each jurisdiction, the largest banks covering up to 80 percent of banking assets are included. Therefore, the simulation does not include the consequences of the scenarios for the solvency of small banks.

[14]The regulatory minimum is the "Pillar 1" requirement—4.5 percent of risk-weighted assets—plus the mandatory buffers required of each global systemically important bank.

Figure 1.13. Banking Sector: Potential Losses in the October 2020 *World Economic Outlook* **Adverse Scenario**

In the adverse scenario, the weak tail of banks is large, especially in emerging markets.

Policy mitigation helps cushion some of the capital depletion and has been stronger in advanced economies.

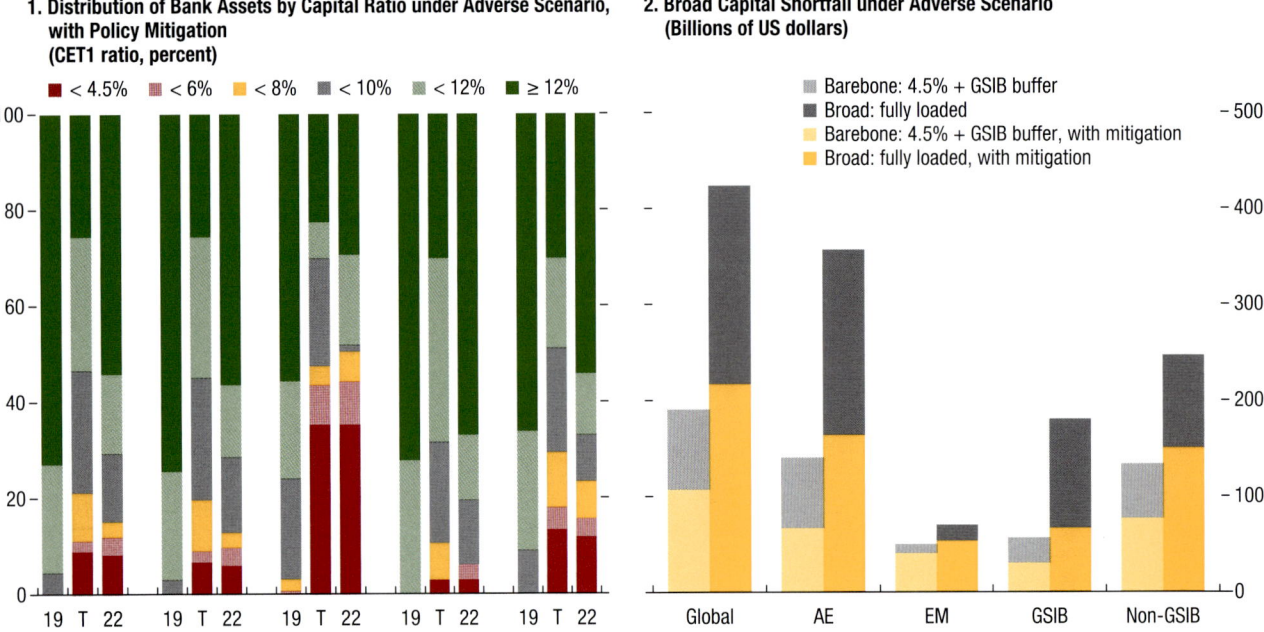

Sources: Bloomberg Finance L.P.; Fitch; IMF, October 2020 *World Economic Outlook*; and IMF staff estimates.
Note: In panel 2, the shortfall is measured against bank-specific and fully loaded capital requirements effective August 2020, which include a minimum CET1 of 4.5 percent, a GSIB buffer, a systemic risk buffer, a stress capital buffer, a conservation capital buffer, and a countercyclical capital buffer, where applicable. AE = advanced economy; CET1 = common equity Tier 1; EM = emerging market; GSIB = global systemically important bank; T = trough year.

households, which effectively reduced bank recapitalization needs ex ante, and which may also adversely affect the fiscal capacity to provide additional support in the future if needed. Furthermore, a more severe adverse scenario that would entail larger losses for the banking sector cannot be ruled out, given the high degree of uncertainty around the depth and duration of the COVID-19 recession.

Fragilities in Nonbank Financial Institutions Remain Elevated

Asset managers in advanced economies entered the pandemic crisis with already elevated vulnerabilities (Figure 1.14, panel 1), including sizable liquidity mismatches (see April 2020 GFSR). After the outbreak, they faced increased credit risk and became more interconnected with banks. Exposures through investment positions, including bank deposits and money market fund shares, have risen. Borrowing from banks has increased, as funds reportedly tapped into credit lines.

In combination with higher credit risk and increased leverage in other financial institutions, this could lead to larger potential losses in the event of renewed market stress.

During the March sell-off, *fixed-income funds* saw a surge in redemptions, which led to selling pressures revealing some weaknesses in market infrastructures and dealers' intermediation capacity (see April 2020 GFSR). Jurisdictions with swing pricing reportedly saw less price pressure from redemptions.[15] Fund flows have generally recovered, reflecting the rebound in asset markets on the back of strong policy support (Figure 1.14, panel 2). *Insurance companies* and *pension funds*, which experienced portfolio losses during the March sell-off, have also seen the value of their portfolios recover.

[15]Swing pricing is the adjustment of a fund's net asset value with the aim to pass on the trading costs generated by purchases or redemptions to the shareholders who initiate those transactions.

Figure 1.14. Vulnerabilities in the Nonbank Financial Sector

Asset managers' vulnerabilities remain elevated in China, the euro area, and the United States, and grew in OFIs in other advanced economies.

During the March 2020 sell-off, fixed-income funds experienced large outflows, which have subsequently reversed.

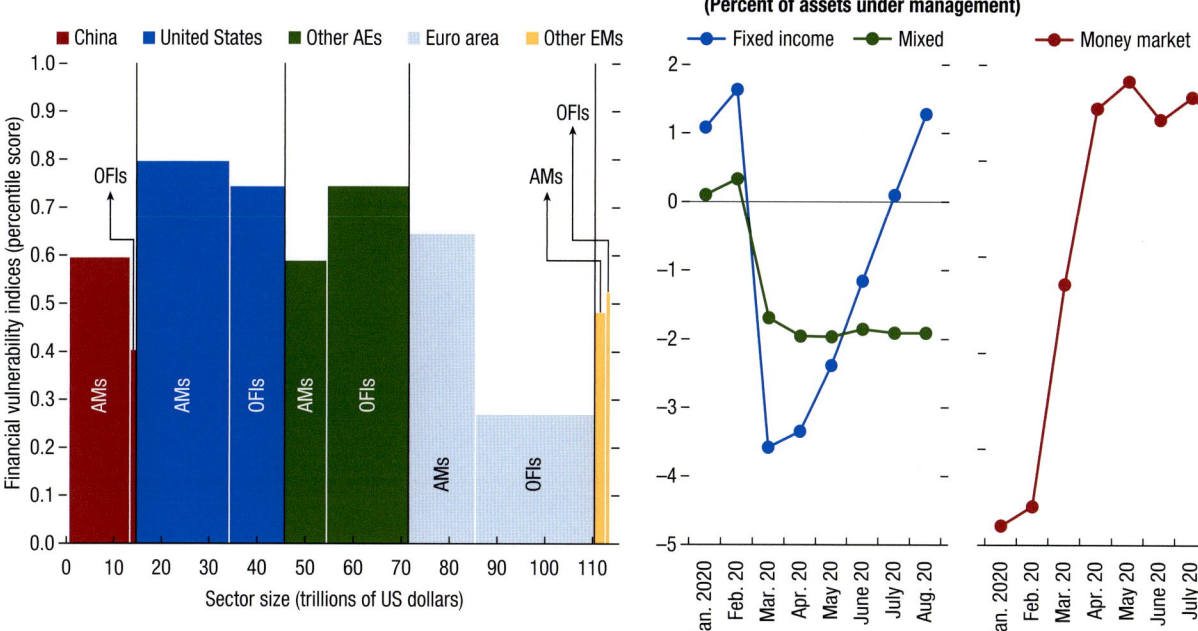

Sources: Banco de Mexico; European Central Bank; Haver Analytics; Morningstar; Reserve Bank of India; Securities and Exchange Commission of Brazil; WIND Information Co.; and IMF staff calculations.

Note: Data in panel 1 are lagged at the end of the series by 18 months for UK AMs, by 15 months for Indian AMs, and by 3 months for Russian AMs as more recent data are not yet available. For OFIs, data are lagged at the end of the series by 15 months for Switzerland and by 3 months for Russia. The financial vulnerability indices reported are the base for the heatmaps reported in Figure 1.9. Panel 2 shows cumulative changes since December 2019. Data included for fixed income funds, mixed funds, and money market funds covered 73%, 57%, and 75% of assets reported by the International Investment Funds Association for the respective global fund sectors (as of end June). AEs = advanced economies; AMs = asset managers; EMs = emerging markets; OFIs = other financial institutions.

Looking ahead, risks from nonbank financial institutions could stem from their portfolio rebalancing in response to investor redemptions and market losses or from their decision to pull back from certain markets. In recent years, nonbank financial institutions have been playing an increasingly important role in credit markets, including in riskier segments (leveraged loans and private debt), which means that they could face sizable credit losses in the event of a surge in defaults and insolvencies (as discussed in Chapter 2 of the April 2020 GFSR). These losses could, in turn, lead them to step back from providing credit to these segments of the corporate sector, which would exacerbate strains on borrowers and lead to worse macro-financial outcomes.

Existing fragilities in the nonbank financial sector (Figure 1.14, panel 1) could have significant implications for the financial system if a more prolonged period of market stress were to occur, possibly

due to or in conjunction with a lack of sufficient policy support:
- *First*, liquidity mismatches in the asset management sector remain elevated, especially in some fragile segments.[16] The analysis of the March sell-off (see Box 1.2) shows that fixed-income funds facing large redemptions reacted primarily by reducing liquid assets, but also by selling less-liquid assets. The sell-off of riskier assets contributed to price dislocations in the underlying markets and could have resulted in larger-scale fire sales had central banks not intervened quickly to backstop the key segments of the financial system. However, these interventions have masked but not eliminated the pressure points. A more prolonged liquidity shock in the future,

[16]See Box 3.1 of the October 2019 GFSR, which presents the liquidity stress test for fixed-income funds in Europe and the United States.

Figure 1.15. Financial Leverage and Global Cross-Asset Correlations

Volatility-targeting investors have been re-leveraging as volatility normalized following the March sell-off.

Cross-asset correlations remain near the historic highs reached during the COVID-19 crisis.

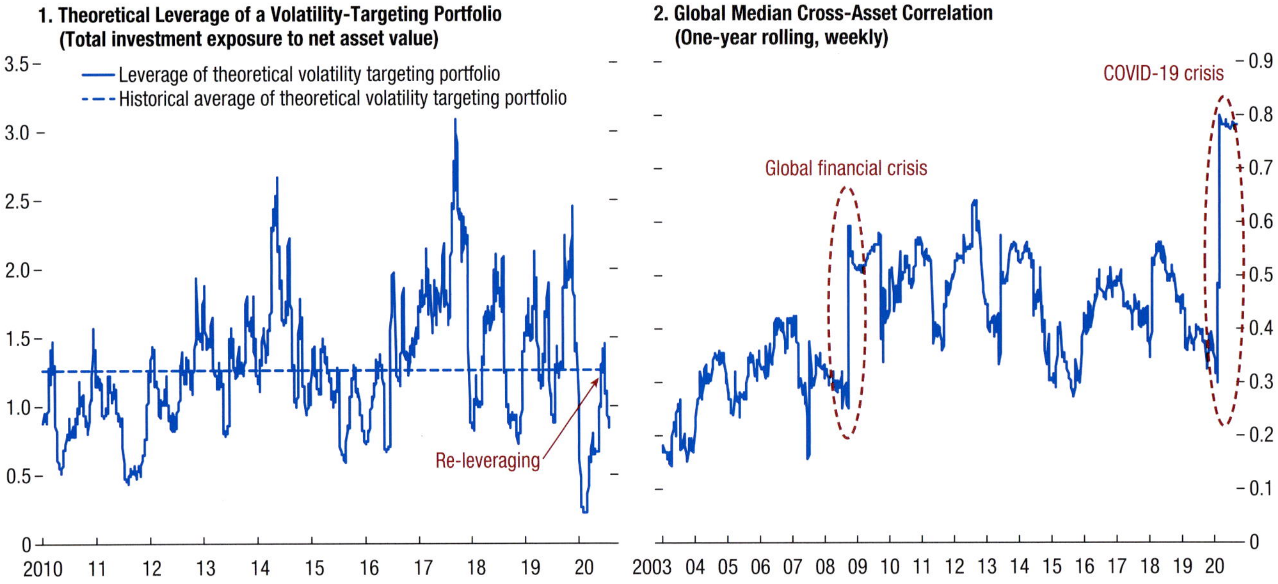

1. Theoretical Leverage of a Volatility-Targeting Portfolio (Total investment exposure to net asset value)

2. Global Median Cross-Asset Correlation (One-year rolling, weekly)

Sources: Bloomberg Finance L.P.; and IMF staff calculations.
Note: In panel 1, the leverage calculation for a theoretical volatility-targeting investment strategy assumes a theoretical investment portfolio consisting of 60 percent global equities/40 percent bonds and an annual return volatility target of 10 percent. Leverage is defined as total investment exposure divided by the net asset value of the portfolio. The MSCI World Equity Index is used as a proxy for equity investments; the Bloomberg Barclays Global Aggregate Total Return Value Unhedged index is used as a proxy for bond investments. Panel 2 shows the median cross-asset correlation across nine global risky assets: global equities (proxied by the MSCI World Equity Index), emerging market equities (proxied by the MSCI Emerging Markets Index), investment-grade credit (proxied by the Bloomberg Barclays Global Aggregate Credit Total Return Index), high-yield credit (proxied by the Bloomberg Barclays Global High Yield Total Return Index), leveraged loans (proxied by the S&P Global Leveraged Loan Index), mortgages (proxied by the Bloomberg Barclays Global Aggregate-Mortgages Index), emerging market sovereign bonds (proxied by the JP Morgan EMBI Global Total Return Index), emerging market corporate bonds (proxied by the JP Morgan Corporate EMBI Broad Diversified Composite Index), and commodities (proxied by the Bloomberg Commodity Index).

should these fragilities remain unaddressed, could potentially lead to larger-scale fire sales.

- *Second*, extremely low yields, compressed market volatility, and the apparent perception that central banks will continue to backstop key markets are likely to create incentives for financial releveraging. For example, volatility-targeting investors that were reportedly forced to liquidate their positions during the March turmoil, thus amplifying the sell-off (see April 2020 GFSR), may have already started to releverage as equity and bond volatility normalized following central bank interventions (see Figure 1.15, panel 1, for a theoretical portfolio).[17] A rapid increase in financial

leverage could contribute to asset price misalignments and increase the risk of a sharp unwinding of positions by leveraged investors during volatility spikes, amplifying asset price declines.

- *Third*, correlations across risk assets remain well above the 2008–09 levels (Figure 1.15, panel 2). These rising correlations may be partly driven by structural changes, including increased central bank presence in a number of markets. Higher correlations tend to reduce portfolio diversification opportunities and could therefore increase contagion risk and propagate losses across investor portfolios during abrupt price corrections.

To sum up, although swift policy actions have mitigated risks to nonbank financial institutions during the March sell-off, fragilities in the sector remain elevated and may lead to larger-scale distress and fire sales in a more prolonged episode of market stress. In addition, increased linkages between nonbank

[17]Volatility-targeting strategies seek to keep expected portfolio volatility to a specific target level. Lower market volatility then means that greater financial leverage is needed to meet volatility targets. Among these, variable annuity funds are the largest, at an estimated $0.5 trillion in assets under management, and are more likely to deleverage quickly when volatility spikes. See the April 2020 GFSR for more details.

Figure 1.16. Sovereign Vulnerabilities and Interconnectedness

Sovereign debt has reached historically high levels in most jurisdictions with systemically important financial sectors ...

... with 6 out of S29 jurisdictions showing elevated vulnerabilities in all three—corporate, banking, and sovereign—sectors.

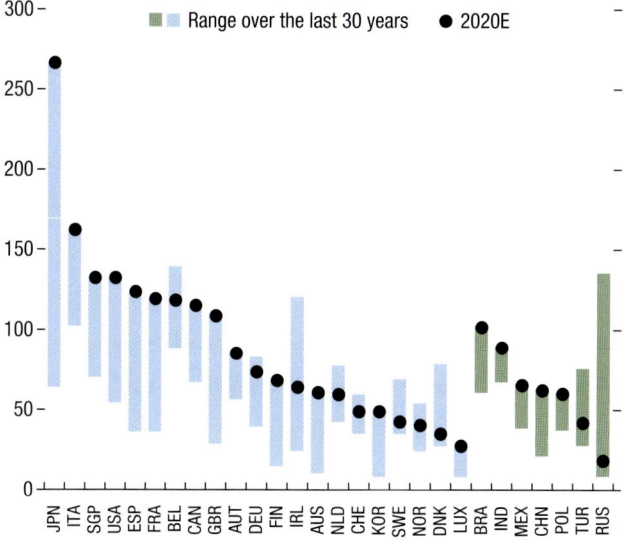

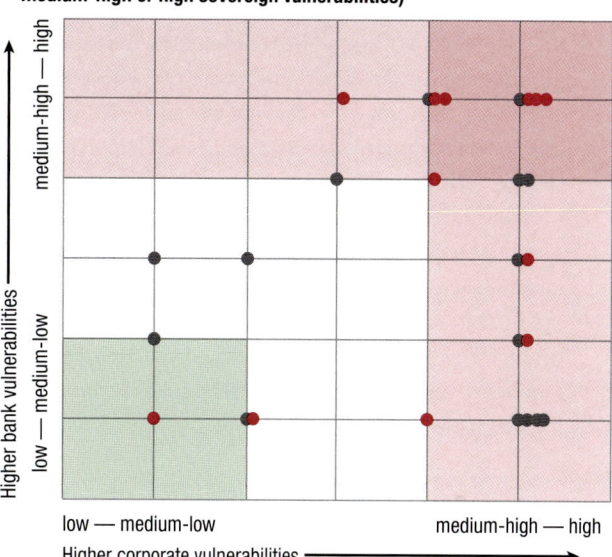

Sources: Bank for International Settlements; Haver Analytics; International Institute of Finance; IMF, October 2020 *World Economic Outlook*; and IMF staff estimates.
Note: Data labels in panel 1 use International Organization for Standardization (ISO) country codes. E = estimated; S29 = euro area economies (Austria, Belgium, France, Germany, Ireland, Italy, Luxembourg, The Netherlands, Finland, Spain), other systemically important advanced economies (Australia, Canada, Denmark, Hong Kong SAR, Japan, Korea, Norway, Singapore, Sweden, Switzerland, the United Kingdom, the United States), and systemically important emerging market economies (Brazil, China, India, Mexico, Poland, Russia, Turkey).

financial institutions and banks imply that fragilities could spread more easily through the financial system. Looking ahead, a prolonged period of low interest rates and high cross-asset correlations may pose further challenges for institutional investors, whereas a widely held belief that central banks will continue to suppress volatility may incentivize investors to take on more risk and increase financial leverage to boost their returns.

Sovereign Debt Levels and Contingent Liabilities Have Increased

The COVID-19 crisis is expected to push global public debt above 100 percent of GDP in 2020, the highest ever (see the October 2020 *Fiscal Monitor*). The large fiscal lifelines in response to the pandemic, coupled with the sharp decline in output and higher automatic stabilizers, have led to rapid expansion of sovereign debt. As a result, public debt reached historic highs in most systemically important economies at the end of the first quarter of 2020 (Figure 1.16, panel 1).

In 2020, headline fiscal deficits in advanced economies are expected to be five times higher than in 2019 (see the October 2020 *Fiscal Monitor*). Emerging markets' fiscal deficits have increased at a more modest pace, largely reflecting financing constraints.

In the baseline scenario, public debt ratios are generally expected to stabilize in 2021, except in the United States and China. Unlike advanced economies, emerging market economies will face greater fiscal challenges, as their ratios of debt service to tax revenue are projected to rise (see the October 2020 WEO). Although accommodative monetary policy could push interest rates lower, hence potentially reducing sustainability concerns at higher debt-to-GDP levels, there could be a feedback loop between high public debt and the risk premium (Alcidi and Gros 2019; Lian, Presbitero, and Wiriadinata 2020). Because private sector financing costs are linked to the sovereign risk premium, central banks in emerging market economies where sovereign debt levels are already high may face greater challenges in easing financial conditions when they need to cushion the impact of an adverse shock on the economy and the financial system. This is because a sharp increase in the sovereign risk premium could offset the central banks' efforts to lower market interest rates.

In addition, sovereigns may be facing a sharp rise in contingent liabilities. With the outbreak of the pandemic, vulnerabilities have increased across multiple sectors (as shown in Figure 1.9), with 6 out of S29 jurisdictions now showing elevated vulnerabilities in the corporate, banking, and sovereign sectors (Figure 1.16, panel 2).[18] Furthermore, bank holdings of government debt have increased in most countries, again tightening sovereign-bank linkages. The simultaneous increase in vulnerabilities in the private and public sectors can also raise financial stability risks through sovereign-corporate linkages at the local government level, as is illustrated by the analysis presented for the case of China (see Box 1.3).

Some Emerging and Frontier Markets May Face External Financing Challenges

Local currency government bond issuance—the primary source of funding for many emerging market sovereigns—picked up pace as the global backdrop improved and domestic financial conditions in many economies eased. Several emerging market economies, such as Chile, Colombia, and Thailand, have managed to fund large portions of their projected deficits for 2020–21 (see Figure 1.17, panel 1), but many other economies still face significant financing requirements. Concerns about future debt supply and weak domestic fundamentals have curtailed demand by nonresident investors, and portfolio flows into local currency bond funds remain weak since the COVID-19 sell-off (Figure 1.17, panel 2).[19] As a result, many emerging markets (India and Mexico, among others) have delayed new local debt issuance to

the second half of the year; some have increased their reliance on foreign currency debt,[20] whereas elsewhere (Indonesia, Poland) central banks have purchased bonds in the secondary market (see Chapter 2). Countries where the domestic investor base may not be deep enough to absorb the additional supply could face some financing challenges.

The extraordinary level and speed of portfolio outflows from February to April 2020 created significant disruptions for emerging markets. Aggregate portfolio flows to emerging markets have recovered since then, driven primarily by hard currency bond issuance, though more than half of emerging market economies have continued to experience outflows over the past three months, suggesting that investors are differentiating across countries based on economic fundamentals and policy frameworks. IMF staff analysis based on the capital-flows-at-risk methodology (see the April 2020 GFSR) points to an improvement in the short- and medium-term outlook on the back of easy global financial conditions, with the probability of outflows over the next three quarters falling from about 60 percent at the peak of market turmoil (black line in Figure 1.17, panel 3) to about 25 percent in September (red line in Figure 1.17, panel 3), though still above the pre–COVID-19 level. Even before the pandemic, emerging market economies had elevated debt vulnerabilities (see the October 2018 GFSR) and were dependent on portfolio flows (see the April 2020 GFSR). Increased fiscal deficits and external funding needs (relative to exports) have made some emerging markets even more vulnerable to shifts in external financing conditions, and these challenges are unlikely to moderate in the near term (see Figure 1.17, panel 4).

Frontier market economies face considerable financing challenges. Even before the global recession, the share of frontier market economies in debt distress or at high risk of debt distress was relatively high (see the October 2019 GFSR). The COVID-19 shock pushed borrowing costs for many of these economies to prohibitive levels (Figure 1.18, panel 1). The Group of Twenty debt service suspension initiative sought to help some 73 countries deal with financing pressures by allowing them to temporarily stop debt payments to official creditors. The recent improvement in market

---

[18]The sovereign vulnerability indicators behind Figures 1.9 and 1.17 include standard balance-sheet indicators, such as government debt-to-GDP ratio, primary balance, maturity profile, etc. The assessment relies on the comparison of the latest values of these indicators with those of a panel of peer countries (cross-section and across time) (see annex to the April 2019 GFSR on the Indicator Based Framework [IBF]). The objective of the IBF is to assess the extent of financial vulnerabilities, which tend to contribute to distress, in different countries and sectors. The forward-looking assessments of the risk of distress (typically presented in the IMF debt sustainability assessments) are not part of the IBF.

[19]This is consistent with the findings of the April 2020 GFSR that domestic fundamentals tend to influence local currency bond flows more than hard currency bond flows.

[20]Foreign-law foreign currency sovereign debt issuance has taken place at a record pace thus far in 2020. Some issuers have also relied on increased local-law foreign currency debt issuance, such as Turkey reflecting greater investor demand. Other countries with high foreign currency debt issuance in total government debt include Argentina and Ukraine.

Figure 1.17. Emerging Market Financing: Challenges, Options, and Risks

Government financing burdens remain steep in some countries with issuance still lagging.

Investor flows into local currency bond funds remain weak.

1. Local Currency Government Bond Gross Issuance Complete Relative to Estimated Total Issuance
(Percent of total)

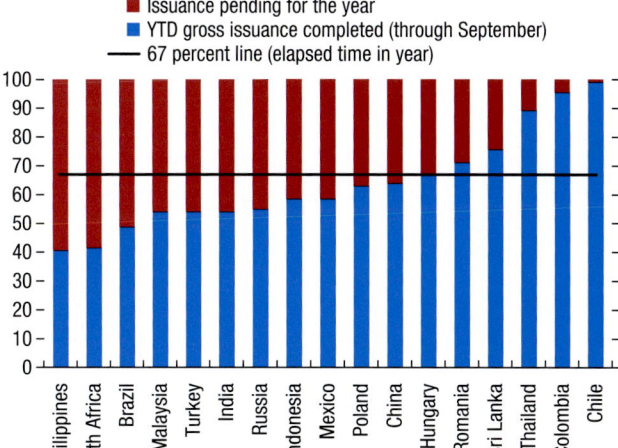

2. EPFR Global Emerging Market Debt Dedicated Fund Flows and Returns
(Cumulative, year to date, billions of US dollars, left scale; percent, right scale)

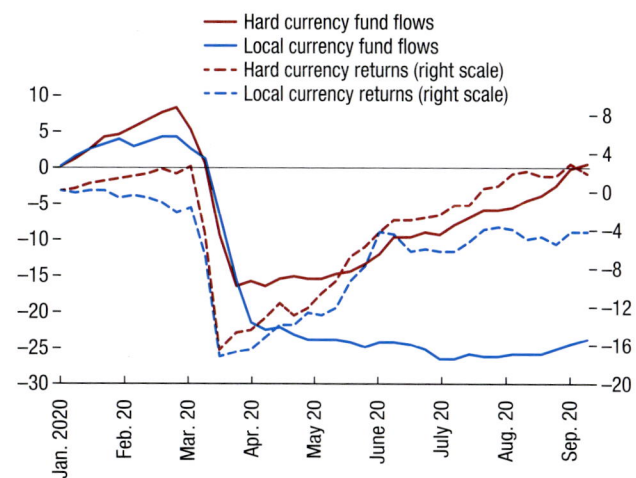

The outlook for portfolio flows remains challenging, with nearly 25 percent probability of outflows next year.

The COVID-19 pandemic has exacerbated existing vulnerabilities, which are likely to remain elevated.

3. Capital Flows at Risk: Near-Term Portfolio Flow Forecast Densities
(Probability Density)

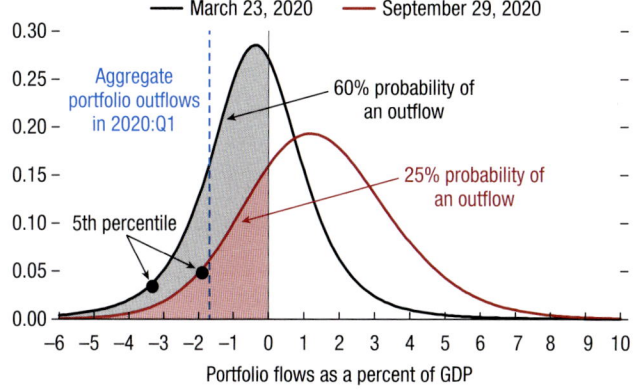

4. Evolution of Sovereign Debt and External Financing Requirements for EMs
(Percentile rank since 1990)

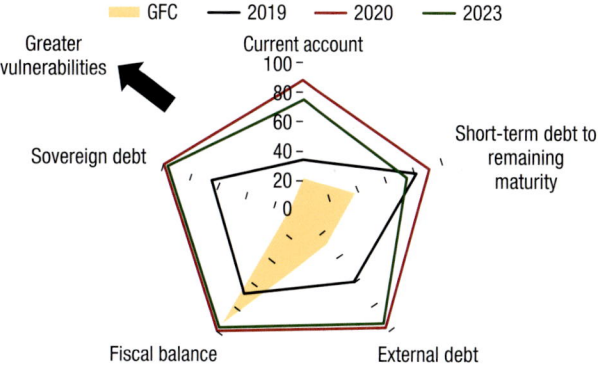

Sources: Bloomberg Finance L.P.; Haver Analytics; HSBC analyst estimates; IMF, World Economic Outlook database; JP Morgan estimates; national sources; and IMF staff estimates.
Note: In panel 1, data are not adjusted for inflation-linked debt. In panel 3, the analysis consists of portfolio flows (including both debt and equity components), based on the model introduced in the April 2020 *Global Financial Stability Report*. The sample consists of 19 large and liquid emerging markets (Brazil, Bulgaria, Chile, Colombia, Egypt, Hungary, India, Indonesia, Korea, Malaysia, Mexico, Peru, Philippines, Poland, Romania, Russia, South Africa, Thailand, Turkey). The capital flows at risk (measured as the 5th percentile of the distribution) stands at −1.9 percent of GDP according to the latest assessment, which compares with −3.3 percent of GDP on March 23 and realized portfolio outflows of almost 2 percent of GDP in 2020:Q1. In panel 4, the indicators are scaled by GDP. The figure plots the percentile rank of the median value of the respective indicators across 71 major emerging markets in the corresponding year. The percentile rank is calculated since 1990. 2020 and 2023 estimates are based on World Economic Outlook database estimates. EMs = emerging markets; GFC = global financial crisis; YTD = year to date.

Figure 1.18. Emerging and Frontier Market Economy Spreads and Market Access

The COVID-19 pandemic pushed spreads of lower-rated economies to prohibitive levels ...

... bringing into focus the large refinancing needs of several frontier market economies.

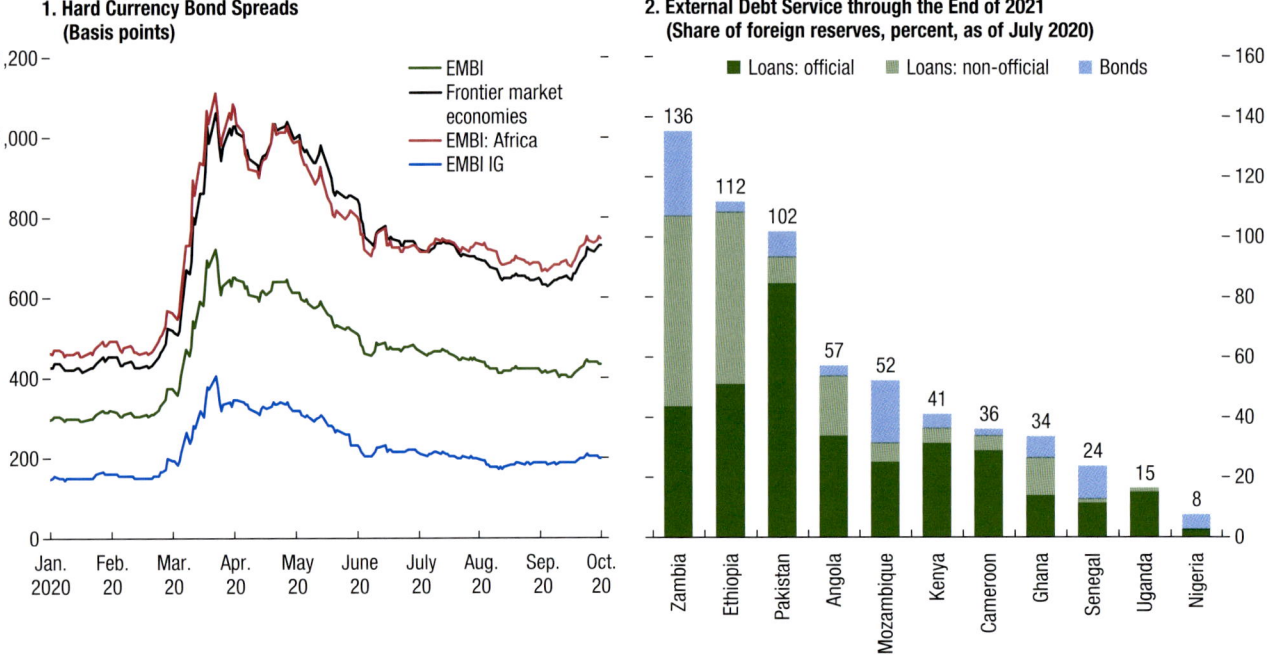

Sources: Bloomberg Finance L.P.; World Bank Debtor Reporting System; and IMF staff calculations.
Note: EMBI = JP Morgan Emerging Markets Bond Index; IG = investment grade.

conditions has reduced these pressures, but many low-income countries with marketable debt have large rollover needs (Figure 1.18, panel 2). This includes some that are eligible for the debt service suspension initiative but are still unable to access international markets at pre–COVID-19 spreads (see Chapter 2 for discussion of the role of creditor composition).

In late July and early August, Argentina and Ecuador reached restructuring deals with bondholders. These deals marked the end of protracted negotiations over both legal and financial terms and were a positive milestone for debt restructuring frameworks going forward.

Policies Need to Focus on Supporting a Sustainable Recovery

The pandemic has led to the worst global recession since the Great Depression, and decisive and timely policy actions have so far cushioned its impact on households and firms, and managed to prevent economic stress from escalating into a full-fledged financial crisis. As the economic recovery takes hold,

the policy focus will shift from dealing with liquidity pressures to *managing a gradual reopening of the economy* and *supporting the recovery*. Table 1.1 provides a road map for monetary and financial sector policies at different stages of the crisis.

Policy Priorities during Gradual Reopening Under Uncertainty

During this phase, which corresponds to the current situation in a number of countries, lockdown measures are eased, but uncertainty remains high, and containment measures may need to be reimposed if there is a resurgence in cases. The priority for the gradual reopening phase is to ensure that policy support is maintained for the recovery to take hold and become sustainable.

- *Monetary accommodation should be maintained.* After aggressively cutting policy rates early in the crisis, most advanced economies are now facing effective lower bounds for conventional monetary policy, though there is still room for further policy cuts in many emerging markets. Central bank balance

Table 1.1. Monetary and Financial Policy Road Map

Policy Areas	Great Lockdown	Gradual Reopening under Uncertainty	Pandemic under Control
Monetary Policy	Ease monetary policy, including use of unconventional monetary policy tools	Maintain monetary policy accommodation	Maintain monetary policy accommodation until the policy objectives (for example, inflation target) are achieved
Liquidity Support to Core Funding Markets	Provide support to maintain market functioning and liquidity	Maintain support, but adjust pricing as appropriate to incentivize and prepare the ground for exit from use of central bank facilities	Gradually withdraw support, as warranted
Liquidity Support to Financial Institutions	Provide support to alleviate liquidity stress and support monetary policy accommodation	Maintain support, but adjust pricing as appropriate to incentivize the return to normal market funding	Maintain liquidity support only as required to support monetary policy accommodation
Measures to Maintain the Flow of Credit	Release macroprudential buffers, allow the use of capital and liquidity buffers, and apply regulatory flexibility as appropriate Suspend the distribution of banks' profits (dividend payouts and share buybacks) Provide financing support to households and businesses (see below)	Continue allowing the use of capital and liquidity buffers Suspend the distribution of banks' profits (dividend payouts and share buybacks)	Rebuild capital and liquidity buffers gradually over time while ensuring continued financial institutions' capacity to extend credit
Measures to Address Problem Assets	Provide guidance on asset classification and provisioning	Maintain prudential standards to incentivize the recognition and handling of problem assets	Require banks to develop credible plans to reduce problem assets over an appropriate period of time Handle weak banks that experience significant credit losses Foster the development of markets for distressed assets
Financing Support to Business	Provide credit guarantees (or other risk mitigation) and term funding to support new lending	Maintain financing support if containment measures are reintroduced, but tighten eligibility criteria to better target illiquid but solvent firms	Withdraw unwarranted support
Debt Restructuring for Businesses and Households	Introduce repayment moratoria	Extend repayment moratoria only if necessary to prevent widespread insolvencies Facilitate debt restructuring that reduces debt overhang and/or adjust repayment schedule Provide solvency support to viable systemic firms, grants for smaller firms Ensure efficient out-of-court agreements, with fast-track procedures to support debt restructuring	Facilitate debt restructuring that reduces debt overhang

Source: IMF staff.

sheets have also grown significantly since March 2020. Some emerging market central banks have launched asset purchase programs to stabilize local markets and ease financial conditions, but in some cases, these purchases have also facilitated financing of government deficits. In such cases, transparency and clear communication of the policy objectives are crucial to minimize risks to central bank credibility and the perception that these programs are used for monetary financing—especially in countries with weaker institutional and governance frameworks (see Chapter 2).

- *The necessary liquidity support to financial markets and institutions should be maintained.* A number of backstops remain in place.[21] Many central bank programs were designed to provide support at prices that were attractive in stressed markets but are at a premium in normal conditions. This feature creates incentives for financial institutions to return to markets as funding conditions normalize. The presence of these facilities still provides support to markets, even if actual use is limited.

- *Banks should be encouraged to continue lending.* Whereas banks should continue to make use of the flexibility built into regulatory frameworks, prudential and accounting standards for loan classification and provisioning should be maintained.[22] Timely and reliable recognition of loan losses based on the expected credit loss framework (under International Financial Reporting Standard 9) is essential, but country authorities may want to delay the impact of additional provisions on regulatory capital, with adequate disclosure of fully loaded capital positions. Supervisors should provide guidance on how banks should deal with restructured loans, including those resulting from moratoria on loan repayments. For example, in commercial real estate markets, extended forbearance and foreclosure moratoriums could help limit contagion across commercial property markets (see Box 1.1). Guidance on the usability of bank buffers, including the optimal pace of rebuilding these buffers once the recovery becomes

sustainable, should be balanced against the need for banks to continue providing credit to the economy during both reopening and recovery phases.

- *Policymakers should develop effective strategies to deal with corporate and household solvency pressures.* Measures to alleviate liquidity stress can provide only temporary relief. Financing support will further increase indebtedness, whereas firms and households may still face some financing difficulties after the moratoria on debt repayments are lifted. Policymakers should shift their focus to solvency support. For instance, solvency support for firms deemed strategic or systemic could mitigate adverse macro-financial consequences. For SMEs, which account for a large share of employment in some countries, governments could consider providing grants (see the October 2020 WEO).

- *Emerging and frontier market economies facing financing difficulties may require official support.* Financing widening fiscal deficits could be a challenge because of deteriorating public finances and shallow domestic markets.[23] The IMF has proactively provided financing support to member countries during the COVID-19 crisis (80 countries to date).[24] However, public debt may become unsustainable in some countries, and debt restructuring with international creditors would be needed to safeguard macro-financial stability.

Policy Responses if Recovery is Delayed

- *In the event of a deterioration of the economic outlook (for example, due to new outbreaks), policymakers should be prepared to scale up liquidity support but in a more targeted manner.* Targeted fiscal measures would be an efficient way to help the most vulnerable firms and individuals (see the October 2020 *Fiscal Monitor*). Eligibility criteria would need to be gradually tightened to ensure that most of the support goes to viable firms.[25] This would help prevent a buildup of debt overhang further down the road, support necessary business adjustments and debt restructuring, and facilitate post-pandemic reallocation of resources. Moratoria on repayments,

---

[21]For example, the Federal Reserve extended its support programs until the end of 2020.

[22]According to the Financial Stability Board, there have been a few cases of measures that went beyond the flexibility of the standards (reducing certain credit risk capital and leverage ratio requirements, lowering liquidity requirements, and postponing the application of the large exposure framework), but most of these measures are temporary and will be reversed as the crisis abates.

[23]For guidance on how sovereign debt managers handle financing challenges, see IMF (2020c).

[24]For an overview of policy responses to maintain macro-financial stability in emerging market and developing economies, see IMF (2020d).

[25]For guidance on how to provide liquidity support to businesses, see IMF (2020b).

which provide temporary relief, should be extended only if necessary to prevent widespread insolvencies stemming from renewed lockdowns.

- *Monetary policy may have to be eased further as needed to support the flow of credit to the economy.* Emergency lending and unconventional monetary policy easing may have to be reactivated or expanded, depending on country circumstances, if the economy slips into an adverse scenario in coming months.
- *Policymakers should provide solvency support to mitigate systemic risk.* Targeted transfers and tax relief could be provided to hard-hit businesses and households. In addition, governments could scale up the solvency support to viable firms that are deemed strategic or systemic individually or collectively to mitigate adverse macro-financial consequences.

Policy Priorities once Pandemic Is under Control

Once the virus is fully under control, policymakers should build on the policy actions taken during the gradual reopening phase, but with a greater focus on tackling solvency issues to ensure a sustainable recovery and completing the structural transformation of the economy to the new post-pandemic normal.

- *Monetary policy accommodation should be maintained until central bank objectives are achieved.* Given expectations of continued low inflation (see Online Annex 1.1) and the likelihood of a pronounced decline in real interest rates for many years, central banks (including the US Federal Reserve and the European Central Bank) are considering adjustments to their monetary policy frameworks and communications to ensure policy efficacy, especially at the effective lower bounds.[26]
- *Liquidity support should be withdrawn as warranted once conditions improve.* Term funding provided to banks may be maintained as needed to support credit flows and ensure a sustainable recovery.[27] Prolonged central bank support in key financial markets may distort price discovery and affect

market liquidity as well as encourage excessive risk taking if it becomes embedded in investor expectations. Systemwide liquidity support should be withdrawn as market conditions normalize. Protracted liquidity support, including financing support to businesses and moratoria on repayments, could keep nonviable borrowers afloat. This could delay the business restructuring, balance sheet correction, and resource reallocation that are necessary to restore macro-financial resilience.

- *Banks should be encouraged to proactively clean up nonperforming loans.* Banks with high levels of nonperforming loans should be required to develop and implement credible action plans to reduce nonperforming loans within an appropriate time frame. To underpin confidence, authorities should ensure that banks maintain transparency on the performance of their loan portfolios, the materiality of loan restructuring, and any material adjustments made to risk management and accounting policies. Some banks may face capital shortfalls as they recognize credit losses. Supervisors may consider suspending automatic triggers for corrective actions and instead require banks to present credible plans to restore their capital.[28] Exceptional measures taken to support distressed borrowers should be phased once conditions allow.
- *Policymakers should develop effective strategies to deal with private debt overhang.* Well-functioning insolvency frameworks can help ensure efficient exit of nonviable firms and facilitate the necessary structural transformation. Firms facing solvency challenges should be recapitalized, restructured, or resolved:
  - *Recapitalization* could be an option for firms deemed viable (for example, with earnings sufficient to cover interest expenses). In such cases, equity-like support could prove more useful than liquidity support (as liquidity support leads firms to accumulate more debt). Modalities could vary depending on firms' characteristics (SMEs, for example, as discussed previously) and would need to account for country-specific institutional and legal frameworks.
  - *Restructuring* of debt could be suitable for firms facing structural challenges (because of the

[26]For example, Jordà, Singh, and Taylor (2020) found that past pandemics were followed by sustained periods of depressed investment opportunities and/or increased precautionary saving.

[27]Some central banks are beginning to withdraw support with no impact on market functioning. Examples include a reduction in the size and frequency of open market operations in most advanced economies and moderation of the pace of purchases of government securities in some advanced economies.

[28]For discussion of banking regulatory and supervisory issues in response to the COVID-19 crisis, see IMF (2020a).

COVID-19 pandemic). In such cases, adjustments to firms' business models would be required to restore viability. Simplified, standardized procedures should be developed to facilitate out-of-court agreements on debt restructuring.

o *Resolution*, or facilitation of an orderly exit, should be applied to unviable firms that cannot be saved through restructuring. Fostering the development of markets for distressed assets would facilitate their disposal.

- *Policymakers should prepare to deal with the implications of corporate and household insolvencies for banks and nonbank financial institutions, as well as for sovereigns.* Bank and nonbank financial institutions will need to absorb credit losses, and some regulated financial institutions may experience capital shortfalls. Country authorities should ensure that banks have credible recovery strategies in place and develop (or update) contingency plans for institutions displaying substantial fragilities. Resolution tools, which have been strengthened since the global financial crisis, should be used as necessary to resolve failing banks in an orderly way. At the sovereign level, steps should be taken to develop a credible medium-term fiscal strategy to ensure debt sustainability in the medium term, considering that prolonged policy support could translate into significant fiscal costs.

- *Policymakers should adopt policies to encourage more proactive management of climate-change-related risks.* The pandemic, despite substantial negative effects on firms' environmental performance (see Chapter 5), presents an opportunity to engineer a green recovery. Policymakers should encourage the appropriate pricing of climate-change-related risks through gradual and well-communicated implementation of carbon taxes, better disclosure of climate-change-related risks, and increased use of climate stress tests for financial institutions. This could in turn generate the right incentives to reduce exposures to physical risk and expedite the transition.

- *Policymakers should adopt policies to encourage greater digital investment to enhance financial sector efficiency and inclusion.* The pandemic may have accelerated the transition of the economy toward digitalization. Digital investment should enable the financial

system to cut expenses (for example, physical branches) and extend services to underserved populations, thereby increasing financial inclusion. Digital currencies in particular could offer substantial efficiency gains, especially in cross-border payments, and reach unbanked populations. However, they need to be carefully regulated to ensure financial stability and integrity, operational safety, market contestability, and consumer protection.

Post-Pandemic Financial Reform Agenda

To safeguard global financial stability and promote inclusive, sustainable growth in the post-pandemic era, the regulatory reform agenda should focus on strengthening the regulatory framework for nonbank financial sector and stepping up prudential supervision to curb excessive risk taking in the lower-for-longer interest rate environment:

- *Strengthening the regulatory framework for the nonbank financial sector:* In light of lessons learned during the COVID-19 crisis—including central banks' need to backstop essential segments of financial markets—policymakers should assess the effectiveness of prudential tools that are currently available and consider strengthening the prudential regulation as well as broadening the regulatory perimeter of nonbank financial institutions.

o The operational frameworks for central counterparty clearing houses (CCPs) have to be adjusted in light of the crisis experience (see April 2020 GFSR). While CCPs played an important role in cushioning the impact of market stress during the March sell-off, policymakers should examine options for prudently limiting procyclicality in margin calls as well as ensuring derivatives counterparties are able to anticipate and prepare for them.

o To enhance the global financial system's resilience, a more robust liquidity risk management framework should be adopted for *investment funds* (International Organization of Securities Commissions 2018), including a broad set of tools to better manage redemptions as well as to identify related risks early (see the October 2019 GFSR). The usability of liquidity buffers in crisis times—which has proven key in the banking sector this year—could be more actively considered. To the extent the swing pricing has been successful in helping to contain redemptions, a wider adoption would be advisable, particularly in jurisdictions with sizable asset management sectors. Given jurisdiction-specific institutional and legal arrangements, however, swing pricing will likely have to be phased in over time, requiring modifications to the existing operational infrastructure. An internationally harmonized measurement of leverage in investment funds (International Organization of Securities Commissions 2019) should help with the timely recognition and mitigation of respective financial stability risks.

- *Implementing micro- and macroprudential measures to curb excessive risk taking in the lower-for-longer interest rate environment:* With market participants anticipating interest rates to remain very low for the foreseeable future, investor search for yield is likely to resume and may lead to excessive risk taking. Given the existing balance sheet weaknesses, a further buildup of leverage in the post-pandemic world should be contained appropriately. The macroprudential policy framework should be strengthened to ensure adequate capital and liquidity buffers in banking systems, to contain excessive risk taking in the nonbank financial sector and to create macroprudential space that could be used to cushion the impact of adverse shocks on the economy and financial system.[29] Prudential authorities could implement measures such as loan-to-value ratio and debt-to-income ratio to prevent excessive risk taking that could inflate property prices, including in the commercial real estate segment (see Box 1.2).

---

[29]For instance, the ECB emphasized in its recent Financial Stability Review the importance of creating the macroprudential space in the euro area in the form of releasable countercyclical capital buffers (CCyBs) to help sustain credit in a downturn.

Box 1.1. Are Financial Stability Risks Rising in Commercial Real Estate Markets?

Market participants and policymakers have increasingly pointed to the commercial real estate sector as a potential source of financial stability risks because of its notable size, procyclicality, and systemic nature. In several economies, commercial real estate loans constitute a significant part of banks' lending portfolio, especially at local and regional banks.[1] Commercial mortgage-backed securities issuance has also recovered since the global financial crisis, with the total volume exceeding $100 billion in 2019 (Figure 1.1.1, panel 1). Historically, volatility in the commercial property market has often been an amplifier of macro-financial instability—for example, in the United States in 2008.

In recent years, the riskiness of the commercial real estate sector has increased globally. Over 2009–19, commercial property asset valuations rose, on average, 4.5 percent a year to reach historical highs in several economies.[2] Concurrently, capitalization rates—which measure rental income relative to the value of the property—fell to their lowest levels (Figure 1.1.1, panel 2).

The COVID-19 crisis has inflicted significant pain on the sector. Worldwide commercial property transactions slumped by about 50 percent in the second quarter of 2020 relative to last year, as containment measures imposed in response to the pandemic adversely affected economic activity and reduced the demand for commercial properties. Within the sector, retail and hospitality businesses have been the most affected, with sales down by 60 percent and 80 percent, respectively (Figure 1.1.1, panel 3). Available price data also point to a significant decline, especially in the retail sector, with the retail sector price index falling by about 18 percent and 23 percent in July,

year over year, in the European Union and the United States, respectively (Figure 1.1.1, panel 4).

Stress in funding markets early this year reverberated through the commercial real estate sector. Funding costs increased sharply in mid-March, with the spread on BBB-rated commercial mortgage-backed securities and commercial mortgage-backed security indices remaining much higher in June relative to the pre-pandemic level (Figure 1.1.1, panel 5). Syndicated commercial real estate lending dropped by about 50 percent in North America, 70 percent in Europe, and 40 percent in Asia in the second quarter of 2020, year over year. Whereas the slowdown in lending may partly be a result of a drop in demand, increasing delinquency rates and tightening of credit conditions for bank loans, as is evident from the US Senior Loan Officer Opinion Survey, may have also played a role (Figure 1.1.1, panel 6).[3]

Looking ahead, there is considerable uncertainty about the outlook for the commercial real estate sector. As economies open up, activity in the sector is likely to pick up. However, based on current projections from rating agencies, the commercial mortgage-backed securities default rates are expected to more than double in the third quarter of 2020, suggesting that the sector may remain under pressure for a while. Moreover, segments such as retail could continue to face headwinds even after the pandemic is over because of the ongoing increased shift toward e-commerce. The demand for office space may also drop as companies experiencing cost savings of work-from-home arrangements consider extending them into the future.[4] All in all, these shifts could induce significant volatility in commercial property markets and bear close monitoring to limit broader macro-financial stability risks.

The authors of this box are Andrea Deghi and Salih Fendoglu.
[1] In the United States and the euro area, for example, commercial real estate loans constituted 50 percent and 23 percent, respectively, of total bank lending to nonfinancial corporates in 2019.
[2] In some economies, for example Hong Kong SAR, Sweden, and the United States, commercial real estate valuations more than doubled between 2009 and 2019.

[3] In the United States, 5.8 percent of commercial mortgage-backed securities loans were delinquent in the second quarter of 2020, an increase of more than 200 basis points relative to the previous year.
[4] For example, a recent corporate survey by Green Street Advisors shows that the propensity of staff to work from home in the medium to long term has increased by about 30 percentage points since the pandemic crisis.

Box 1.1 *(continued)*

Figure 1.1.1. Trends and Developments in Commercial Real Estate Markets

CMBS issuance has increased since the global financial crisis ...

1. CMBS Issuance
(Billions of US dollars)

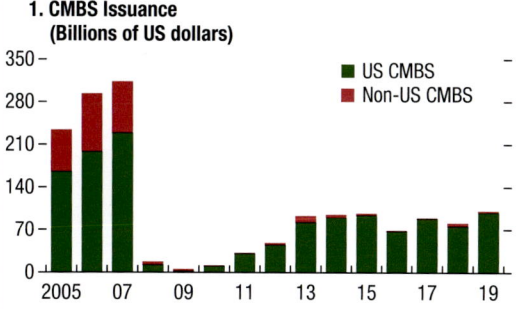

... whereas capitalization rates have continued to fall.

2. Capitalization Rates for Selected Economies
(Percent)

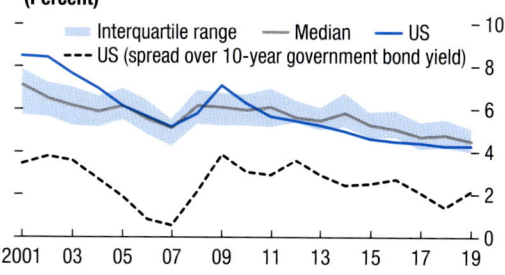

Global commercial property transactions fell sharply in 2020:Q2 ...

3. Change in CRE Transaction Volumes
(Percent, 2020:Q2 versus 2019:Q2)

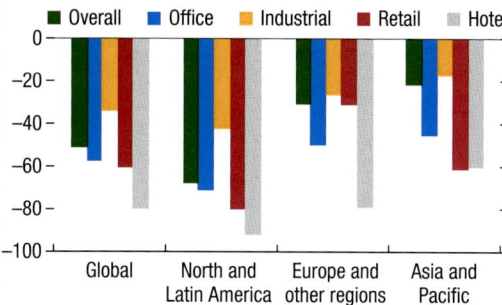

... with prices also dropping, especially in the retail sector.

4. Change in CRE Prices across Sectors
(Percent, July 2020 versus July 2019)

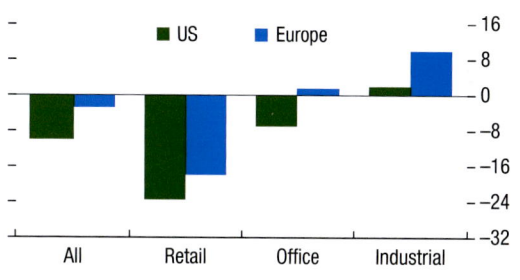

Funding costs in the CMBS market have increased sharply ...

5. CMBS Funding Conditions in the United States
(Basis points)

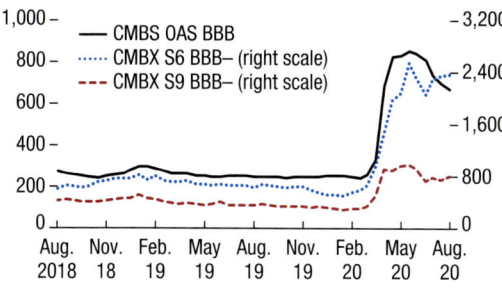

... whereas lending standards have tightened, and delinquency rates have inched up in 2020:Q2.

6. Credit Standards and Delinquency Rates in the US CMBS Market
(Percent)

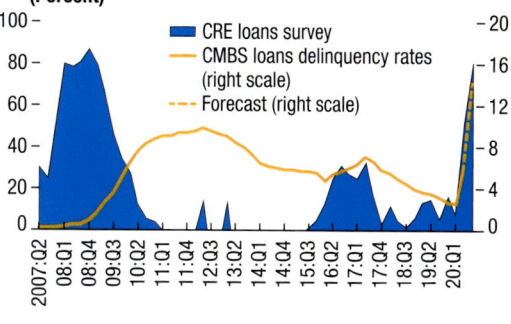

Sources: Bloomberg L.P.; Commercial Mortgage Alert; Federal Reserve Bank; Green Street Advisors; Moody's; MSCI Real Estate; Real Capital Analytics; and IMF staff calculations.
Note: Panel 1 shows the total issuance of CMBS for the United States and other countries. Panel 2 shows the capitalization rate for the United States and other selected economies and the spread of the US capitalization rate over the 10-year US government bond yield. Selected economies are Australia, Austria, Belgium, Canada, China, the Czech Republic, Denmark, Finland, France, Hungary, Hong Kong SAR, Indonesia, Ireland, Italy, Japan, Korea, Malaysia, The Netherlands, New Zealand, Norway, Poland, Portugal, Singapore, South Africa, Spain, Sweden, Taiwan Province of China, Thailand, and the United Kingdom. Panel 3 shows the change in global real estate sales (single asset, portfolio, entity) in 2020:Q2 relative to 2019:Q2. Panel 4 shows the change in the commercial property price index in July 2020 relative to July 2019 for different CRE sectors and for the overall market. Panel 5 shows the spreads over the Treasury yield curve for the Bloomberg Barclays Global Aggregate BBB index and the CMBX S6 and CMBX S9. Panel 6 shows the percent of respondents in the US Senior Loan Officer Opinion Survey indicating a tightening in CRE lending standards and CMBS loan delinquency rates (historical and projected to 2020:Q3). CMBS = commercial mortgage-backed security; CMBX = commercial mortgage-backed security index; CRE = commercial real estate; OAS = option-adjusted spread; US = United States.

Box 1.2. The Behavior of Investment Funds during COVID-19 Market Turmoil

In March 2020 the global investment fund sector and, in particular, fixed-income and nongovernment money market funds experienced a short period of intense withdrawals as investors redeemed shares following a sharp increase in valuation uncertainty in many asset classes, including debt securities (Figure 1.14, panel 2).[1] The market liquidity of securities held by fixed-income funds deteriorated substantially, as evidenced by the near doubling in the average bid-ask spreads of securities held in their portfolios (Figure 1.2.1, panel 1).[2] Though liquidity declined for almost all fund portfolios, average bid-ask spreads more than tripled temporarily for the most affected portfolios, indicating that a few funds bore the brunt of the liquidity impact, while on average the industry proved resilient.

With only a handful of funds suspending redemptions,[3] most fixed-income funds resorted to a mix of strategies to deal with outflows. First, the most afflicted funds used their relatively ample liquidity buffers and shed liquid assets such as cash, cash equivalents, and US Treasuries to cover redemptions, whereas funds receiving inflows hoarded cash and delayed investments, presumably because of uncertain market conditions (Figure 1.2.1, panel 2). Second, despite large outflows, some funds were willing to purchase assets at high bid-ask spreads, possibly using cash reserves to take advantage of depressed prices of potentially illiquid assets (Figure 1.2.1, panel 2). Third, with their investors more sensitive to performance and less amenable to increased corporate exposures, fixed-income funds were less inclined to retain their relatively high exposures to corporate bonds, especially if they were anticipating more redemptions (Figure 1.2.1, panel 3). In addi-

tion, swing pricing may have helped funds manage redemptions.[4]

As a result, fixed-income funds that were forced to sell assets in response to redemption pressures seem to have had some adverse effect on both asset prices and market liquidity. In March 2020 the bid-ask spreads of assets sold most heavily by fixed-income funds facing large redemptions increased more than the bid-ask spreads of assets not facing such selling pressure. Similarly, during March 2020 cumulative returns of assets under selling pressure declined more than assets experiencing no pressure (Figure 1.2.1, panel 4). Hence, funds' sales of liquid assets are likely to have contributed to price pressures and liquidity strains observed in fixed-income markets. Similarly, increased incentives for funds to sell corporate bonds may have amplified the price dislocations observed in risky credit markets in March 2020. Some funds, however—even some of those experiencing large outflows—may have helped to mitigate price pressures, as they were willing to absorb relatively illiquid assets even under uncertain market conditions (Figure 1.2.1, panel 2, right side, and panel 4).

The behavior of fixed-income funds and their clients during the March 2020 redemption stress episode highlight some fragilities in this industry. Selling relatively liquid assets first might have further intensified funds' liquidity mismatches, if liquidity conditions had not improved so rapidly. The weakening in the average liquidity profile of funds facing outflows may have also made them more susceptible to future redemption or valuation shocks. The sale of less liquid assets has contributed to price dislocations in the underlying asset markets. In combination with fund investors' increased sensitivity to fund performance, this could have generated feedback loops resulting in larger-scale fire sales had central banks not stepped in so quickly with asset purchase programs and liquidity facilities.

Looking ahead, a comprehensive review of available prudential tools in the investment fund sector, including considering a more widespread adoption of swing pricing, would help to mitigate vulnerabilities revealed during the COVID-19 market turmoil.

The authors of this box are Frank Hespeler and Felix Suntheim.

[1] These outflows are still lower than those assumed under the liquidity stress presented in Box 3.1 of the October 2019 *Global Financial Stability Report*.

[2] Based on a sample of 323 fixed-income funds with available information on individual securities held in their portfolios.

[3] Fitch reported for 2020 that mutual funds suspended a total of $62 billion year to date, a mere 0.11 percent of the sector's total assets (Fitch Ratings 2020).

[4] Data limitations did not allow for an analysis of the effectiveness of swing pricing during the March 2020 turmoil period. However, Jin and others (2019) provide respective evidence for UK corporate bond funds during stress periods.

Box 1.2 *(continued)*

Figure 1.2.1. Vulnerabilities of Fixed-Income Funds Exposed during the March 2020 Market Turmoil

During March 2020, the liquidity of the fixed-income funds' portfolios deteriorated substantially.

Funds facing redemptions reduced cash buffers and sold liquid assets, but in some cases also purchased illiquid assets, taking advantage of illiquidity discounts.

1. Bid-Ask Spreads of Fixed-Income Funds' Portfolios
(Percent)

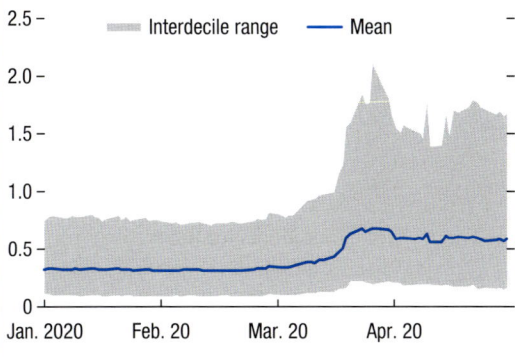

2. Portfolio Shares of Cash and Fund Flows (left panels) and Bid-Ask Spreads of Assets Bought and Sold by Funds (right panel), by Flow Quintile
(Percent)

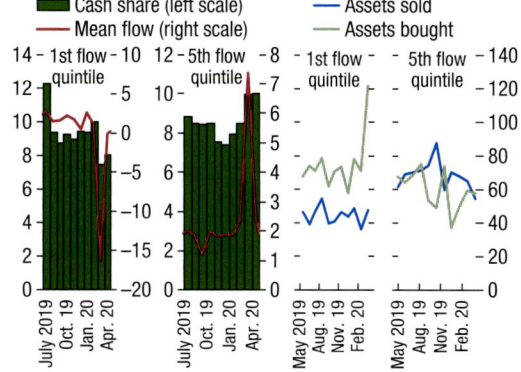

Funds facing outflows saw their investors become more sensitive to performance and were less keen to hold on to corporate bonds ...

... adding to asset sales as well as lower performance and liquidity of assets under high selling pressure compared with other assets.

3. Quantile Regression Coefficients of Fund Flows on Returns and Corporate Bond Exposures
(Percent)

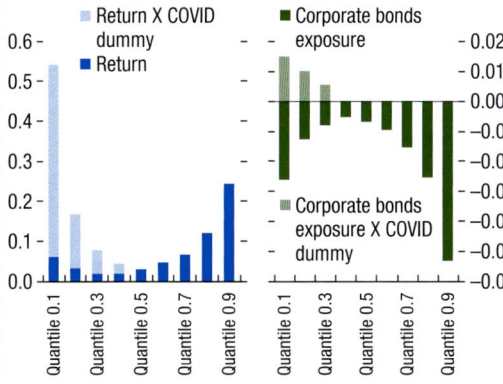

4. Bid-Ask Spreads and Cumulative Returns of Securities under Selling Pressure Held by Fixed-Income Funds
(Percent)

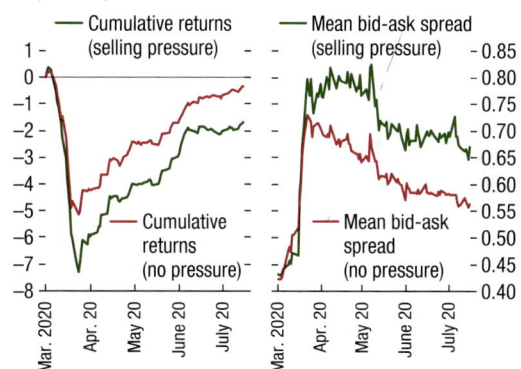

Sources: Bloomberg Finance L.P.; Morningstar; Refinitiv; and IMF staff calculations.
Note: Panel 1 is based on 323 fixed-income funds providing information on securities held in their portfolios. The graph on the left in panel 2 reports average shares of cash and cash equivalents in fixed-income funds with assets over $0.5 billion in extreme flow quintiles. The graph on the right in panel 2 shows the bid-ask spread of the assets bought and sold in a given month, relative to the bid-ask spread of the fund's portfolio. The bid-ask spread of assets sold and bought is the average bid-ask spread in the month the assets were sold or bought. Panel 3 reports coefficients significant at the 5 percent level from unconditional panel quantile regressions of fund flows on portfolio shares of cash, corporate bonds, and sovereign bonds and on returns, fund size, fund age, a quarter dummy, and a coronavirus disease dummy, as well as interactions of the latter with cash, corporate bonds, sovereign bonds, and returns and a set of macro-financial variables, including the Chicago Board Options Exchange Volatility Index, a term spread, a credit risk spread, a proxy for US interest levels, and a basket of major exchange rates versus the US dollar. Fund fixed effects are included. Samples include available monthly data for fixed-income funds with assets over $0.5 billion from January 2015 to May 2020. Panel 4 is based on detailed portfolio holdings data of 390 fixed-income funds holding approximately 13,000 identifiable securities in March 2020. Prices and bid-ask spreads are computed based on Refinitiv composite end-of-day bid and ask prices. Pressure of security in March 2020 is defined similarly to the definition in Coval and Stafford (2007) as the fraction of flow-motivated trading in a security's average monthly trading volume. Flow-motivated trading is the difference between a security's purchases by funds experiencing higher inflows than 90 percent of their peers and the sales by funds facing outflows higher than 90 percent of their peers. The mentioned fraction defines a security as experiencing high selling pressure if it is in the bottom decile of the ratio's distribution across all securities; it is considered to experience no pressure if this ratio exceeds 0.

Box 1.3. Interlinkages among Local Government, Corporate, and Bank Vulnerabilities in China

In China, debt vulnerabilities at the local government level have increased in recent years. Direct borrowing by local governments was first permitted in 2015 but has risen quickly to 24 percent of GDP, significantly outpacing growth in local government tax revenues (Figure 1.3.1, panel 1). Direct borrowing growth has accelerated during the COVID-19 crisis as it became a key funding source for macroeconomic countercyclical measures, including for investment, spending, and even bank recapitalization. This direct debt is considered low risk by investors, reflecting perceptions of central government guarantees.

Local governments also remain exposed to debt owed by off-balance-sheet entities known as local government financing vehicles (LGFVs) and, indirectly, to debt of local government-owned enterprises (local state-owned enterprises [SOEs]). LGFVs are involved primarily in quasi-fiscal projects such as infrastructure, but in recent years have expanded financial linkages to local SOEs and in some cases to private firms, in the form of credit guarantees and capital injections. Entities identifying as LGFVs in bond prospectuses have outstanding debt equivalent to 39 percent of GDP (Figure 1.3.1, panel 1).

Local governments' growing direct debt burdens may affect financial stability by weakening the credibility of their backstop for LGFV and other local debt. This linkage can tighten financial conditions for the corporate sector, transmitting risks from the government to the corporate sector, and ultimately to the banking sector, which is the lender for most corporate debt.

Bond market data show that borrowing conditions for LGFVs and lower-rated non-LGFVs appear sensitive to local governments' direct indebtedness. With weak revenue, LGFVs rely on implicit or explicit government guarantees to access credit. LGFVs in provinces with financially weaker local governments have seen bond market credit spreads widen notably relative to other provinces, whereas overall debt growth has slowed or contracted (Figure 1.3.1, panel 2).

Lower-rated non-LGFV firms appear to be similarly affected by government debt. Province-level bond market credit spreads for this segment saw

sharply increased differentiation based on government direct debt loads in 2019 (Figure 1.3.1, panel 2, bottom-right chart). Increased government debt may weaken backstops for local SOEs and government-backed credit guarantee institutions, indirectly tightening financial conditions for private firms, which often rely on guarantees to access credit. Non-LGFVs may also be weakened by reduced LGFV activity given the significant linkages between them.

Investor concerns about local government debt may have also limited the effectiveness of authorities' COVID-19–related credit measures in financially weaker provinces. Net new credit to the household and corporate sectors in the first half of 2020 was equivalent to 18 percent of 2019 GDP, but 40 percent of that increase occurred in just three provinces. Provinces with worse debt-to-revenue ratios saw significantly weaker credit impulses than the national average (Figure 1.3.1, panel 3).

A large proportion of LGFV and local SOE debt is likely unserviceable, implying significant further deterioration in these local fiscal backstops. Roughly 75 percent (RMB 26 trillion) of outstanding LGFV debt is likely unserviceable, defined as owed by LGFVs with a net-debt-to-earnings ratio of more than 15 or negative earnings. Local SOEs owe another RMB 10 trillion in similarly defined debt. If local governments assume this unserviceable debt, it will more than double existing debt loads and increase by tenfold the debt owed by provinces with debt-to-revenue ratios above 400 percent (Figure 1.3.1, panel 4).

The potential for spillovers to banks is also considerable. Banks are the primary creditors to LGFVs and local SOEs. If these debts develop into nonperforming loans, there will be a large negative spillover effect on banks' asset quality.

Linkages between local governments, firms, and banks could pose significant financial stability risks and underscore the urgency of accelerating structural reforms in China, even as authorities seek to support the recovery from COVID-19. Key priorities should be to strengthen the intergovernmental fiscal coordination framework, introduce bank and corporate restructuring frameworks in line with international best practices, and address remaining gaps in financial supervision and regulation.

This box was prepared by Henry Hoyle.

Box 1.3 *(continued)*

Figure 1.3.1. Interlinkages among Local Government, Corporate, and Bank Vulnerabilities in China

Direct local government debt has been rising faster than indirect debt incurred via local government financing vehicles, outpacing growth in local tax revenues.

Bigger government debt loads may weaken backstops for local firms, resulting in increased credit risk premiums and deleveraging for firms with weaker stand-alone debt servicing capacity.

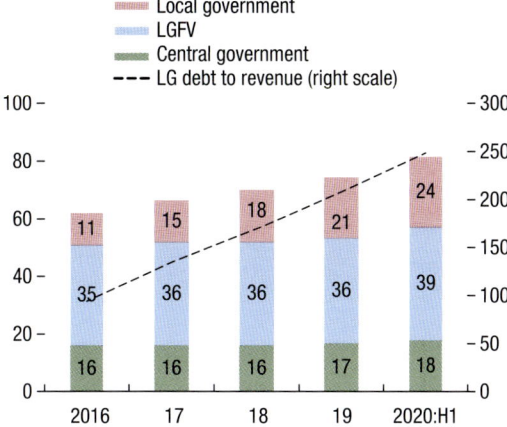

1. China: Government Debt by Type: Local Government Debt to Total Revenue (Percent of GDP; ratio)

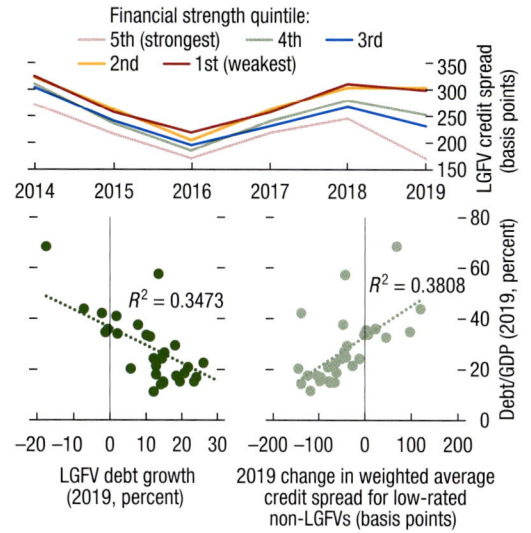

2. China: Selected Measures of Corporate Borrowing Conditions, by Province Quintile

Policy-driven credit growth acceleration in response to the COVID-19 pandemic has disproportionately benefited provinces with more manageable government debt loads.

Much of the LGFV and local SOE debt local governments are exposed to is unserviceable, implying significant further deterioration in backstops.

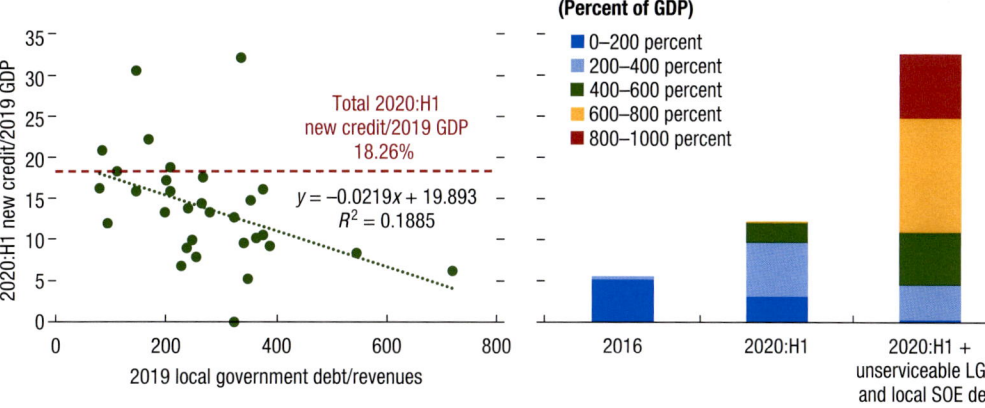

3. China: Province-Level Household and Corporate Credit Growth and Ratio of Government Debt to Revenue (Percent)

4. China: Local Government Direct Borrowing and Unserviceable LGFV and Local SOE Debt, by Ratio of Debt to Revenue (Percent of GDP)

Sources: Bloomberg Finance L.P.; CEIC; and IMF staff calculations.
Note: In panel 1, LGFV debt is based on financial statements of 1,852 firms with bonds designated as urban investment vehicle bonds. 2020:H1 LGFV total borrowing is estimated as the 2020:Q1 level multiplied by the 2020:Q1 quarterly growth rate. In the top chart of panel 2, each line is a quintile of provinces based on equally weighted ranking of fiscal deficit and debt-to-GDP ratio. In the bottom charts of panel 2, each point represents a province. Borrowing cost measures are based on weighted average bond coupons. In the bottom-right chart of panel 2, change is the 2019 average minus the 2018 average. In panel 4, unserviceable debt is defined as debt held by firms with a net debt to EBIT ratio above 15 (or negative earnings). Consolidated firm earnings are added to local government revenues. EBIT = earnings before interest and taxes; LG = local government; LGFV = local government financing vehicle; SOE = state-owned enterprise.

References

Alcidi, Cinzia, and Daniel Gros. 2019. "Public Debt and the Risk Premium: A Dangerous Doom Loop." Centre for European Policy Studies, Brussels.

Coval, Joshua, and Erik Stafford. 2007. "Asset Fire Sales (and Purchases) in Equity Markets." *Journal of Financial Economics* 86 (2): 479–512.

Durham, J. Benson. 2002. "The Extreme Bounds of the Cross-Section of Expected Stock Returns." https://ssrn.com/abstract=333362

Fitch Ratings. 2020. "Global Mutual Fund Redemption Suspensions Highlight Liquidity Mismatches: Application of Extraordinary Liquidity-Management Tools Becoming More Common." https://www.fitchratings.com/research/fund-asset-managers/global-mutual-fund-redemption-suspensions-highlight-liquidity-mismatches-application-of-extraordinary-liquidity-management-tools-becoming-more-common-21-06-2020

International Monetary Fund (IMF). 2020a. "Banking Sector Regulatory and Supervisory Response to Deal with Coronavirus Impact (with Q and A)." IMF Special Series on COVID-19, International Monetary Fund, Washington, DC, May 13.

————. 2020b. "Considerations for Designing Temporary Liquidity Support to Businesses." IMF Special Series on COVID-19, International Monetary Fund, Washington, DC, May 8.

————. 2020c. "Debt Management Responses to the Pandemic." IMF Special Series on COVID-19, International Monetary Fund, Washington, DC, May 6.

————. 2020d. "Monetary and Financial Policy Responses for Emerging Market and Developing Economies." IMF Special Series on COVID-19, International Monetary Fund, Washington, DC, June 8.

International Organization of Securities Commissions (IOSCO). 2018. "Recommendations for Liquidity Risk Management for Collective Investment Schemes." Final Report FR01/2018, The Board of the International Organization of Securities Commissions, Madrid.

————. 2019. "Recommendations for a Framework Assessing Leverage in Investment Funds." Final Report FR18/2019, The Board of the International Organization of Securities Commissions, Madrid.

Jin, Dunhong, Marcin T. Kaperczyk, Bige Kahraman, and Felix Suntheim, 2019. "Swing Pricing and Fragility in Open-end Mutual Funds." IMF Working Paper 19/227, International Monetary Fund, Washington, DC.

Jordà, Òscar, Sanjay Singh, and Alan Taylor. 2020. "Long-Run Economic Consequences of Pandemics." NBER Working Paper 26934, National Bureau of Economic Research, Cambridge, MA.

Lian, W., Andrea Presbitero, and Ursula Wiriadinata. 2020. "Public Debt and r-g at Risk." IMF Working Paper 20/137, International Monetary Fund, Washington, DC.

Panigirtzoglou, Nikolaos, and Robert Scammell. 2002. "Analysts' Earnings Forecasts and Equity Valuations." Bank of England Quarterly Bulletin, Spring, London.

A GREATER SET OF POLICY OPTIONS TO RESTORE STABILITY

Chapter 2 at a Glance

- To mitigate stress in local bond and currency markets, many emerging market central banks used foreign exchange (FX) interventions and, for the first time, asset purchases.
- This *Global Financial Stability Report* (GFSR) presents a novel *local stress index* (LSI) to measure the stress in local bond and currency markets.
- Asset purchase programs (APPs) helped lower government bond yields, did not lead to FX depreciation, and eventually reduced market stress. Asset purchases may have a role to play going forward, but ongoing evaluation of the risks is also needed.
- Strategies to address debt distress in frontier markets need to consider the impact of the expected treatment of different creditors in future debt restructurings on investor perception of risk.

The pandemic has hit emerging and frontier market economies hard, but the policy response has been equally strong. Policymakers have taken steps to soften the hit to economic activity, ease financial conditions, and reduce stress in domestic markets. For the first time, many emerging market central banks have launched asset purchase programs to support the smooth functioning of financial markets and the overall economy. Asset purchases have been effective in reducing bond yields and have not contributed to currency depreciation, but they appear to have taken longer to reduce broader domestic bond market stress. This chapter examines the effectiveness of these unconventional policy measures and concludes that asset purchases with credible monetary policy frameworks and good governance may be a useful addition to the policy toolkit of central banks in emerging and frontier market economies, although a careful ongoing evaluation of associated risks is needed, especially for open-ended programs. In frontier market economies, the policy focus has been on addressing the effect of the pandemic while dealing with high debt. This chapter examines the potential impact on investor perception of sovereign risk as a result of the expected treatment of different classes of creditors in future debt restructurings.

Prepared by staff from the Monetary and Capital Markets Department (in consultation with other departments): The authors of this chapter are Dimitris Drakopoulos, Rohit Goel, Evan Papageorgiou (team leader), Dmitri Petrov, Patrick Schneider, Can Sever, and Jeff Williams, under the guidance of Fabio Natalucci and Anna Ilyina. Magally Bernal and Andre Vasquez were responsible for word processing and the production of this report.

The Global Pandemic Has Required Bold Action

Emerging market economies have responded forcefully to the coronavirus disease (COVID-19) crisis. As a result of the sudden and unprecedented shock to economic activity, most governments have increased spending for emergency measures and transfers (Figure 2.1, panel 1). Over 90 percent of central banks have cut policy rates since March—some to all-time lows—and many have taken measures to provide liquidity to the banking system (Figure 2.1, panels 2 and 3). As a result of these measures and buoyant global risk appetite, financial conditions have eased considerably (see Chapter 1).

This chapter discusses the historic policy responses of emerging market policymakers to the global pandemic and the financial stability implications of those policies. The "FX Intervention by Emerging Market Central Banks" section considers the use and effectiveness of FX interventions during the peak of the crisis and reviews central bank asset purchases—a new policy tool for emerging market economies—including an examination of their effectiveness and lessons to evaluate their risks in the two sections that follow. "The Role of the Official Sector in Frontier Market Economy Debt Restructuring" section discusses many frontier market economies' loss of market access because of COVID-19 and the potential impact of different classes of creditors on debt restructurings and on investor perception of sovereign risk. Building on the findings of the chapter, the final section

Figure 2.1. Emerging Market Policy Response to the COVID-19 Pandemic

The need for emergency spending and the hit to revenues from the sharp economic shock of the COVID-19 crisis increased budget deficits ...

... and most central banks have aggressively cut rates, some to all-time lows.

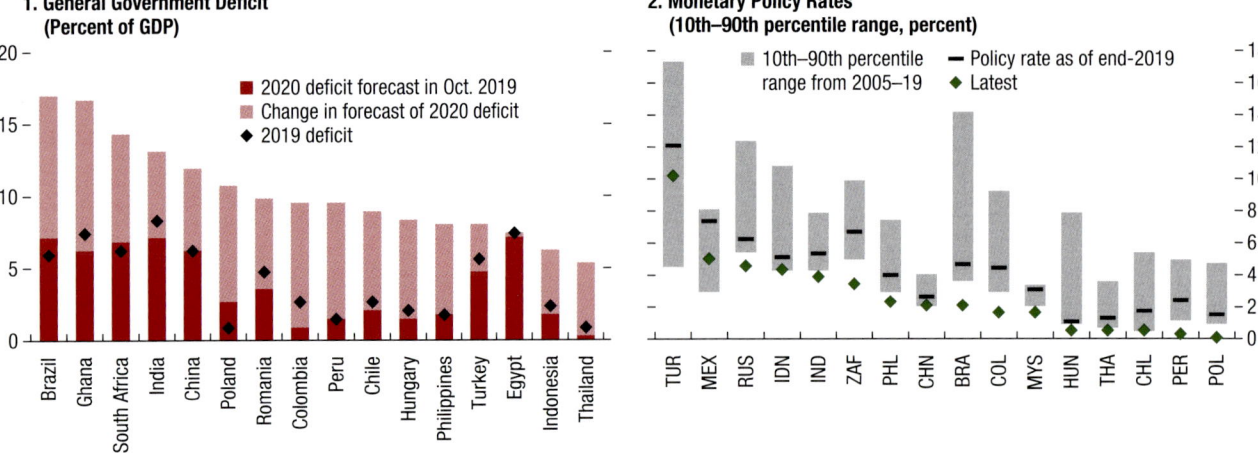

In addition to rate cuts, central banks have responded forcefully to the COVID-19 crisis with an array of measures to boost market liquidity and stabilize economic and financial conditions.

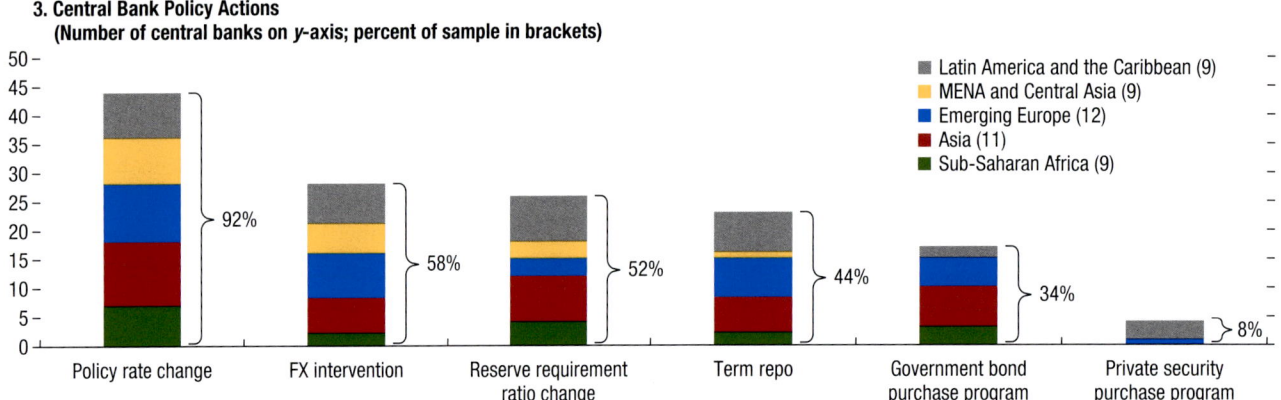

Sources: Bloomberg Finance L.P.; IMF, World Economic Outlook database; national authorities; and IMF staff calculations.
Note: In panel 3, countries are counted only once per action (for example, multiple policy rate cuts are counted once). The sample comprises 50 central banks and does not include any advanced economies. The sample is defined in Online Annex 2.1 and is quantified by region in parentheses. Data labels in panel 2 use International Organization for Standardization (ISO) country codes. FX = foreign exchange; MENA = Middle East and North Africa.

offers policy recommendations. The apparent absence to date of capital flow management measures during the COVID-19 crisis and China's policy challenges in maintaining supportive financial conditions are briefly examined as well (Online Annex Boxes 2.1 and 2.2).

FX Intervention by Emerging Market Central Banks

FX interventions, including in some cases through forward contracts, were widespread at the height of the crisis in March, as policymakers sought to insulate their

economies from external movements in the pricing of risk. While many countries intervened, surpassing recent stress episodes in absolute size (Figure 2.2, panel 1), the use of reserves (as a share of total international reserves) was about two-thirds the magnitude observed during the global financial crisis for the median country (Figure 2.2, panel 2). The limited and short-lived use of reserves can potentially be attributed to a relatively short duration of the stress episode due to a quick turnaround in global risk sentiment, which has also likely reduced the need for the capital flow management measures (see Online Annex Box 2.2).

IMF staff analysis shows that global factors, including Federal Reserve rate cuts and global risk appetite (proxied by the Chicago Board Options Exchange Volatility Index [VIX][1]), played a significant role in driving currency surprises[2] during the COVID-19 sell-off (Figure 2.2, panel 3). Domestic policy rate cuts and FX interventions, on the other hand, had a relatively insignificant impact. This contrasts with the 2015 sell-off, which was more specific to emerging markets and not driven by exogeneous global shocks, and during which emerging market currencies were significantly affected by domestic FX interventions and policy rate cuts (Figure 2.2, panel 4).

The New Game in Town: Central Bank Asset Purchases

During the COVID-19 crisis, for the first time on a broad basis, at least 18 emerging market central banks adopted unconventional policies through the use of asset purchase programs[3] targeting government or private sector bonds in local currency. In several cases the purchases were sterilized, which alleviated downward pressure on exchange rates. The scope and motivation of these programs varied across economies (see Table 2.1 and Figure 2.3, panel 1), and the objectives were often multifaceted, but a view toward the available conventional monetary policy space allows for the identification of three broad groups:

- Central banks with *policy rates well above zero* tended to use asset purchase programs as a tool to improve bond market functioning (India, Philippines, South Africa) and provide liquidity to the financial sector. In some cases, central banks may have seen nominal policy rates below a certain level as counterpro-

ductive, primarily because of fears over portfolio outflows and ineffective policy transmission.

- Central banks with *policy rates closer to their lower bound* (Chile, Hungary, Poland) have partially sought to use asset purchase programs for somewhat similar reasons as advanced economies, to ease financial conditions, provide additional monetary stimulus, and exert greater influence on longer maturity bond yields. It is worth noting that in most cases market functioning and liquidity objectives were prominently featured.

- Some central banks explicitly stated that one of their objectives was to temporarily *ease government financing pressure* in the face of the once-in-a-generation global pandemic (Ghana, Guatemala, Indonesia, and the Philippines through its repurchase agreement).

Central bank purchases of government securities played an important role in some domestic bond markets during the acute phase of the sell-off. Beginning in February 2020 (Figure 2.3, panel 2), almost all economies faced sizable local currency bond outflows. Central bank asset purchases varied substantially in size, but in most cases they helped the domestic investor base absorb much of the outflow pressure and deal with the government's increased financing needs. For example, in Poland between the end of February and June the central bank purchased more than 2 percent of GDP in government bonds in the secondary market compared with outflows of 0.7 percent of GDP, alongside an increase in net domestic issuance of 4.4 percent of GDP. In some countries that did not launch asset purchase programs, debt management offices limited the local bond supply to avoid further deterioration of already stressed local bond markets. Instead, they relied on alternative sources of financing (for example, the use of cash buffers in Brazil, increased external issuance in Mexico, and pension funds in some Latin American countries) or back-loaded issuance to the second half of the year.

Local Market Stress Is Greater in Bonds than in Currencies

This GFSR introduces a novel market conditions index designed to assess the level of stress in local bond and currency markets. The *local stress index* (LSI) summarizes conditions into an indicator that can help guide central bank decisions regarding the need for interventions to support local market functioning. Unlike financial conditions indices, which can loosen or

---

[1]Other policy variables, such as announcements by the Federal Reserve of additional purchases, credit facilities, and swap lines, must have also affected emerging market currencies indirectly, but a significant part of that impact should be reflected through global risk appetite.

[2]The results are broadly consistent even when simple currency changes are considered. For more details, see Online Annex 2.1. All annexes are available at www.imf.org/en/Publications/GFSR.

[3]For the purpose of this GFSR, an APP is the expansion of the central bank balance sheet via purchases of various type of securities. APPs include quantitative easing programs that aim to ease financial conditions and provide monetary stimulus, more limited programs that aim to improve market functioning, and purchases in primary markets that aim to assist with government financing requirements. Some countries in the sample set up new purchase programs (for example, Chile and Hungary); others adjusted their existing open market operations (for example, Malaysia and Turkey).

Figure 2.2. FX Interventions and Reserve Operations

Reserve operations were substantial and widespread in dollar terms ...

... though as a share of reserves they never reached the level of the global financial crisis and receded quickly.

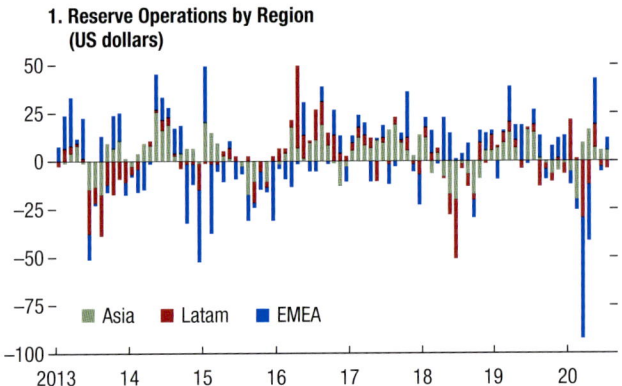

1. Reserve Operations by Region (US dollars)

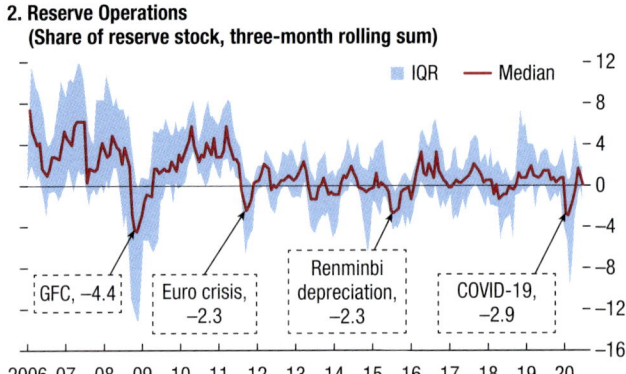

2. Reserve Operations (Share of reserve stock, three-month rolling sum)

Global factors played a significant role in driving emerging market currency surprises during the COVID-19 sell-off ...

... in sharp contrast to the 2015 emerging market sell-off, when domestic factors played a significantly more important role.

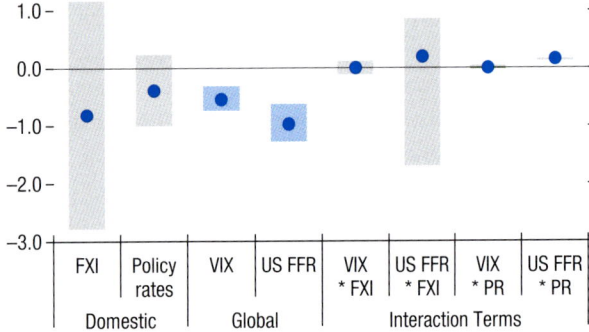

3. Coefficients for the Drivers of the EM FX Surprise during the COVID-19 Sell-off (January 2020–May 2020)

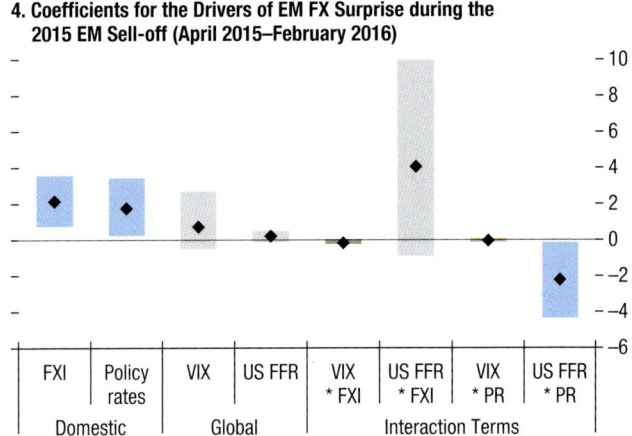

4. Coefficients for the Drivers of EM FX Surprise during the 2015 EM Sell-off (April 2015–February 2016)

Sources: Data set from Adler and others (forthcoming); Bloomberg Finance L.P.; Haver Analytics; International Institute of Finance; and IMF staff calculations.
Note: In panel 1, data exclude China. In panels 1 and 2, data are as of end-August 2020. Data from May onwards include estimates for operations only in the spot market, while data for April and earlier include estimates for operations in spot as well as derivatives markets. Operations in derivatives markets do not represent a drag on the reserve stock but are included in the calculations to estimate the size of the intervention. These estimates do not adjust for foreign exchange bond sales/purchases, so they may represent a partial picture in a few cases (for example, Mexico). In panels 3 and 4, the sample consists of 14 emerging markets with panel data at monthly frequency (see Online Annex 2.1 for more details). The dependent variable is the forecast error between the spot currency value and the value forecast by the previous month's forward contracts. A positive value implies that the currency appreciated versus market expectations, assuming parity holds. In reality, the forward values might vary from spot for an extended period of time, but the changes in this metric will still highlight currency pressures, albeit only partially. The results hold broadly true even if the dependent variable is taken as foreign exchange appreciation. Foreign exchange intervention (FXI) is calculated as valuation-adjusted changes in reserves and the intervention as taken in the derivative markets. A positive value means active intervention. Country fixed effects are included. Coefficient estimates are shown with two standard error confidence intervals. In panels 3 and 4, blue bars are the statistically significant coefficients, while gray bars are not statistically significant. EM = emerging market; EMEA = Europe, Middle East, and Africa; FFR = Federal funds rate (effective); GFC = global financial crisis; IQR = interquartile range; Latam = Latin America; PR = policy rate; VIX = Chicago Board Options Exchange Volatility Index.

Table 2.1. Asset Purchase Programs in Response to COVID-19 in Emerging Market Economies

Country	Primary Objectives	Asset Type	Target or Limit Size (local currency unless specified)	Market	Total Purchases (percent of GDP)	Program Duration (observed or explicit)	Significant Program Announcement Dates	General Government 2020 Deficit (percent of GDP)	Government Debt (percent of GDP)
Colombia	Provide liquidity to the financial sector	Government, private sector bonds	10 tn private, up to 4 tn government	Secondary	1.1	Mar.–Apr.	Mar. 23	–9.5	68.2
Chile	Facilitate monetary policy transmission, ease financial conditions	Bank, central bank, and government bonds*	$16 bn	Secondary	2.9*	Mar.–present	Mar. 16, Mar. 31, Jun. 16, Aug. 12	–8.7	32.8
Croatia	Stabilize domestic bond market	Government bonds	Not specified	Secondary	4.9	Mar.–Jun.	Mar. 13	–8.1	87.7
Ghana	Finance budget deficit	Government bonds	5.5 bn (up to 10 bn)	Primary	1.4	May	May 15	–16.4	76.7
Guatemala	Finance budget deficit	Government bonds	11 bn	Both	1.9	Apr.–Aug.	Apr. 8	–5.6	32.2
Hungary	Facilitate monetary policy transmission at longer maturities, provide financial sector liquidity	Government, mortgage bonds (MBs)	No upper limit, but technical revision after 1 tn in government, 300 bn in MBs	Both (only MBs in primary)	1.4	May–present	Apr. 7, Apr. 28, Jul. 21, Aug. 25	–8.3	77.4
India	Stabilize domestic bond market	Government bonds	Not specified	Secondary	1.0	Mar.–present	Mar. 18	–13.1	89.3
Indonesia	Stabilize domestic bond market, provide liquidity to the financial sector, finance budget deficit	Government bonds	Initially not specified, with direct "burden sharing" of 397.6 tn later announced	Both	3.8**	Mar.–present	Mar. 31, Jul. 7	–6.3	38.5
Malaysia	Provide liquidity to financial sector	Government bonds	Not specified	Secondary	0.6	Mar.–Jun.	Mar. 25	–6.5	67.6
Philippines	Provide liquidity to financial sector, stabilize bond market, finance budget deficit (repurchase agreement)	Government bonds, including repurchase agreement	Secondary market purchases not specified, repurchase amount limited to about 850 bn	Both	4.3 (7.3)***	Mar.–present	Mar. 23, Apr. 10, Oct. 2	–8.1	48.9
Poland	Strengthen monetary policy transmission at longer maturities, stabilize domestic bond market, provide liquidity to financial sector	Government, SOE bonds	Not specified	Secondary	4.6	Mar.–present	Mar. 17, Apr. 8	–10.5	60.0
Romania	Provide liquidity to financial sector	Government bonds	Not specified	Secondary	0.5	Mar.–present	Mar. 20	–9.6	44.8
South Africa	Stabilize domestic bond market	Government. bonds	Not specified	Secondary	0.7	Mar.–present	Mar. 25	–14.0	78.8
Thailand	Stabilize domestic bond market	Government, central bank bonds	Not specified	Secondary	1.0	Mar.–Apr.	Mar. 19, Mar. 22	–5.2	50.4
Turkey	Provide liquidity to financial sector, strengthen monetary policy transmission mechanism, secure credit conditions	Government bonds	Not specified, but OMO portfolio limited to 10 percent of balance sheet	Secondary	1.6	Mar.–present	Mar. 31	–7.9	41.7

Sources: Local media; national authorities; and IMF staff estimates.

Note: Total purchase amounts are estimates of March through latest available as of publication process (late September). Program dates are not exhaustive, but generally reflect a significant program announcement or first purchase date. Poland includes purchases of bonds from the State Development Bank (BGK) and State Development Fund (PFR). For Chile, only assets purchased under the Special Asset (June) and Bank Bond (March) Purchase Programs that were in direct response to the COVID-19 crisis were included, and not the Nov. 2019 crisis were included here. Papua New Guinea, Jamaica, Sri Lanka, and the Central African Economic and Monetary Community (through the Bank of Central African States) are not included in the table but announced asset purchases of various forms. Brazil outlined plans to purchase corporate bonds in June, but had yet to do so. The BSP (Philippines) opened its purchase window in March prior to written public announcement in April. bn = billion; OMO = open market operations; tn = trillion.

*Chile's central bank did not gain the legal ability to purchase government bonds until August 12.

**Indonesia includes staff estimates of secondary market purchases, primary market purchases prior to July, and the full 397.6 tn July burden sharing agreement, though only about 60 percent of the agreed purchases had been completed through mid-September.

***Philippines includes staff estimates of secondary market purchases and the three-month repurchase agreement of 540 bn (3.0% of GDP) with the central government added in parentheses, and the BSP closed out a previous 300 bn repurchase agreement in September.

Figure 2.3. Central Bank Asset Purchases in Emerging Markets

Asset purchase programs in emerging markets differ in scope, size, and duration from those in advanced economies and are often used with higher policy rates.

Central bank purchases helped offset portfolio outflows during the crisis period in some economies.

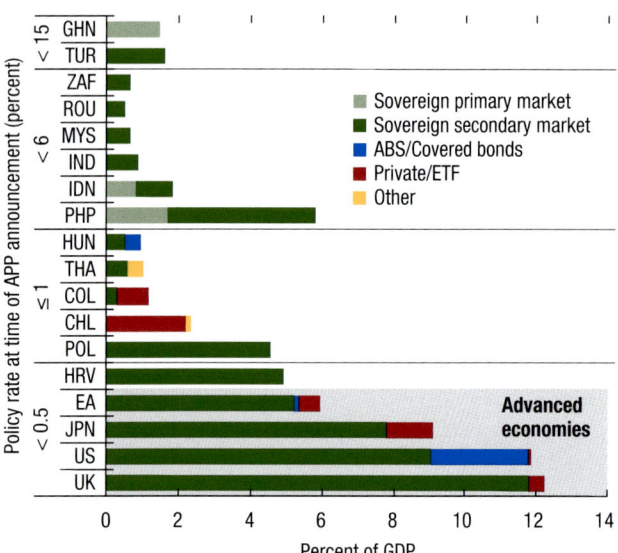

1. Central Bank Asset Purchases through August
   (Percent of GDP)

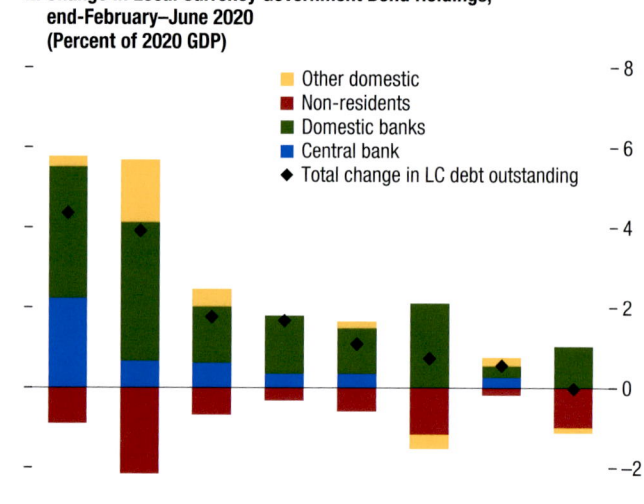

2. Change in Local Currency Government Bond Holdings,
   end-February–June 2020
   (Percent of 2020 GDP)

Sources: Bloomberg Finance L.P.; Haver Analytics; national sources; World Bank; and IMF staff calculations.
Note: Data in panel 1 and panel 2 may in some cases have different sourcing related to definitional and availability reasons. Asset purchases in Hungary did not begin until May. In panel 1, sovereign purchases for Poland include those from the state development bank (BGK) and the state development fund (PFR), which are excluded in panel 2. Purchases for Chile include only those under Special Asset (June) and Bank Bond (March) Purchase Programs. Primary market purchases for the Philippines refer to the 300 bn (~1.6% of GDP) repurchase agreement in April 2020, which was repaid in September. In panel 1, Indonesia primary market purchases include only the share of the burden sharing agreement completed through August, not the entirety of the 397.6 trillion plan. In panel 2, total change for South Africa differs slightly from aggregated holdings as it includes Treasury bills separately. Data are not adjusted for inflation-linked bonds. Indonesia central bank holdings are defined as net of monetary operations. Data labels use International Organization for Standardization (ISO) country codes. ABS = asset-backed securities; APP = asset purchase program; ETF = exchange-traded fund.

tighten as a result of changes in policy rates or external spreads—as a reflection of the cost of funding—the LSI focuses on local market liquidity and stress indicators (such as bid-offer spreads, realized volatility, and other risk premium measures).[4]

The level of stress in local markets during the COVID-19 sell-off, as measured by the LSI, was comparable to that of the global financial crisis, but the period of stress was considerably shorter. In aggregate (Figure 2.4, panel 1), the level of stress was well above that of previous episodes, such as the 2013 taper tantrum and 2014–15 stress episodes. However, markets have been normalizing much faster than during previous episodes (Figure 2.4, panel 2).

A large part of the increase (and subsequent partial reduction) in stress in local bond markets originated from

developments in the global financial markets. In line with past episodes of sharp tightening in global financial conditions, the spillovers in FX markets emanating from the United States and the European Union rose sharply (Figure 2.4, panel 3) as currencies played their role as shock absorbers.[5] However, unlike what happened during past tightening episodes, the spillovers to local bond markets were more pronounced (Figure 2.4, panel 4). Most emerging markets have seen a large increase in nonresident participation in their local bond markets since the global financial crisis, which may have exacerbated increased volatility spillovers during the recent sell-off.

The stress in FX markets was lower than during 2008–09, with less noticeable demand for dollar liquidity.

---

[4]For details, see Online Annex 2.1, available at www.imf.org/en/Publications/GFSR.

[5]Spillover indices in Figure 2.4, panel 1, are calculated using the approach in Diebold and Yilmaz (2012), in which time-varying spillovers are constructed using rolling generalized forecast error decompositions. The index is the contribution from a shock to market X to the overall variability in any other market Y.

Figure 2.4. Stress in Local Currency Bond and FX Markets

The COVID-19 shock led to significant market dysfunction comparable to that of the 2008 global financial crisis.

1. Emerging Market Local Stress Index
(Index)

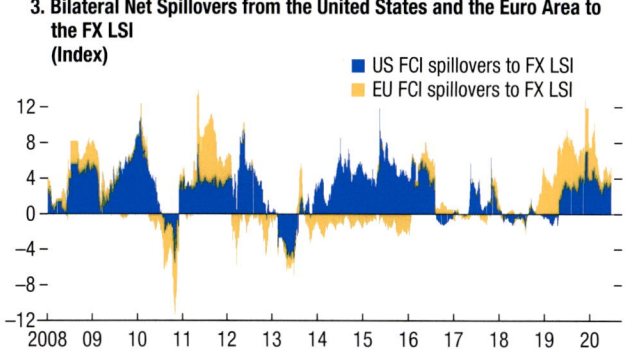

Stress dissipated faster than in previous episodes but remains elevated.

2. Emerging Market Local Stress Index
(Dates in parentheses correspond to day = 0 on x-axis)

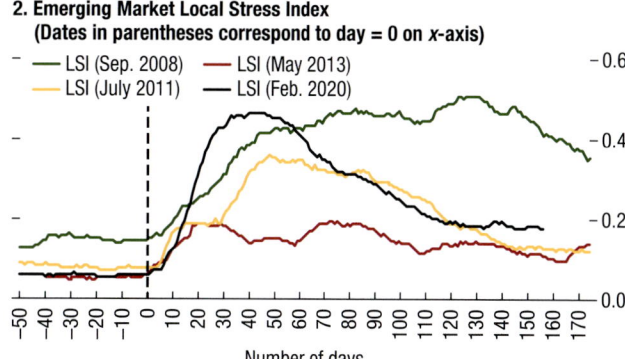

Number of days

The spillovers of tightening US/EU financial conditions to emerging market currencies were of the same magnitude as in the past ...

3. Bilateral Net Spillovers from the United States and the Euro Area to the FX LSI
(Index)

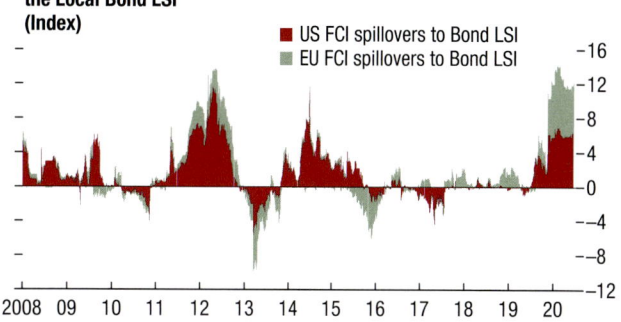

... while the spillover to emerging market bond market conditions is far more pronounced now than in the past.

4. Bilateral Net Spillovers from the United States and the Euro Area to the Local Bond LSI
(Index)

Policy actions in FX markets normalized conditions quickly, but ...

5. FX LSI and Components
(Index)

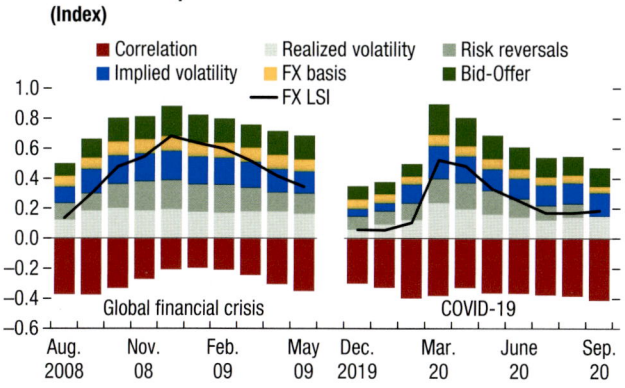

... local bond markets have remained more dysfunctional, triggering asset purchase programs.

6. Local Bond LSI and Components
(Index)

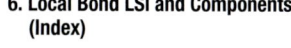
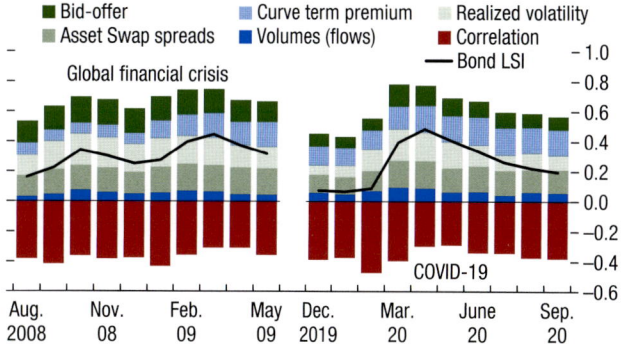

Sources: Bloomberg Finance L.P.; and IMF staff calculations.
Note: The local stress index (LSI) is calculated from the country LSIs of 16 countries. For more information see Online Annex 2.1. FCI = financial conditions index; FX = foreign exchange; GFC = global financial crisis.

For example, increases in measures such as risk reversals, which indicate the level of hedging demand for a sharp depreciation against the dollar, have been more muted.[6] In addition, the wider cross-currency basis—a measure of dollar funding liquidity stress (Figure 2.4, panel 5)—was more short-lived. These developments were likely a result of:

- The rapid establishment of central bank swap line facilities and bond repo facilities for foreign central banks by the Federal Reserve and the European Central Bank.[7]
- Structural shifts in the operation of FX markets since the global financial crisis (Schrimpf and Sushko 2019),[8] including increased turnover in emerging market currencies and electronic trading and a larger set of market-making institutions.

Unlike FX markets, local bond markets became more stressed and triggered policy responses in the form of asset purchase programs. A notable aspect is the increase in the risk premiums of long-end government bonds relative to short-end bonds and onshore swap rates (Figure 2.4, panel 6). Despite the positive impact of asset purchase programs on market conditions (see next subsection), stress levels have been more elevated, likely as a result of:

- High local bond supply risks that weigh on yields through risk premiums.
- Weak foreign flows to local bond markets, which had a negative impact on liquidity.
- Relatively limited depth of local currency government bond markets. Unlike FX markets, local bonds are still traded largely domestically, and market depth has not matched higher foreign participation, which could induce volatility (see Chapter 3 of the April 2020 GFSR). In countries with a shallower domestic investor base (see "Looking Ahead: Trade-offs of Asset Purchase Programs" section), domestic banks are the sole liquidity providers in times of stress.

---

[6]In fact, during the early stages of the shock in February, the depreciation pressures in emerging markets were more acute against the euro, likely because of unwinding of euro-funded carry trades relative to high-yield currencies, such as the Russian ruble and the Mexican peso.

[7]The IMF flexible credit lines for Chile and Peru in the second quarter of 2020, and the renewal of the flexible credit line for Colombia, also boosted confidence and provided insurance against downside risks.

[8]Another structural shift worth noting is the shift toward more flexible exchange rate regimes since the 2008 global financial crisis (for example, in Russia).

Domestic Asset Purchases Eventually Helped Reduce Market Stress

The announcement of asset purchase programs in the second half of March did not have an immediate impact on local stress indices, given that global financial conditions were very tight and market conditions were hampered by illiquidity, strong risk aversion, and fiscal concerns (Figure 2.5, panel 1).[9] However, as external conditions started to improve in April and countries stepped up implementation of asset purchase programs, country-level local stress indices showed some improvement and differentiation.[10] A large part of the improvement was seen in market liquidity measures, such as bid-offer spreads and a reduction in intraday volatility. Yet term premiums in some local bond markets remain elevated as investors are facing bond supply risks over a longer horizon given the uncertainty of pandemic-related government financing requirements.

Evaluating the effectiveness of asset purchase programs with respect to their stated goal of improving market conditions is complex, and more work is needed. Asset purchase programs helped reduce market stress, eventually, and several factors contributed to this reduction. The size of announced asset purchase programs in emerging markets has been small overall (except in Chile, Indonesia, the Philippines, and Poland) and short-lived, as is evident in the slowdown of asset purchases since May for most countries (Figure 2.5, panel 2). In addition, announcements and implementations of asset purchase programs can affect market conditions differently, and the lack of local currency bond inflows had a negative impact on market liquidity, especially in markets with a large foreign presence. The introduction of asset purchase programs at the height of the crisis is likely to have served as a useful circuit breaker, preventing further escalation of stress. Purchases of government bonds and other assets signaled that emerging market central banks were ready to stand as buyer of last resort (Arslan, Drehmann, and Hofmann 2020). Moreover, the empirical analysis presented in the following section suggests that asset

---

[9]This is in line with developments in the United States, where the Federal Reserve's March 15 announcement of additional US Treasury purchases did not relieve market stress.

[10]Figure 2.5, panel 1, aggregates countries that have different characteristics, which could be the main driver of the results rather than APPs. Online Annex 2.1 presents event studies around the asset purchase announcements that show country-level developments.

Figure 2.5. Bond Stress and Asset Purchase Programs in Emerging Market Economies

Stress has eased somewhat faster for countries with asset purchase programs than for those that do not have them.

Emerging market asset purchases rose significantly in March and April but moderated thereafter.

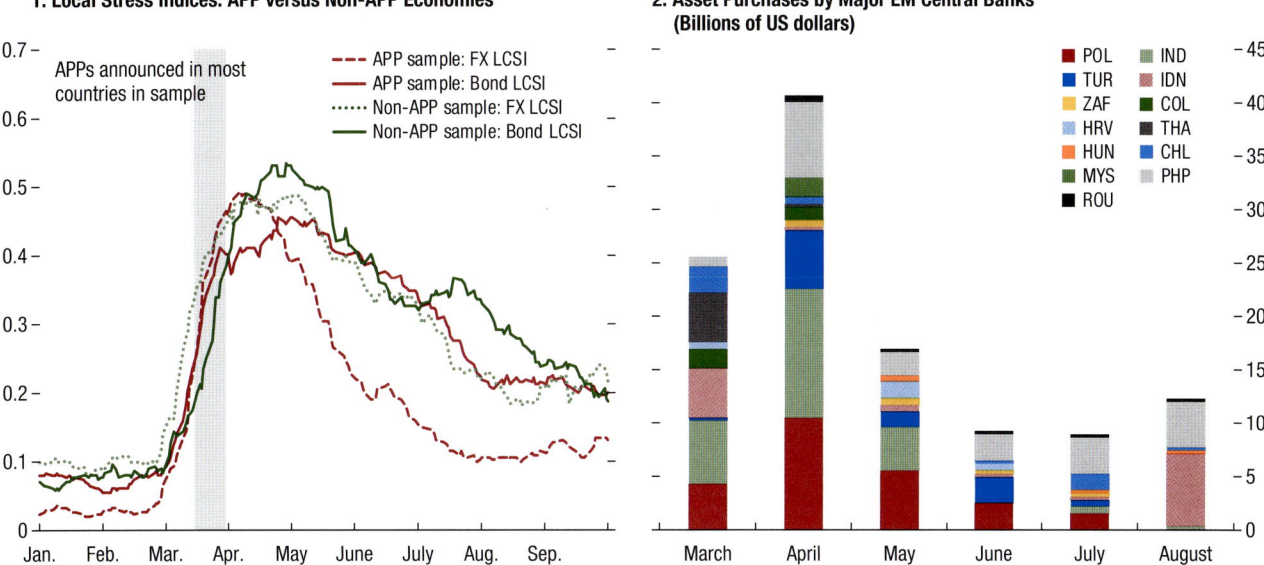

Sources: Bloomberg Finance L.P.; Haver Analytics; JPMorgan Chase and Co.; national authorities; and IMF calculations.
Note: Non-APP economies are Brazil, Chile, China, Mexico, Peru, and Russia. In panel 2, Indonesia uses change in gross holdings as proxy for asset purchases. Monthly purchases are IMF staff estimates otherwise. Data labels in panel 2 use International Organization for Standardization (ISO) country codes. APP = asset purchase program; EM = emerging market; FX = foreign exchange; LCSI = local currency stress index.

purchase program announcements had a positive impact on yields on the announcement date and several days beyond, even after controlling for external factors. Nevertheless, large-scale APPs, especially when open-ended, carry risks and may negate their initial effectiveness.

Domestic Asset Purchases Lowered Bond Yields and Had Little Effect on Currencies

Event studies show that asset purchase program announcements[11] had a significant immediate impact on asset prices and helped turn sentiment around.[12] Financial conditions were tightening going into the announcements but were inflected following the announcements, with a corresponding sharp reduction in government bond yields (Figure 2.6, panel 1) and term premiums (Figure 2.6, panel 2), but with

relatively limited impact on currencies (Figure 2.6, panel 3). The reaction seen in intraday data for selected countries—to control for the effect of global and exogenous factors on end-of-day levels—shows a similar trend, with declining government bond yields but relatively less impact on currencies (Figure 2.6, panel 4; Arslan, Drehmann, and Hofmann 2020).

This section discusses empirical analysis of the effect of domestic asset purchase program announcements on local currency government bond yields.[13] The model controls for policy rate cuts by emerging market central banks and global factors, such as the VIX and the VIX rate of change and asset purchase program announcements by the Federal Reserve. The analysis uses daily data from 13 emerging market economies from January to mid-May 2020 and controls for unobserved country-specific factors using country fixed effects (see Online Annex 2.1). The analysis is based on the local projections method (Jordà 2005; Teulings and Zubanov 2014), which capture the full dynamics of sovereign bond yields in the aftermath of

[11]The size of the announced programs may also have influenced the market reaction, although it is not considered (in line with the literature) given the lack of consistency across announcements and divergent market expectations.
[12]Results in this section draw upon Drakopoulos and others (forthcoming).

[13]Drakopoulos and others (forthcoming) discusses also the effect of APPs on equity markets.

Figure 2.6. Market Reaction to Domestic Asset Purchase Program Announcements

Event studies around emerging market asset purchase program announcements show a significant change following the event, including a decline in sovereign bond yields and a decline in term premiums, but a relatively small and short-lived impact on EM currencies.

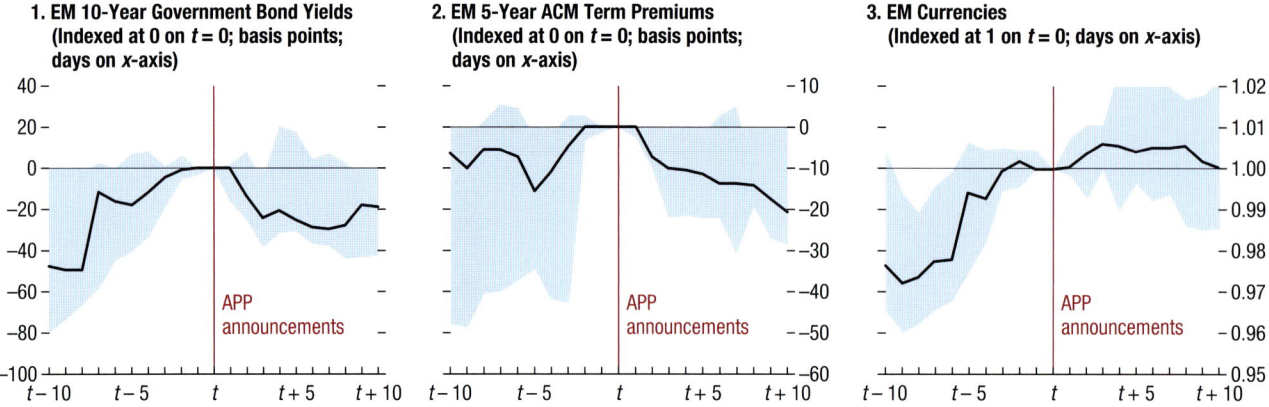

Intraday price reaction showed a similar trend, with government yields reacting very sharply, but relatively limited impact on emerging market currencies.

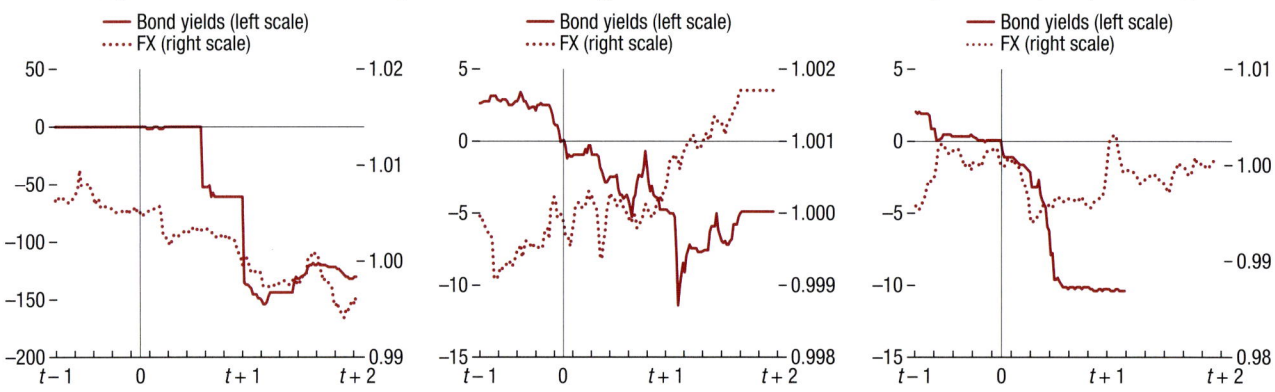

Sources: Bank for International Settlements; Bloomberg Finance L.P.; BNP Paribas; national authorities; and IMF staff calculations.
Note: In panel 2, term premium calculations are based on the methodology detailed in Adrian, Crump, and Moench (2013). In panels 3 and 4, a declining trend in the foreign exchange lines implies an appreciation of the local currency versus the US dollar. In panels 1–3, the black line denotes the median across our sample, while the blue range highlights the interquartile range across the events. The sample comprises Chile, Colombia, Hungary, India, Indonesia, Malaysia, the Philippines, Poland, South Africa, and Turkey (across a total of 16 dates). ACM = Adrian, Crump, and Moench (2013); APP = asset purchase program; EM = emerging market; FX = foreign exchange.

the announcements by central banks.[14] The dependent variable is the cumulative change in bond yields, and the main variable of interest is the indicator for the dates of asset purchase program announcements (Figure 2.7). A challenge in this analysis is to isolate the impact of asset purchase program announcements on bond yields from the effect of policy rate cuts and announcements by the Federal Reserve around the same time. To that end, two empirical specifications

are presented to account for the direct effect of the additional asset purchase announcement by the Federal Reserve (Figure 2.7, panels 1, 3, and 5) and the VIX as a proxy for global risk appetite (Figure 2.7, panels 2, 4, and 6). Both specifications control for domestic policy rates.

Both specifications find that emerging market central bank asset purchase program announcements reduce long-end bond yields in a significant and persistent way (Figure 2.7, panels 1 and 2), even controlling for the Federal Reserve asset purchase program announcement (Figure 2.7, panel 1) or the change in global risk appetite (Figure 2.7, panel 2). The size

[14]Some evaluations of the effectiveness of asset purchases by the Federal Reserve use the surprise announcement of 10-year equivalents on term premiums, but such an approach is beyond the scope of the analysis here.

Figure 2.7. Asset Purchase Program Announcements and Sovereign Bond Yields

Panels 1, 3, and 5 show the impulse response functions to APP announcements by emerging market central banks, controlling for Federal Reserve actions and emerging market rate cuts.

Panels 2, 4, and 6 show the impulse response functions of APP announcements by emerging market central banks, controlling for the VIX as a proxy for global risk appetite and emerging market rate cuts.

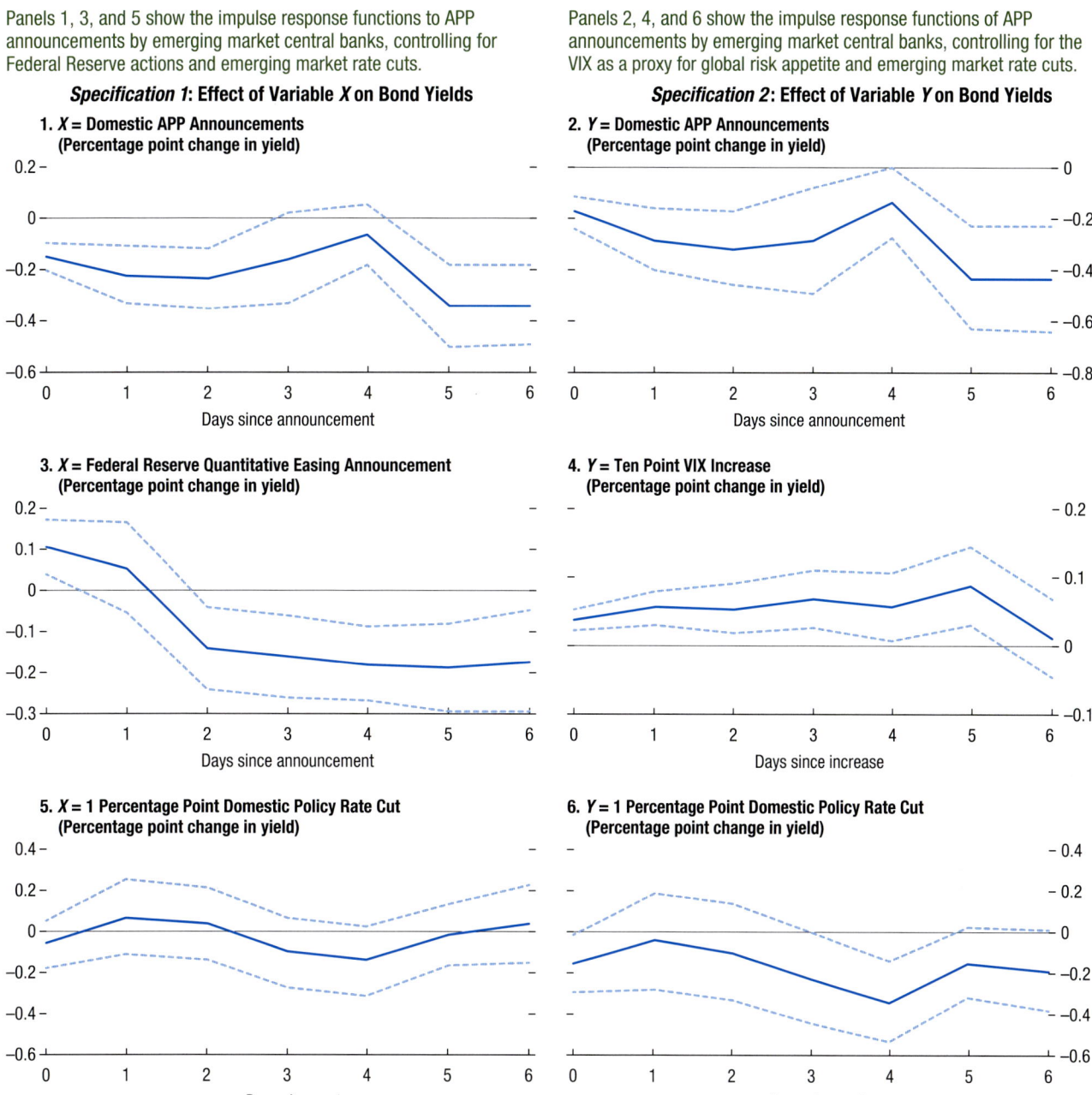

Source: IMF staff calculations.
Note: Results are based on the local projections method (Jordà 2005; Teulings and Zubanov 2014) using panel data from 13 emerging markets at daily frequency from the beginning of January to mid-May 2020. The dependent variable is the cumulative change (in percentage points) in local currency sovereign bond yields. The first specification controls for the APP announcement by the Federal Reserve and domestic rate cuts (panels 1, 3, and 5). The second specification controls for the Chicago Board Options Exchange Volatility Index (VIX) and domestic rate cuts (panels 2, 4, and 6). Country fixed effects are included in both specifications. Coefficient estimates are reported with one standard error confidence interval. The x-axes represent the number of trading days following each episode. See Online Annex 2.1 for more details. APP = asset purchase program; VIX = Chicago Board Options Exchange Volatility Index.

Figure 2.8. Asset Purchase Program Announcements and Domestic Currencies

Announcements of asset purchase programs did not lead to a significant depreciation of emerging market currencies.

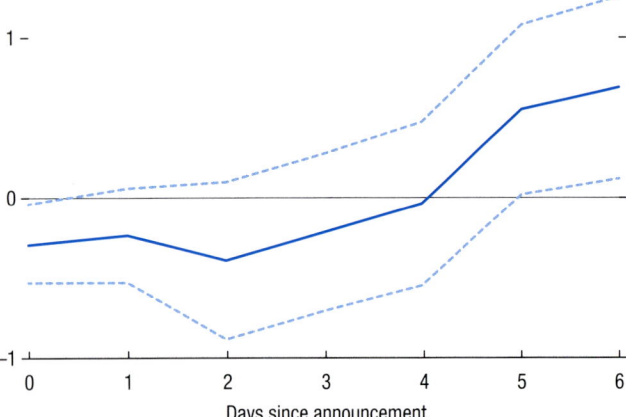

Emerging Market Currencies
(Percent change)

Source: IMF staff calculations.
Note: Results are based on the local projections method (Jordà 2005; Teulings and Zubanov 2014) using panel data from 13 emerging markets at daily frequency from the beginning of January to mid-May 2020. The dependent variable is the cumulative change (in percent) in the value of domestic currencies vis-à-vis the US dollar. The specification controls for the asset purchase program (APP) announcement by the Federal Reserve and domestic rate cuts, as well as country fixed effects. Coefficient estimates are reported with a one standard error confidence interval. The x-axis shows the number of trading days following each episode. See Online Annex 2.1 for more details.

of the impact of domestic asset purchase program announcements on yields ranges from 20 to 60 basis points and is statistically significant within one standard error confidence interval. The size of the effect is in the range of Arslan, Drehmann, and Hofmann (2020) and Hartley and Rebucci (2020). By contrast, in both specifications, domestic rate cuts do not appear to have a significant effect on yields, controlling for other factors, such as asset purchase programs[15] (Figure 2.7, panels 5 and 6).

The improvement in external conditions also had a significant and persistent impact on lowering long-end yields. Both the Federal Reserve asset purchase program announcement on March 23 (Figure 2.7, panel 3) and the improvement in global risk appetite

[15]This might also reflect that the rate cuts were already priced in or that risk premiums remained high.

(Figure 2.7, panel 4) had a positive effect on decreasing yields, reflecting the sensitivity of domestic bond yields to global factors (April 2020 GFSR). This is also consistent with the finding by Beirne, Renzhi, and Sugandi (2020) of evidence of spillovers to emerging market bond yields from quantitative easing by central banks in advanced economies (see Chapter 1). The magnitudes of the effect of the asset purchase program announcements by emerging market central banks and the Federal Reserve are broadly similar.

Announcements of asset purchase programs did not lead to a significant depreciation of emerging market currencies (Figure 2.8), in line with intraday event studies (Figure 2.6, panel 4). This may reflect the relatively small size of the programs and the fact that the purchases were sterilized in many cases. Furthermore, the restoration of stability and the decisive actions taken by advanced and emerging market central banks may have also contributed to investor confidence and reversal of the earlier considerable FX sell-off.

Looking Ahead: Trade-offs of Asset Purchase Programs

The experience with emerging market asset purchase programs has been largely positive so far, though further expansion of duration or size could create risks and thus warrant an ongoing evaluation of risks. APPs had a catalyzing effect on lowering local currency government bond yields without indications of immediate risks to financial stability. In some cases, purchases may have intermediated an orderly exit of investors from local currency bond markets, but this was likely done in the interest of preserving investor confidence and avoiding more costly and widespread market disruptions. Central bank communication and benign market perception in terms of the scope, timing, and temporary nature of these programs were essential in containing perceived risks of fiscal dominance that would likely have led to higher bond yields and weaker currencies.

Beyond the pandemic, this positive experience may motivate more emerging market central banks to consider unconventional monetary policy as a key additional part of their policy toolkit, especially where conventional policy space becomes limited.[16]

[16]For a deeper discussion of the use of unconventional monetary policy in emerging market economies see Hofman and Kamber (forthcoming).

Figure 2.9. Considerations for Asset Purchase Programs

The depth of the domestic investor base and its ability to repatriate foreign assets may affect the need for APPs.

Credible monetary policy frameworks and sound governance are prerequisites for APPs.

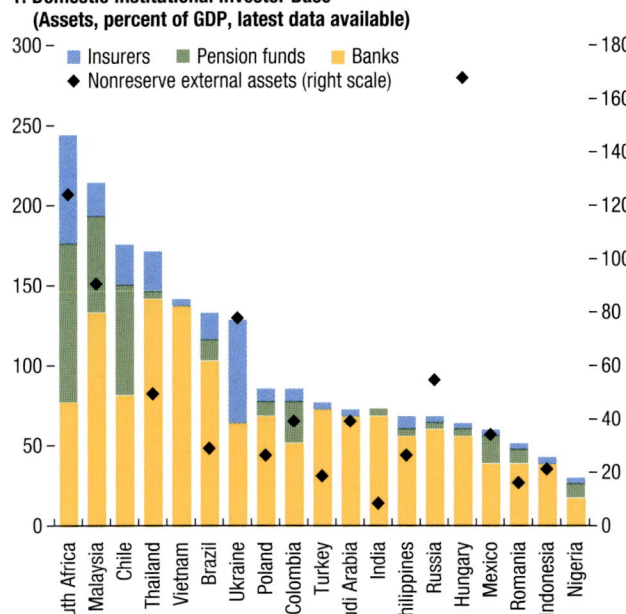

1. Domestic Institutional Investor Base
   (Assets, percent of GDP, latest data available)

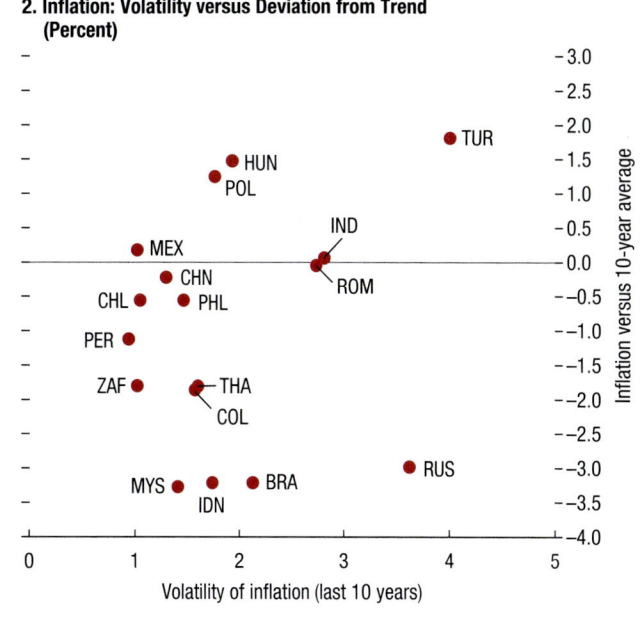

2. Inflation: Volatility versus Deviation from Trend
   (Percent)

Sources: Bloomberg Finance L.P.; Haver Analytics; World Bank; and IMF staff calculations.
Note: In panel 1, data are as of latest vintage available, though gaps exist for select countries and series. Data labels in panel 2 use International Organization for Standardization (ISO) country codes. APPs = asset purchase programs.

APPs may be suitable for countries constrained by their own effective lower bound, with inflation expectations steady, where the concern over capital outflows and FX depreciation is low or where the domestic absorption capacity of new bond supply is limited (Figure 2.9, panel 1). The goal of an APP in such cases is to exert control over the medium- to long-end of the yield curve (even when policy rates remain substantially above zero) to lower government financing costs and to temporarily ease pressure on domestic investors when there is increased issuance or foreign investor outflows. There are important caveats when it comes to this goal, however. Longer-term yields play a less central role in most emerging market economies than they do in advanced economies. Similarly, the fragilities behind higher short-term rates are likely to limit the scope for attempts to lower longer-term yields.

Policymakers should consider both the benefits and potential significant costs of APPs with respect to monetary policy and financial stability. If large-scale APPs are used beyond the current pandemic-related extraordinary situation, the following risks could arise,

especially for open-ended programs (see Figure 2.9, panel 2, for select country characteristics to take into consideration while deploying APPs, and Hofman and Kamber, forthcoming):

- **Institutional and central bank credibility may be weakened.** Credible monetary policy frameworks and sound governance are prerequisites for effective unconventional policy actions such as APPs. Early evidence suggests that APPs by central banks with higher institutional quality tended to have a greater reduction of their bond local stress index, introduced earlier in this chapter. Increased balance sheet exposure to long-term debt may raise concerns about the central bank's ability to raise interest rates when conditions warrant or to achieve price stability.

- **Asset purchases may invite concerns about fiscal dominance.** When central banks become buyers of last resort, with large-scale and open-ended APPs in economies with weak monetary and fiscal policy frameworks, it can lead to fiscal dominance, resulting in higher risk premiums and steeper government bond yield curves.

- *APPs may intensify capital outflow pressure, especially in countries with weaker fundamentals.* Expectations of large-scale APPs may put downward pressure on long-term yields and foreign exchange rates, putting capital flows at risk, especially during risk-off periods, when emerging market assets are seen as risky. Investors may decide to rebalance their portfolios more decisively if APPs result in an excessive gap between domestic and peer-group risk premiums.
- *The lasting presence of central banks as buyers in the local currency bond market may distort market dynamics.* APPs can end up substantially increasing the role of the central bank as a market maker, impairing the price discovery process, especially in primary markets,[17] and the development of the financial market. Considerations should also be given to the effect of APPs on collateral availability in the banking system and its impact on the policy rate transmission (Singh and Goel 2019) as well as possible overvaluation of assets.

The motivation, effectiveness, and associated risks of APPs vary considerably from country to country and depend on additional considerations, such as the structure and liquidity of capital markets, availability of high-quality domestic assets, extent of foreign investor participation, and level of development of the financial sector (Hofman and Kamber, forthcoming). Focused use of APPs as part of the crisis toolkit of emerging and frontier market economy central banks with credible monetary policy frameworks and good governance has a role to play. But continuing evaluation is needed as more data become available on the effectiveness of unconventional monetary policy in emerging markets, especially for open-ended programs.

The Role of the Official Sector in Frontier Market Economy Debt Restructuring

Frontier market economies[18] entered the pandemic in a vulnerable position, with a number of countries

already deemed to be at a high risk of debt distress (see the October 2019 GFSR) and with relatively little policy space compared with major emerging market economies. The postcrisis period of easy global financial conditions allowed frontier market economies to raise unprecedented amounts of capital in private markets (Figure 2.10, panel 1), all the while increasing their rollover risk. Markets reflected these concerns, as bond spreads rose to their highest level since the global financial crisis during the initial stages of the market sell-off, but spreads have since erased a significant amount of the widening (Figure 2.10, panel 2).

To help alleviate the strains facing frontier economies, the Group of Twenty (G20) announced the Debt Service Suspension Initiative (DSSI) to temporarily ease the financing constraints of the poorest countries by freeing up scarce money that they can use to mitigate the human and economic impact of the COVID-19 crisis. While some countries have already begun to participate in the initiative, some have been reluctant, in part because of fears of loss of market access (see also Chapter 1).

Markets, however, are not pricing in a significant risk from DSSI participation, despite concerns about possible negative actions by the credit rating agencies. On average, spreads of countries eligible for the DSSI have outperformed those of other frontier countries, even excluding countries eligible for the DSSI that do not intend to participate (Figure 2.10, panel 3). This outperformance could be a result of investor expectations that the initiative can allow these countries to better weather the outcome of the pandemic. For now, the initiative is providing relief primarily through a moratorium on bilateral debt, whereas private sector groups have begun assessing potential ways to assist. Even though the DSSI helps free up scarce money to mitigate the human and economic impact of COVID-19, once the impact of the pandemic becomes clearer, official sector relief may prove insufficient for some countries. Overall, bilateral creditors represent about one-third of debt payments owed by countries eligible for the DSSI over the next few years (Figure 2.10, panel 4). For many countries, private sector debt represents a much larger proportion of their external debt (Figure 2.10, panel 5).

For some countries, to achieve a necessary debt reduction, it is impractical for only the official sector to proactively alleviate the debt burden. Putting off debt relief by private sector creditors may eventually

---

[17]In markets that lack financial depth and where the government has large crisis-related short-term financing needs, there may be scope for the central bank to provide, under conditions, temporary support directly to the primary market to assist with the absorption of large issuance.

[18]Frontier economies comprise 43 countries, defined in Online Annex 2.1, the bulk of which are part of JP Morgan's Next Generation Markets Index.

Figure 2.10. Frontier Economies Have a Challenging Road Ahead

Frontier economies have become more dependent on private sector debt in recent years.

1. Frontier Market Debt: Creditor Composition
(Percent of GDP and billions of US dollars)

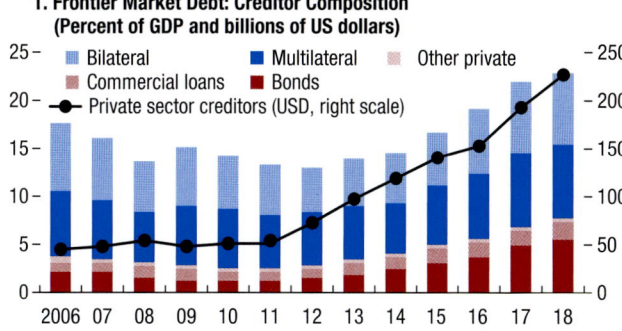

Market conditions have deteriorated substantially since the onset of the COVID-19 crisis.

2. Bond Spreads of Frontier Economies during the COVID-19 Crisis
(Basis points)

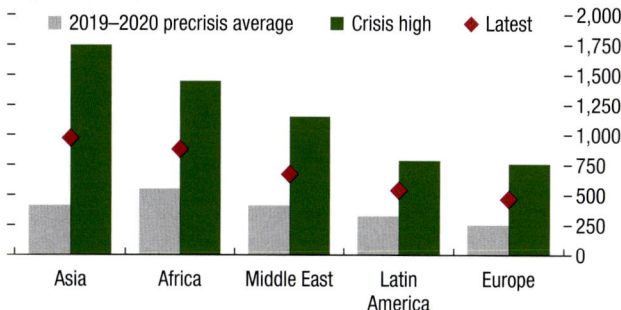

Countries eligible for the Debt Service Suspension Initiative have outperformed somewhat since April.

3. Normalized Spreads of Frontier Market Economies
(Index; January 1, 2020 = 100)

Bilateral creditors, primarily non–Paris Club creditors, represent about a third of debt payments over the next few years ...

4. Debt Service Payments by Creditor for a Sample of Frontiers
(Share of total, percent)

... but for several countries, private creditor debt is significant.

5. Debt Outstanding: Private versus Official Creditors
(Public external debt outstanding, percent of GDP)

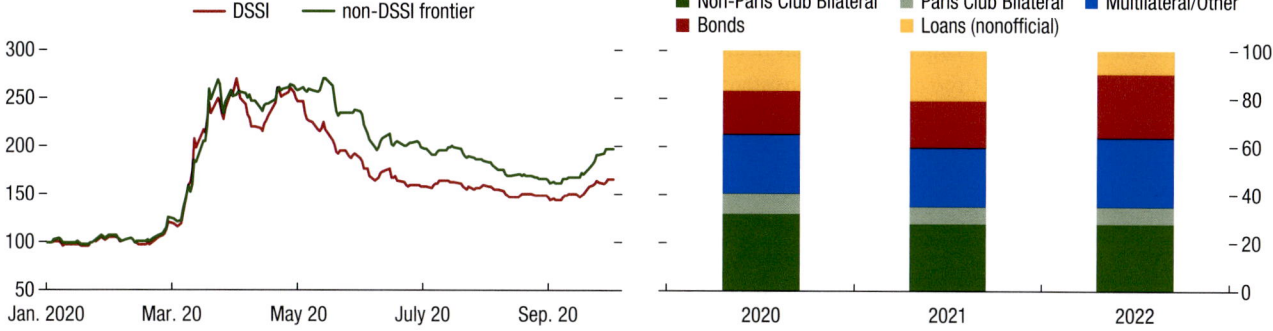

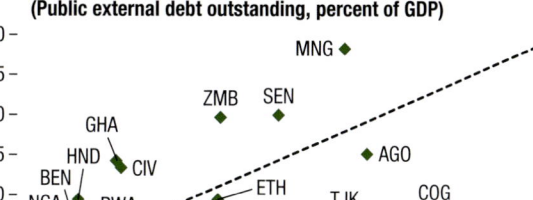

Sources: Bloomberg Finance L.P.; Bond Radar; JPMorgan Chase and Co; World Bank; and IMF staff estimates.
Note: Panel 1 refers to public and publicly guaranteed debt. Panel 4 comprises a sample of 22 frontier economies that are DSSI-eligible. The broad frontier universe comprises 43 countries defined in Online Annex 2.1. Panel 5 uses data from the World Bank as of 2018. Data labels in panel 5 use International Organization for Standardization (ISO) country codes. DSSI = Debt Service Suspension Initiative; Latam = Latin America.

call for a larger debt write-down, which could disproportionately affect private sector debt. Markets appear to perceive already that, in a default situation, they would be forced to take a larger haircut than bilateral creditors would.

Why this would drive higher spreads can be demonstrated in a hypothetical example. If a country requires a given overall debt reduction to make its debt sustainable, but one class of creditors is treated as senior, other creditors would need to take a greater burden (Figure 2.11, panel 1). Panel 2 of Figure 2.11 demonstrates the impact that different levels of senior debt would have on a bond's spreads at given levels of expected probability of default.[19] A country whose debt is entirely "junior," or private sector, would have a much lower spread than one for which half of the debt is considered senior. This spread impact increases as the credit quality decreases (higher expected default probability). A model for sovereign bond spreads shows that investors do expect a larger haircut than bilateral creditors.[20] The results of the model are consistent with investors expecting that bilateral creditors would take a 30 percent haircut in the case of a country that requires an overall 40 percent haircut. This analysis does not consider differences among groups of bilateral creditors or whether the impact is less or more for Paris Club creditors. Considering that bilateral loans are often extended at concessional levels, or at times when countries are not able to consistently borrow from private markets, it is not surprising that they would be expected to receive more favorable treatment in a restructuring scenario.

Policies for Recovery and Resilience

Unprecedented policy measures put in place by advanced and emerging market policymakers after the onset of the COVID-19 pandemic averted the worst outcome and helped stabilize domestic financial conditions. Emerging market central banks actively used available and new tools to soften the blow from

the spike in global risk aversion and intervened to smooth excess volatility of domestic currencies and contain the spillovers of tighter global financial conditions to domestic financial conditions. Appropriate use of FX intervention, macroprudential policies, and capital flow management measures in the face of shocks, such as the global pandemic, can contribute to financial stability and enhance monetary policy autonomy.

This chapter finds that global factors played a more important role in driving currencies than FX intervention did, probably because of the global nature of the shock. The short-lived FX intervention is consistent with using the currency as a key shock absorber when other vulnerabilities are in check. Countries with shallow FX markets may experience macroeconomic destabilization after such shocks, and FX interventions to lean against market illiquidity to mute excessive volatility can be appropriate (IMF 2020a).

Most notably, many emerging and frontier market central banks for the first time embarked on APPs to ensure the smooth functioning of bond markets and provide accommodation in an environment of very low policy rates. The apparent success in helping reduce bond yields without risking financial stability so far prompts the question of whether APPs should be part of the emerging and frontier market policy toolkit in the future.

For *central banks with APPs in progress*, transparency and clear communication[21] are crucial to minimize risks to their credibility—especially in countries with weaker institutional frameworks. In most cases, APPs should be limited in time and scale and should be linked to clear objectives. This chapter's findings suggest that APPs can be helpful, but that they are not a panacea to improve market conditions. They appear to be more effective when used jointly as part of a broader macroeconomic policy package.

Central banks considering APPs for the first time or seeking to restart them should design programs that aim to affect segments of the yield curve that are an effective pricing benchmark to maximize transmission to the real economy. Purchases should preferably be made in secondary markets, as purchases in the primary market or at below market rates can disrupt the price

---

[19]This stylized exercise assumes a 10-year bond with an 8 percent coupon.

[20]This is based on a variant of the emerging market hard currency bond valuation model introduced in the October 2019 GFSR. The domestic fundamentals include expectations for growth and inflation, current account balance, external debt, net issuance of foreign currency government debt, and foreign currency reserves. External factors include global risk-appetite and growth expectations. The model was modified to also include the share of bilateral and multilateral debt.

[21]Communication and transparency regarding the cost of sterilization can also be crucial, especially in cases where central bank purchases are done below market rates. Large sterilization costs can increase concerns about central bank losses and monetary policy independence.

Figure 2.11. Large Shares of Senior Creditors Could Lead to Higher Spreads

If one class of creditors receives smaller haircuts, other creditors need to bear a greater burden.

Investors pricing a larger required haircut in case of default could meaningfully impact spreads.

1. Stylized Example of Issuer Requiring a Total 40 Percent Haircut with Debt Evenly Split

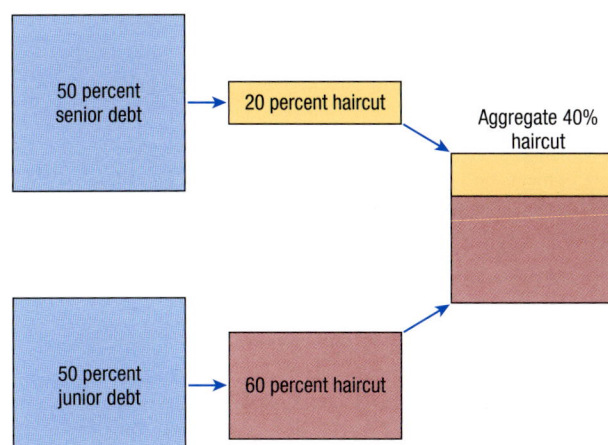

2. Bond Spread under Different Recovery Assumptions and Expectations of Default (Basis points)

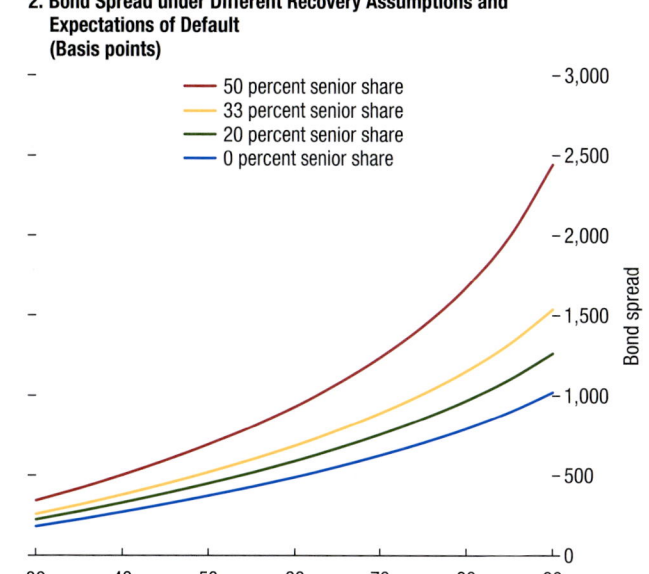

Source: IMF staff calculations.
Note: Panel 2 assumes a bond with an 8 percent coupon and 10-year maturity. It assumes that an overall debt reduction of 40 percent is required, with senior debt holders accepting only a 20 percent haircut.

discovery process and invite fiscal dominance. APPs should take into consideration the efficacy of the portfolio balance channel and whether investors have the ability to allocate their investments in other domestic assets, such as corporate or covered bonds. In the absence of such domestic alternatives, both foreign and domestic investors might choose to exit their country position altogether, which could increase the sensitivity of the exchange rate to APP policies. The resultant currency depreciation in countries with large currency mismatches in private sector balance sheets could at least partly offset the stimulatory effect of APP policies by tightening overall financial conditions. The experience of advanced economy central banks with exit strategy plans may also be important for emerging market central banks to consider, particularly when the size of the program is meaningful.

APPs should be designed so as not to become barriers to the development of domestic capital markets or the growth of a stable and diversified local investor base. In countries with relatively small bond markets, large and prolonged APPs could end up substantially increasing the role of the central bank as a market

maker in bond markets, impairing the price discovery process and financial market development. Specific measures for further local market development include (1) developing efficient money market frameworks; (2) strengthening primary market practices to enhance transparency and predictability of issuance; (3) bolstering market liquidity, including the use of repo facilities for local dealers in times of stress; and (4) developing a robust market infrastructure, including local clearing and settlement and other services (as detailed in IMF 2020b). For countries with adequate preparation in terms of legal barriers and market infrastructure, authorities should work toward enabling settlement and clearance of local currency debt in international capital markets so that domestic markets can benefit from access to wider liquidity pools.

Frontier market economies with unsustainable debt dynamics, limited market access, and high external financing requirements should preemptively and cooperatively seek debt resolution with their creditors. Countries that maintain market access at reasonable rates should decrease rollover risks as part of their debt management strategy.

References

Adler, Gustavo, Kyun Suk Chang, Rui Mano, and Yuting Shao. Forthcoming. "Foreign Exchange Intervention: A Data Set of Public Data and Proxies." International Monetary Fund, Washington, DC.

Adrian, Tobias, Richard K. Crump, and Emanuel Moench. 2013. "Pricing the Term Structure with Linear Regressions." Federal Reserve Bank of New York Staff Report 340, revised April 2013, New York.

Arslan, Yavuz, Mathias Drehmann, and Boris Hofmann. 2020. "Central Bank Bond Purchases in Emerging Market Economies." BIS Bulletin 20, Bank for International Settlements, Basel.

Beirne, John, Nuobu Renzhi, and Eric Alexander Sugandi. 2020. "Financial Market and Capital Flow Dynamics during the COVID-19 Pandemic." Working Paper 1158, Asian Development Bank Institute, Washington, DC.

Diebold, Francis X., and Kamil Yilmaz. 2012. "Better to Give than to Receive: Predictive Directional Measurement of Volatility Spillovers." *Economic Journal* 199: 157–71.

Drakopoulos, Dimitris, Rohit Goel, Evan Papageorgiou, and Can Sever. Forthcoming. "Effects of Emerging Market COVID-19 Asset Purchase Program Announcements on Financial Markets." IMF Working Paper, International Monetary Fund, Washington, DC.

Hartley, Jonathan S., and Alessandro Rebucci. 2020. "An Event Study of COVID-19: Central Bank Quantitative Easing in Advanced and Emerging Economies." NBER Research Paper 27339, National Bureau of Economic Research, Cambridge, MA.

Hofman, David, and Gunes Kamber. Forthcoming. "Unconventional Monetary Policy in Emerging Market and Developing Economies." Special Series on COVID-19, International Monetary Fund, Washington, DC.

International Monetary Fund (IMF). 2020a. "Toward an Integrated Policy Framework." Washington, DC.

———. 2020b. "Staff Note for the G20 IFAWG: Recent Developments on Local Currency Bond Markets in Emerging Economies." Washington, DC.

Jordà, Òscar. 2005. "Estimation and Inference of Impulse Responses by Local Projections." *American Economic Review* 95 (1): 161–82.

Schrimpf, Andreas, and Vladyslav Sushko. 2019. "FX Trade Execution: Complex and Highly Fragmented." *BIS Quarterly Review* (December).

Singh, Manmohan, and Rohit Goel. 2019. "Pledged Collateral Market's Role in Transmission to Short-Term Market Rates." IMF Working Paper 19/106, International Monetary Fund, Washington, DC.

Teulings, Coen N., and Nikolay Zubanov. 2014. "Is Economic Recovery a Myth? Robust Estimation of Impulse Responses." *Journal of Applied Econometrics* 29 (3): 497–514.

LIQUIDITY STRAINS CUSHIONED BY A POWERFUL SET OF POLICIES

Chapter 3 at a Glance

- In the Group of Seven (G7) economies, nonfinancial corporate borrowing surged in March and during the second quarter of 2020, benefiting from unprecedented policy support as a consequence of the coronavirus disease (COVID-19) crisis.
- Credit supply conditions across the G7 were generally favorable during the second quarter, yet the buoyancy of the bond market in the United States stood in sharp contrast to tighter loan market lending standards in that country.
- Among listed firms, those vulnerable to liquidity shocks suffered relatively more financial stress in the early stages of the COVID-19 crisis, and residual signs of strain remained as of the end of June.
- Premature withdrawal of policy support could jeopardize the success achieved so far in broadly meeting the nonfinancial corporate sector's liquidity and funding needs.

The COVID-19 pandemic has adversely affected nonfinancial corporate sector cash flows, generating liquidity and solvency pressures. In the G7 economies—Canada, France, Germany, Italy, Japan, the United Kingdom, and the United States—corporate borrowing surged in March and into the second quarter of 2020, thanks to credit line drawdowns and unprecedented policy support. This allowed firms to build cash buffers to cope with a period of reduced cash flow and high uncertainty. In the United States, the bond market has been buoyant since the end of March, but credit supply conditions for bank loans and the syndicated loan market have tightened. In other G7 economies, credit supply conditions eased somewhat across markets during the second quarter. Among listed firms, entities with weaker solvency or liquidity positions before the onset of COVID-19, as well as smaller firms, suffered relatively more financial stress in some economies in the early stages of the crisis. However, residual signs of strain remained as of the end of June, when the stock market underperformance of French, UK, and US firms with pre–COVID-19 liquidity vulnerabilities ranged between 4 and 10 percentage points. Policy interventions, especially those directly targeting the

corporate sector, had a beneficial effect overall. Looking ahead, premature withdrawal of policy support could jeopardize the success achieved so far in broadly meeting the nonfinancial corporate sector's funding needs.

Introduction

The COVID-19 pandemic has triggered a deep global economic crisis. Closures and restrictions imposed by governments to contain the spread of the virus, as well as social distancing, have severely disrupted business activity and clouded the economic outlook amid heightened uncertainty. Corporate cash flows have been heavily impaired in many industries, with adverse implications for corporate liquidity and solvency.

In the major advanced economies, severe disruptions to corporate funding markets became apparent amid a sharp tightening of financial conditions early in the year following the onset of the COVID-19 crisis, as corporate bond funds, loan funds, and prime money market funds faced large outflows. This led to a collapse in the issuance of nonfinancial corporate bonds, syndicated loans, and commercial paper, and to a jump in corporate spreads. Many firms turned to their existing credit lines to secure funds in a "dash for cash."

In response, policymakers in these economies quickly announced a wide range of powerful policy measures to support markets and address corporate

The authors of this chapter are Andrea Deghi, Ken Zhi Gan, Tom Piontek, Dulani Seneviratne, Tomohiro Tsuruga, and Jérôme Vandenbussche (team leader), with contributions from Germán Villegas Bauer, under the guidance of Fabio Natalucci and Mahvash Qureshi. Jeremy Stein served as an expert advisor.

funding needs (see Online Box 3.1 for a brief description of the key measures and their timing). Some of these measures were unprecedented; one example is the new Federal Reserve facilities to support corporate credit. The combination of these fiscal, monetary, and financial policy measures helped normalize financial conditions during the second quarter, as discussed in the June 2020 *Global Financial Stability Report* (GFSR) *Update* and Chapter 1 of this current report. However, corporate spreads remain wider than at the beginning of the year, especially in the high-yield segment, pointing to remaining concerns about default risk.[1]

The degree of eventual economic scarring from the COVID-19 crisis will depend a great deal on how well the financial system—supported to an exceptionally large extent by policies to date—is able to meet the corporate sector's demand for liquidity during the crisis. This means preventing still-solvent firms facing liquidity strains from turning into insolvent entities or being forced to significantly curtail their activities.[2]

Against this backdrop, this chapter assesses whether corporate liquidity needs were met for listed firms in the G7 economies during the first few months of the crisis (from the beginning of February to the end of June).[3] Given the rise in corporate sector leverage in several G7 economies during the period preceding COVID-19, as documented in recent issues of the GFSR, the chapter also examines the impact of high corporate indebtedness on firms' financial stress during the crisis. While the COVID-19 crisis has severely hurt a very large number of unlisted small and medium-sized enterprises, which traditionally face difficulties accessing external financing, lack of recent publicly available data for these firms prevents a thorough analysis of their funding situation during the pandemic.[4]

The chapter seeks to address four broad sets of issues. First, it analyzes the impact of the COVID-19 crisis on aggregate credit volumes in several segments of the corporate debt market as well as the effects of the subsequent policy response on the debt financing choices of large firms. Second, it discusses the evolution of aggregate conditions in credit markets and seeks to quantify the credit supply shocks in these markets. Third, it examines the extent to which ease of access to external finance, or liquidity position, had an impact on firm-level financial performance in the early stages of the crisis, potentially signaling the presence of tighter credit conditions.[5] Acknowledging that such an analysis is a very challenging task, the chapter turns to an examination of the effect of key policy announcements and tries to gauge the impact of various types of policy responses on the supply of corporate credit during the containment phase of the pandemic.[6]

The chapter finds that drawdowns of existing credit lines and unprecedented policy support helped maintain the flow of credit to firms, and that corporate borrowing surged in March and the second quarter of 2020. As a result, firms managed to build cash buffers to cope with a period of reduced cash flow and high uncertainty. Since the end of March, the bond market has been buoyant in the United States, but credit supply conditions for bank loans and syndicated loans have tightened. In Japan, bank lending standards have eased, but bond market supply conditions have tightened somewhat despite a solid year-on-year increase in issuance. In other G7 economies, credit supply conditions have evolved in a more homogeneous manner across markets, with somewhat easier conditions prevailing, on average, during the second quarter. Among listed firms, entities with weaker solvency or liquidity positions before COVID-19, as well as smaller firms, suffered relatively more financial stress in some economies during the early stages of the crisis, and residual signs of strain remained as of the end of June. Policy interventions, especially those directly targeting the corporate sector,

---

[1]As of September 10, 2020, US investment-grade (high-yield) credit spreads had widened 33 basis points (125 basis points) since the beginning of the year. In Europe, investment-grade (high-yield) spreads had widened 9 basis points (101 basis points) on a net basis. Yet with US government bond yields having fallen significantly during the crisis, junk bond yields were at, or close to, record lows.

[2]Several studies on the global financial crisis have documented reductions in credit supply's adverse consequences on employment, investment, and total factor productivity growth (Duchin, Ozbas, and Sensoy 2010; Chodorow-Reich 2014; Duval, Hong, and Timmer 2020).

[3]The focus on G7 economies is dictated by these economies' global systemic relevance and their relatively better data availability.

[4]Chapter 1 of the October 2020 *World Economic Outlook* discusses a model-based analysis of the impact of the COVID-19 crisis on small and medium-sized enterprises, building on work by Gourinchas and others (forthcoming).

[5]The chapter does not aim to project liquidity gaps at the firm level (see Banerjee and others 2020); rather, it aims to provide a quantification of the challenges firms face in accessing debt financing during the containment phase of the COVID-19 crisis. Similarly, the chapter does not aim to provide an account of differences in performance across industries but controls for the heterogeneous effect of the crisis across industries in the empirical analysis.

[6]Data sources and variables used in this chapter are described in Online Annex 3.1. All annexes are available at www.imf.org/en/Publications/GFSR.

had a beneficial effect, on average. These findings can help inform ongoing discussions about the appropriate level of policy support as the global economy moves toward the recovery phase. While trade-offs with other policy objectives need to be considered, especially in a context of limited fiscal space, premature withdrawal of policy support could jeopardize the success achieved so far in broadly meeting the nonfinancial corporate sector's funding needs.

A Surge in Debt Financing and Cash Balances

This section discusses the provision of credit to firms in key segments of the corporate credit market during the containment phase of the crisis. Loans represent the major source of corporate debt funding in the G7 economies, ranging from 58 percent in the United States to 90 percent in Germany, according to the latest available financial accounts data. The remainder is composed of debt securities. In terms of issuance by large firms, the ratio of syndicated loans (which are mostly held by banks post syndication if they are investment grade and by nonbanks if they are non-investment grade) to bonds ranges from two to three.[7]

Despite a period of acute financial stress early in the year, outstanding amounts of bank credit to firms grew significantly in March and in the second quarter in all seven economies analyzed (Figure 3.1, panel 1). On a year-over-year basis, the rate of bank credit growth during the first half of the year was clearly above trend.[8] Part of this dynamic is clearly attributable to sizable credit line drawdowns, especially in the United States (Figure 3.1, panel 2). Listed firms' drawdowns increased more than 40 percent, on average, compared with the first half of 2019. The increase was particularly spectacular in the United States, where net drawdowns at the end of March doubled, representing an increase of $250 billion, which is of the same order of magnitude as the increase in commercial and industrial loans by domestic banks over the same period.[9] Panel 3 of Figure 3.1 shows that these drawdowns were

concentrated in March, with a peak on the last day of the month. Presumably, this reflects firms' desire to secure funds while they were still in compliance with their maintenance covenants and because they expected a sharp deterioration in cash flow during the second quarter. Gross drawdowns in the United States subsided at the beginning of April, resulting in a decline in utilization rates—that is, the share of credit line commitments used. The same reduction can be observed in Canada; drawdown activity in Japan, however, continued during the second quarter, resulting in a utilization rate of 60 percent. Nevertheless, utilization rates across the seven economies remained well below 50 percent, on average, at the end of June, suggesting that liquidity insurance remained significant, at least in the aggregate.[10] Bank credit developments during the second quarter also reflected the implementation of government programs (notably, off-budget credit guarantees) that transferred part—sometimes all—of the credit risk to the sovereign, as well as government-sponsored loans with a significant grant component. These direct support programs to corporate funding represented between 2.6 and 34 percent of GDP as of June 12 (Figure 3.1, panel 4). They complemented other on-budget fiscal measures that directly supported corporate cash flows and solvency, for example, through grants, employment support programs, and reductions in tax liabilities.[11] As of early July, committed amounts appear to have been significantly smaller than announced amounts in European economies (Anderson, Papadia, and Véron 2020).

Syndicated loan issuance during the first half of the year was somewhat more heterogeneous across economies. It was generally stronger than in 2019 in Europe and Japan, but weaker in the United States and Canada, especially during the second quarter. This appears to have been driven by a surge in investment-grade loan issuance in Europe and Japan (Figure 3.2, panel 1) and a drop in leveraged loan issuance outside of Germany and Italy (Figure 3.2, panel 2).[12] The weak recovery in the leveraged loan markets was to a large extent due

---

[7]Syndicated loans include both term loans and credit lines.

[8]Before the pandemic, the volume of nonfinancial corporate bank loans was on a declining trend in Italy.

[9]Acharya and Steffen (2020) and Kapan and Minoiu (2020) discuss credit line drawdowns in the United States in early 2020. In contrast to the experience of the global financial crisis described in Ivashina and Scharfstein (2010), the increase in credit line drawdowns was related to immediate liquidity demand rather than concerns about the health of the US banking sector.

[10]Of course, there is substantial heterogeneity across firms and sectors. In the United States, the utilization rate was significantly above average in wholesale and retail trade at the end of June.

[11]See the IMF's Fiscal Monitor Database of Country Fiscal Measures in Response to the COVID-19 Pandemic, https://www.imf.org/en/Topics/imf-and-covid19/Fiscal-Policies-Database-in-Response-to-COVID-19.

[12]It should be noted that the euro area leveraged loan market is significantly smaller than the US market.

Figure 3.1. Bank Lending to Nonfinancial Firms and Government Liquidity Support

Corporate bank lending grew rapidly from March onward ...

1. Bank Loans to Nonfinancial Firms, Amount Outstanding
(NSA; corresponding period in 2019 = 100)

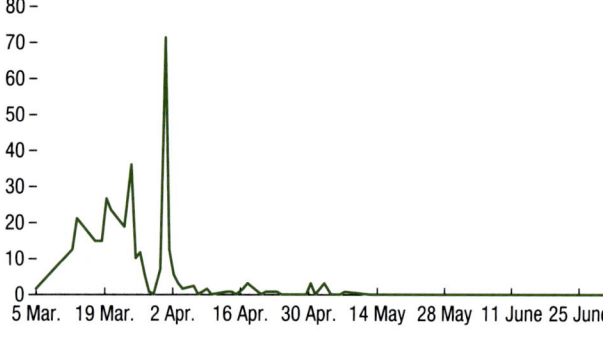

... driven in part by credit line drawdowns ...

2. Listed Nonfinancial Firms' Net Credit Line Drawdowns
(Percent change from same period in 2019)

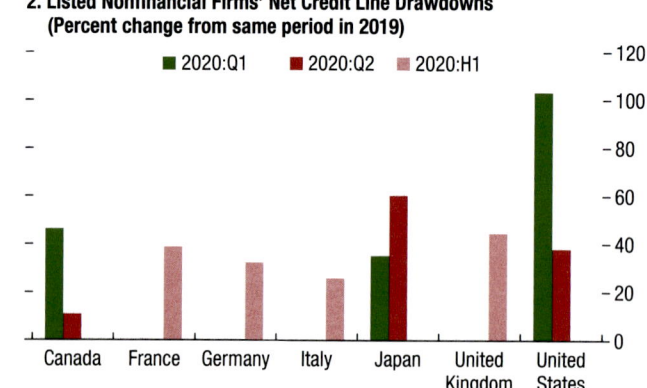

... especially in the United States in March.

3. United States: Gross Credit Line Drawdowns
(Billions of US dollars; March 5–June 30, 2020)

Liquidity support to firms by government was huge, especially in Europe and Japan.

4. Governments' Announced Liquidity Support Measures in Response to COVID-19
(Percent of GDP)

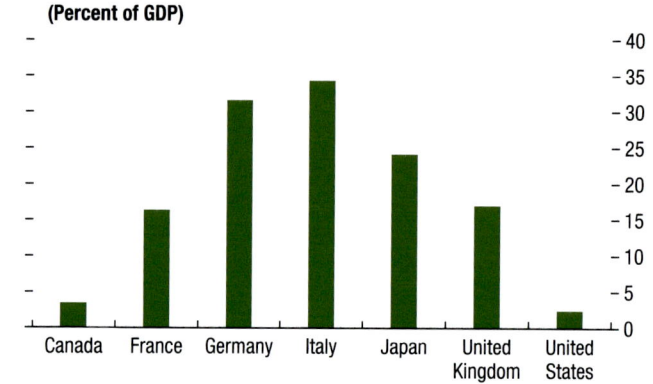

Sources: Federal Reserve; Haver Analytics; IMF, Fiscal Monitor Database of Country Fiscal Measures in Response to the COVID-19 Pandemic (June 2020); S&P Capital IQ; S&P Leveraged Commentary & Data; and IMF staff calculations.
Note: Panel 2 is based on data available as of August 25, 2020. Half-yearly data are used instead of quarterly data for European economies because of scant quarterly reporting (when first half data are not available, but first quarter data are, the latter are used). Panel 4 shows liquidity support (including equity injections, loans, asset purchases or debt assumption, guarantees, and quasi-fiscal operations) per country as a percent of GDP. Amounts do not include above-the-line fiscal measures, such as the US Paycheck Protection Program, which amounts to about 3 percent of US GDP. NSA = not seasonally adjusted.

to subdued demand from the traditional investor base. Collateralized loan obligation (CLO) new issuance has been slow to restart.[13] While activity picked up modestly from March levels, new CLO supply ran at half of last year's pace, while still accounting for more than 70 percent of new leveraged loan demand (Figure 3.2, panel 3). CLO investors were concerned about the wave

of downgrades and defaults (Figure 3.2, panel 4), which may affect lower-rated tranches.

Corporate bond markets in the first quarter were generally more resilient despite coming under intense pressure in mid-March. Policy responses by central banks announced in the second half of March, especially facilities aimed at directly supporting corporate bond markets, appear to have boosted activity in these markets and contributed to a reversal in corporate bond fund flows (including exchange-traded funds). During the second quarter, investment-grade issuance surged to levels twice as large as those in 2019

[13]A collateralized loan obligation is a structured finance product collateralized predominantly by broadly syndicated leveraged loans. See Chapter 2 of the April 2020 GFSR for a discussion of risky corporate credit markets.

Figure 3.2. Developments in Syndicated Loan Markets

During the second quarter, investment-grade loan issuance was much stronger in Europe and Japan than in North America ...

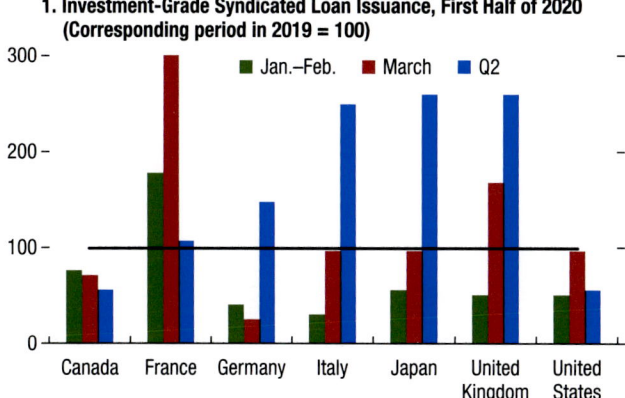

... whereas activity in the leveraged loan market generally dropped sharply.

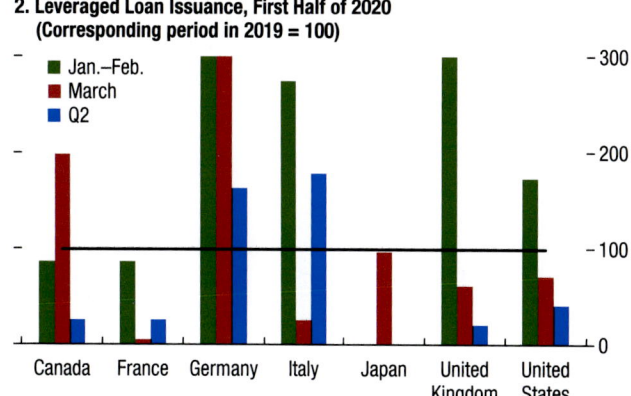

Weaker investor demand suppressed new leveraged loan issuance, such as from slower CLO formation ...

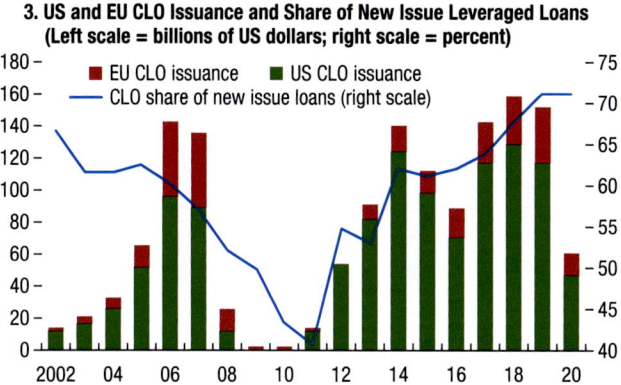

... as underlying asset quality deteriorated.

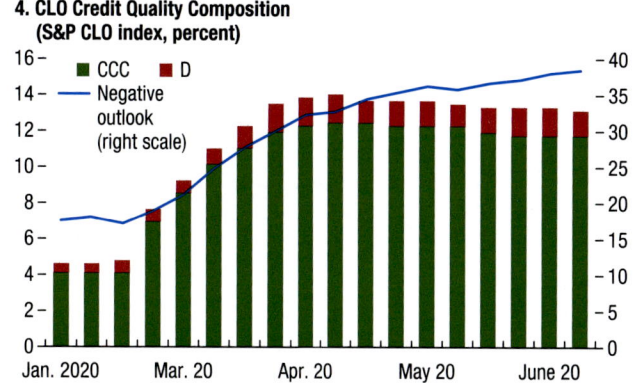

Sources: Dealogic; S&P Capital IQ; S&P Global Ratings; S&P Leveraged Commentary & Data; and IMF staff calculations.
Note: For panel 3, 2020 data are annualized through end-June 2020. Data for individual European countries are not available, so the European Union aggregate is shown. CLO = collateralized loan obligation; EU = European Union.

in France, Germany, the United Kingdom, and the United States (Figure 3.3, panel 1). The response of the high-yield segment was somewhat more muted outside the United States, probably reflecting its relative underdevelopment and the focus of central banks' purchases on the investment-grade segment. For its part, the United States saw high-yield issuance during the second quarter more than double compared with that in 2019 (Figure 3.3, panel 2).

The characteristics of new debt in the high-yield bond market reveal a shift toward higher quality. In G7 economies, nearly 60 percent of high-yield new issues during the first half of the year were BB rated, and more than 30 percent of the bonds were secured, the highest levels for the past 15 years at least

(Figure 3.3, panel 3). By use of proceeds, more than 80 percent of year-to-date supply was for refinancing existing debt as lower yields and strong investor demand encouraged a range of issuers to tap into the market to repay credit lines, or for short-term expenses such as working capital (Figure 3.3, panel 4). Issuances motivated by acquisition and dividends or share repurchases, however, were at their lowest in a decade.

Developments in bond and syndicated loan issuance suggest that, for firms with access to these markets, the bond market clearly was the preferred source of debt financing in the United States, but perhaps not in the other G7 economies. This hypothesis is confirmed by a granular investigation of the

Figure 3.3. Corporate Bond and Commercial Paper Issuance

Unlike for syndicated loans, bond issuance was buoyant during the second quarter in the investment-grade segment ...

1. Investment Grade Bond Issuance, First Half of 2020
(Corresponding period in 2019 = 100)

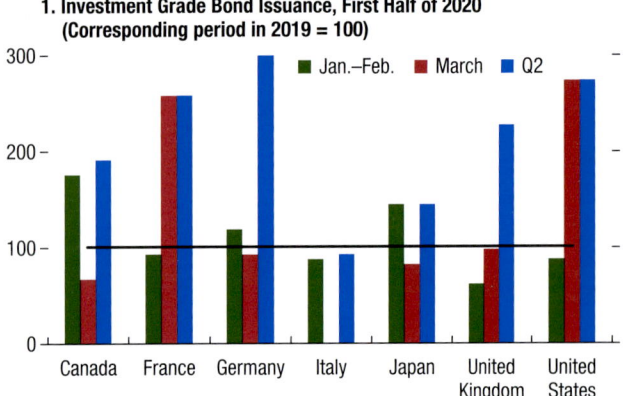

... as well as in the high-yield segment in the United States.

2. High-Yield Bond Issuance, First Half of 2020
(Corresponding period in 2019 = 100)

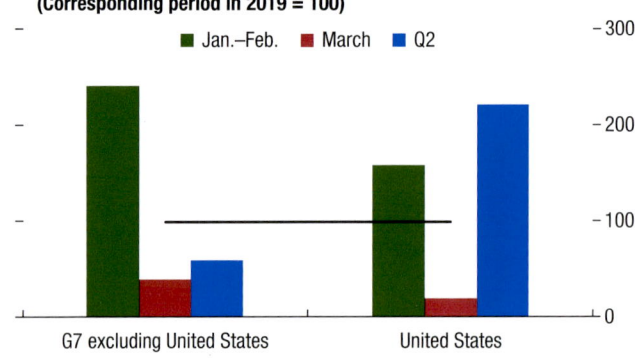

High-yield bond supply shifted to higher quality with more security and stronger ratings.

3. Group of Seven High-Yield Bond Supply by Security and Rating
(Percent)

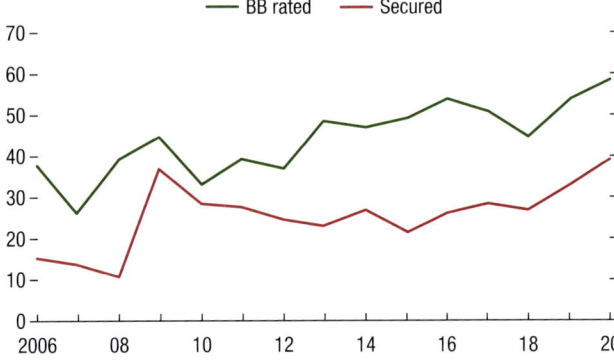

The majority of high-yield bond supply was used for refinancing and for other purposes, such as repayment of credit lines.

4. Group of Seven High-Yield Bond Issuance by Use of Proceeds
(Percent)

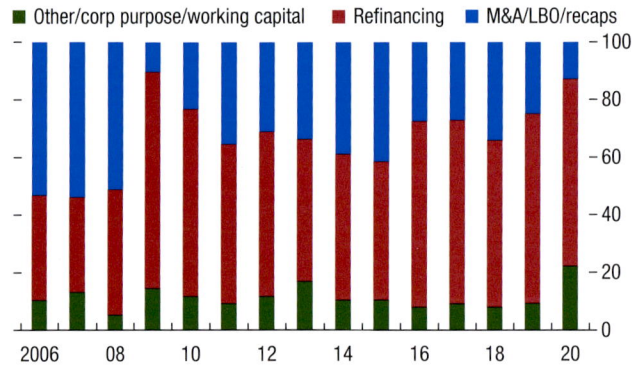

The bond market was clearly more attractive to US firms during the second quarter ...

5. Change in Relative Attractiveness of Bond versus Loan Issuance during the First Half of 2020
(Change in bond issuance probability, percentage points)

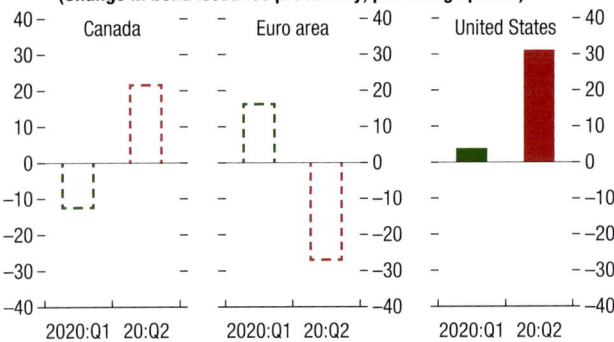

... both in the investment-grade and the high-yield segments.

6. United States: Change in Relative Attractiveness of Bond versus Loan Issuance
(Change in bond issuance probability, percentage points)

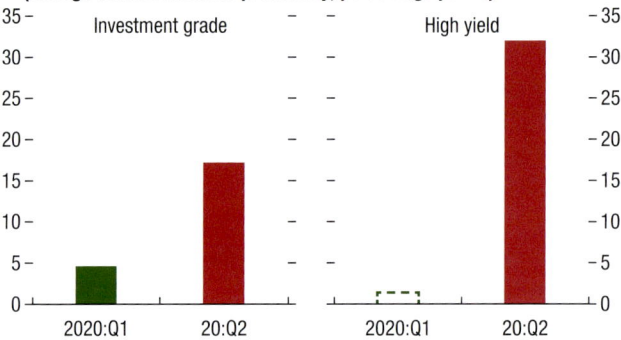

Figure 3.3. Corporate Bond and Commercial Paper Issuance *(continued)*

Volumes in the commercial paper market had opposite dynamics in the United States and the euro area.

Nonfinancial corporate debt growth was strong overall.

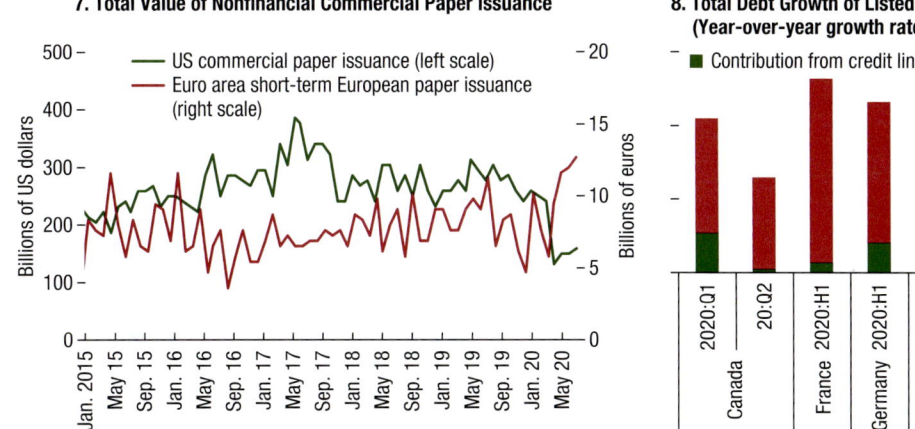

7. Total Value of Nonfinancial Commercial Paper Issuance

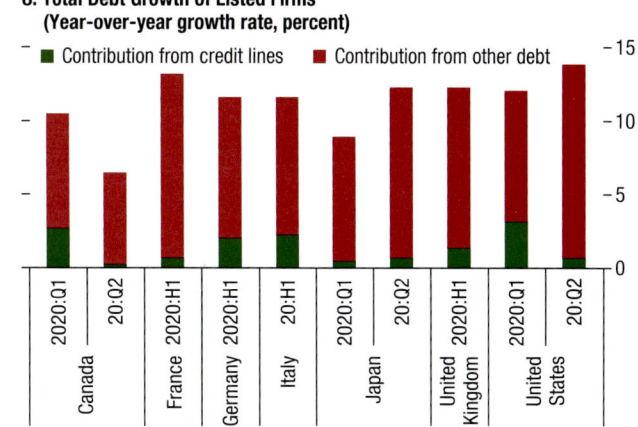

8. Total Debt Growth of Listed Firms
(Year-over-year growth rate, percent)

Sources: Federal Reserve; Haver Analytics; S&P Capital IQ; S&P Leveraged Commentary & Data; and IMF staff calculations.
Note: For panels 3 and 4, 2020 data are through end-June. Euro area refers to three euro area economies (France, Germany, Italy). Panels 5 and 6 show the change in the probability of issuing a bond (versus a loan) for a nonfinancial firm with characteristics equal to the sample mean during the first and second quarters of 2020 compared with before the COVID-19 crisis. Colored bars indicate significance at the 1 percent level. Empty bars indicate lack of statistical significance. See Online Annex 3.2 for methodological details. Panel 8 is based on data available as of August 25, 2020. Data as of the first half of the year are used for European Group of Seven economies to account for semiannual reporting of most firms (when first half data are not available, but first quarter data are, the latter are used). LBO = leveraged buyout; M&A = mergers and acquisitions.

debt financing choice of these firms. Controlling for a large set of firm characteristics and macro-financial variables, the analysis documents a shift toward bond financing in the United States but not in other jurisdictions (Figure 3.3, panel 5).[14] This finding suggests that the Federal Reserve's March 23 announcement of its new corporate credit facilities had a stimulative impact on domestic bond markets.[15,16] That the choice between bond versus loan financing was not affected in other jurisdictions likely partially reflects the presence of central bank corporate bond purchase programs predating the pandemic in these economies (except in Canada).[17] A more detailed analysis for

the United States confirms that the shift toward the bond market happened in both the investment-grade and high-yield segments, with the shift in the former already visible in the first quarter, in line with record investment-grade issuance levels in March (Figure 3.3, panel 6).[18] These shifts in corporate financing choice during the first half of the year also varied, depending on firm characteristics such as leverage and investment opportunities, as discussed in Online Box 3.2.

In contrast to the bond market, volumes in the commercial paper market in the United States have not recovered since their sharp drop in March, when investors shifted funds from prime to government money market funds (Figure 3.3, panel 7), despite the reintroduction of the Federal Reserve's Commercial Paper Funding Facility on March 17 and inflows resuming into prime funds, especially from institu-

---

[14]See Online Annex 3.2 for methodological details.

[15]Thus, a key driver of the shift toward bond financing in the United States appears to be related to policy rather than to the weakness of banks' balance sheets, as was the case at the time of the global financial crisis (Adrian, Colla, and Shin 2013; Becker and Ivashina 2014). The Federal Reserve corporate credit facilities cover the primary bond and loan markets as well as the secondary bond market. As of August 31, no purchases had been made on the primary markets.

[16]The evidence for the US market is consistent with the findings of Acharya and Steffen (2020).

[17]The Bank of Canada announced its first corporate bond purchase program on April 15, 2020.

[18]One factor contributing to the large volume of high-yield bond issuance in the United States in the second quarter was the announcement on April 9, 2020, by the Federal Reserve that the scope of its new corporate credit facilities would be extended to high-yield exchange-traded funds and bonds and loans from firms that lost their investment-grade status after March 22, 2020.

tional investors. It appears that the fall in bond market yields has tempted firms to reduce their refinancing risk and substitute commercial paper with longer-term debt.[19] By contrast, commercial paper issuance in the euro area, supported by the European Central Bank's expansion of its commercial paper purchases through the Asset Purchase Programme and the Pandemic Emergency Purchase Programme, rebounded quickly from the March trough and hit a record high in June. Incentives to substitute commercial paper with longer-term bonds were weaker in the euro area, because the yield differential remained more stable than in the United States.[20]

All in all, the year-over-year growth rate of total debt of listed firms was strong, generally exceeding 10 percent, with notable contributions from credit line drawdowns in Canada and the United States during the first quarter (Figure 3.3, panel 8).

Evidence suggests that this additional borrowing was used mostly to build cash reserves to cope with the uncertainty and the expected reduction in cash flow triggered by the pandemic shock. In contrast to Europe, all listed firms in Canada, Japan, and the United States are required to report quarterly, and their cash flow statements for the first quarter reveal an accumulation of cash and short-term investments of about 0.5 percent of assets in Japan and about 1.5 percent of assets in Canada and the United States. This behavior contrasts sharply with that observed a year earlier and during the peak of the global financial crisis in the fourth quarter of 2008, when no cash accumulation took place (Figure 3.4, panel 1). The change in cash levels can be attributed mostly to an increase in financing in Canada, a reduction in investment in Japan, and a combination of both in the United States relative to 2019. During the second quarter, listed Japanese and US firms built their cash buffers further, whereas listed Canadian firms reduced them somewhat. The accumulation of cash is also visible from nonfinancial corporate deposit data, which reveal

a further large expansion during the second quarter, especially in France and the United Kingdom (Figure 3.4, panel 2).

Shifts in Aggregate Credit Supply Conditions

The large increase in borrowing (net of withdrawals from existing credit lines) in March and the second quarter of 2020 was associated with credit spreads that widened sharply in March and subsequently slowly declined (as discussed in the June 2020 GFSR *Update* and Chapter 1 of this report). A key reason for the wider spreads is obviously the sharp deterioration in corporate fundamentals and concerns about default risk in all seven economies (Figure 3.5, panel 1), but a tightening in credit supply may also have played a role.

To assess how much of the widening in spreads can be attributed to adverse credit supply conditions, this section looks at evidence available in different segments of credit markets. For the commercial bank loan market, useful information is obtained from central banks' quarterly surveys of bank lending officers, which measure officers' perception of the strength of credit demand and of the evolution of their banks' lending standards.[21] For the European and US primary syndicated loan markets, an empirical analysis to disentangle credit supply from demand factors is conducted by making use of publicly available transaction-level issuance data. Specifically, the analysis relies on empirical estimation of a supply and demand system of equations that includes variables capturing lender and borrower characteristics and covers the mid- to late 2000s through the second quarter of 2020.[22] The value of the credit supply shock in each quarter is obtained by computing the time-varying "residual term" of the credit supply equation. For the secondary corporate bond market, a measure of investor risk appetite—the so-called excess bond premium

---

[19]Li and others (2020) suggest that liquidity rules introduced at the time of the 2016 money market fund reform may not have achieved the goal of making the system immune to runs. See also the discussion in Eren, Schrimpf, and Sushko (2020).

[20]The Bank of Canada and the Bank of England also introduced commercial paper purchase programs, whereas the Bank of Japan stepped up its existing program. These countries are not shown on the chart for lack of data.

[21]An important caveat in interpreting results of bank lending officers' surveys is that they do not always clearly distinguish between changes in default risk and changes in credit supply in the definition of lending standards.

[22]The analysis addresses endogeneity concerns by using an identification-through-heteroscedasticity methodology (Rigobon 2003). See Online Annex 3.3 for details.

Figure 3.4. Change in Corporate Cash-to-Assets Ratio and Corporate Bank Deposits

Nonfinancial firms accumulated more cash during the first quarter of 2020 than during the same period of 2019, mostly because of increased external financing in Canada and the United States ...

... and this precautionary behavior continued during the second quarter.

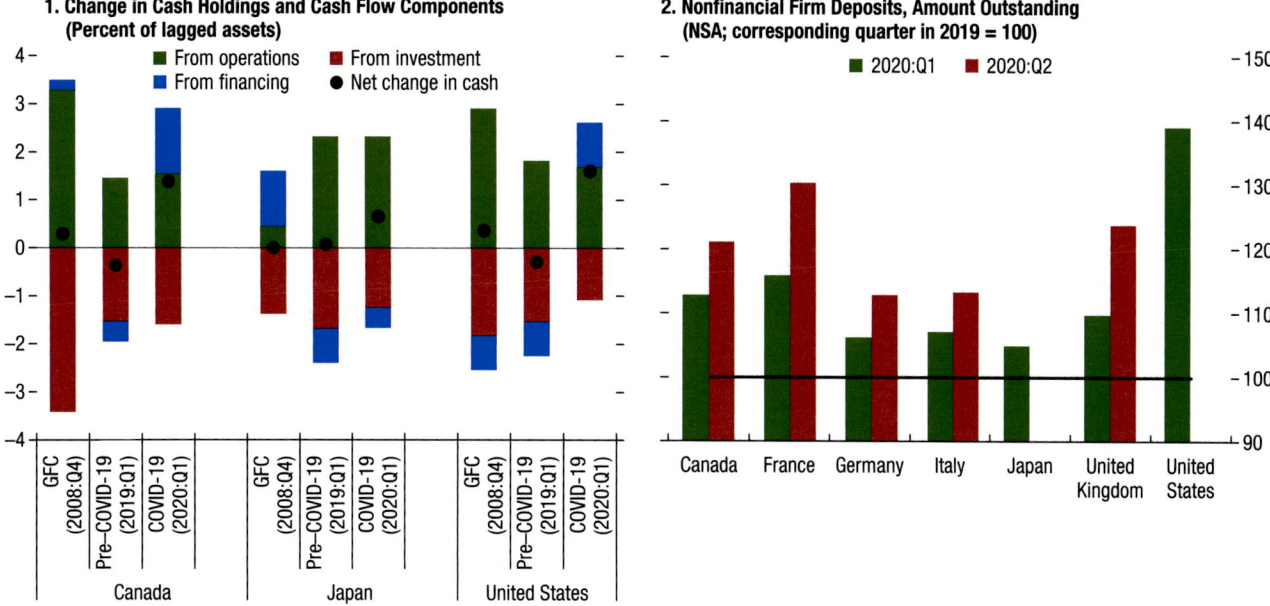

Sources: Bank of Japan; Federal Reserve Board; Haver Analytics; S&P Capital IQ; and IMF staff calculations.
Note: Panel 1 shows the listed nonfinancial firms' quarterly net change in cash as well as the contributions from the three cash flow components. European countries are not shown because of insufficient data for the first quarter. Panel 2 shows the amount of nonfinancial firms' deposits outstanding in the first and second quarters of 2020 compared with the corresponding quarter of 2019. Data for the second quarter are not available for Japan and the United States. GFC = global financial crisis; NSA = not seasonally adjusted.

proposed by Gilchrist and Zakrajšek (2012)—is constructed to gauge shifts in supply.[23,24]

Survey-based evidence indicates that the commercial bank loan market in the United States was an outlier across countries in the second quarter. Credit demand fell and lending standards tightened sharply, while the evolution was generally muted or the opposite in the

other G7 economies.[25] In particular, a large loosening of credit conditions was observed in Japan and the United Kingdom (Figure 3.5, panel 2).[26] This stands in sharp contrast to the experience during the global financial crisis, when surveys indicate that banks tightened lending standards consistently across the board. The situation in the current crisis is likely related to the fact that banks' indicators of funding stress spiked only briefly in late March before normalizing thanks

[23]This measure is constructed in two steps using detailed information on many individual corporate bonds for the period from the mid-2000s (or the first quarter of 2011 for the euro area) through the second quarter of 2020. First, for each bond, a spread to a synthetic risk-free rate that considers information on the duration of the bond is computed. Such a spread is more accurate than the more commonly used "naïve" spreads, whose construction ignores bond duration. Second, the spread is purged of its credit risk component to obtain the excess bond premium, which can therefore be interpreted as an indicator of bond investor risk appetite. See Online Annex 3.4 for methodological details. The series for the United States is from the Federal Reserve Board.

[24]The three euro area economies (France, Germany, Italy) are analyzed as a group to improve sample size, and Canada is not included in the analysis for data availability reasons.

[25]The evolution of the index for the United States indicates only that the tightening of lending standards was widespread, not that it was intense. However, the text describing the survey results makes it clear that lending standards were tight and explains that "banks, on balance, reported that their lending standards across all loan categories are currently at the tighter end of the range of standards between 2005 and the present" (Board of Governors of the Federal Reserve System 2020).

[26]In the United Kingdom, the survey question refers to the "availability of credit" rather than to lending standards per se. The two notions are different in the presence of government loan guarantees, which may explain part of the difference between the United Kingdom and the euro area economies.

Figure 3.5. Evolution of Credit Supply Conditions

As the risk of default increased ...

... bank lending standards tightened in the United States but eased in Japan and the United Kingdom.

1. One-Year Expected Default Frequency of Nonfinancial Firms Rated between Baa1 and B3 at the End of 2019, End of Period, 75th Percentile (Difference from end-2019, percent)

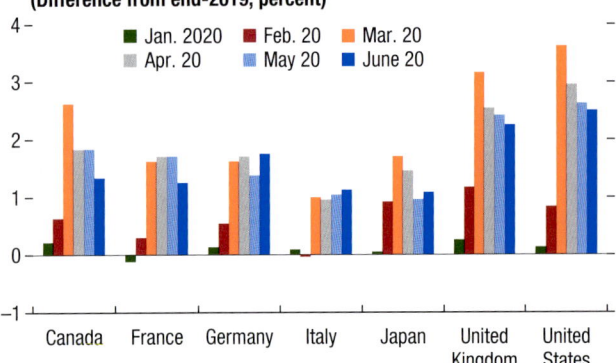

2. Change in Bank Lending Standards (Index; see note for details)

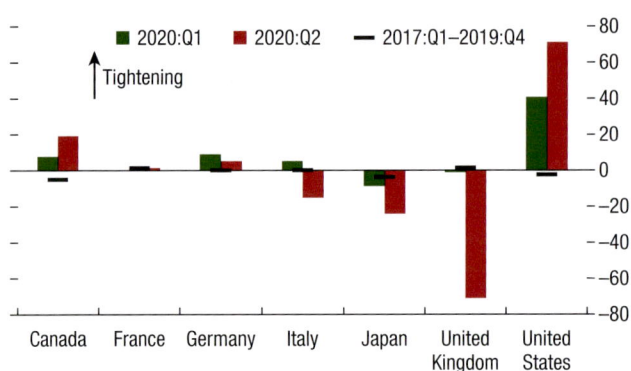

In the United States, credit conditions tightened somewhat in the syndicated loan market, but eased in the bond market after a period of tension in March.

In the United Kingdom, credit conditions also eased in the bond market after the stress in March, while conditions in the syndicated loan market remained neutral.

3. Credit Supply Conditions in the United States
   (Top: syndicated loan market, spread residual, percent—quarterly;
   bottom: bond market, excess bond premium, percent—monthly)

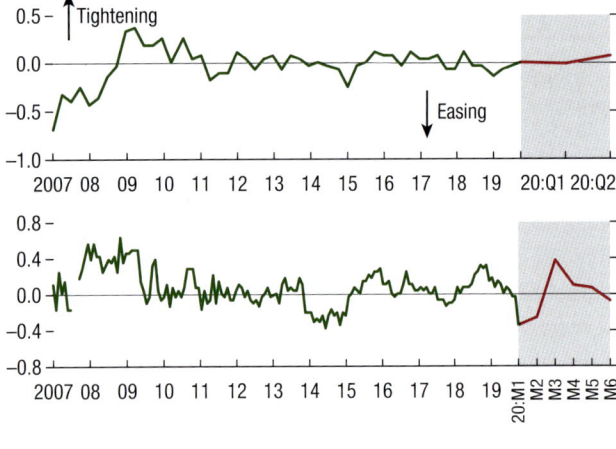

4. Credit Supply Conditions in the United Kingdom
   (Top: syndicated loan market, spread residual, percent—quarterly;
   bottom: bond market, excess bond premium, percent—monthly)

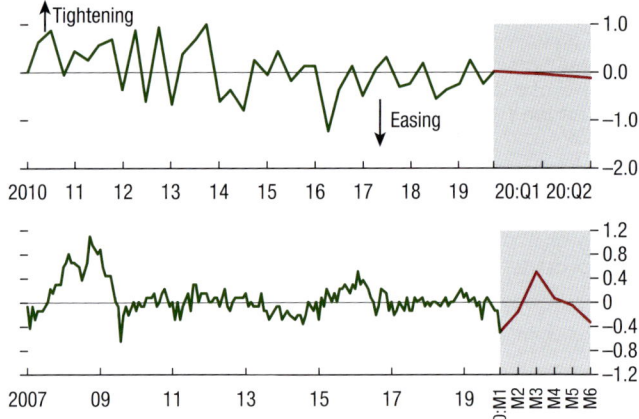

to the speed of policy support to financial markets and the economy, as well as to the effect of government programs to support lending to businesses (Bank of England 2020; European Central Bank 2020).[27]

Turning to supply conditions in the syndicated loan and bond markets, the divergence across the two markets during the second quarter in the United States is striking. The top part of Figure 3.5, panel 3, shows the time series of the credit supply shock in the

syndicated loan market. Credit conditions were neutral in the first quarter, on average, and tightened during the second quarter, bringing the market into a tight position, though not as tight as in the aftermath of the global financial crisis. By contrast, the bottom part of the same panel, which shows supply conditions in the secondary bond market, reveals that a large part of the March tightening was undone during the second quarter. Aside from the stimulative effect of the introduction of the Federal Reserve corporate credit facilities mentioned previously, two supply-side considerations may explain the buoyancy of the US bond market. First, with short-term rates near zero and Treasury

[27]The total amount of credit line drawdowns could also be a factor explaining the tightening of lending standards in the United States because it reduced the amount of bank capital available for new lending (Kapan and Minoiu 2020).

Figure 3.5. Evolution of Credit Supply Conditions *(continued)*

In the euro area, credit conditions eased in the syndicated loan market and remained broadly neutral in the bond market.

5. Credit Supply Conditions in the Euro Area
(Top: syndicated loan market, spread residual, percent—quarterly; bottom: bond market, excess bond premium, percent—monthly)

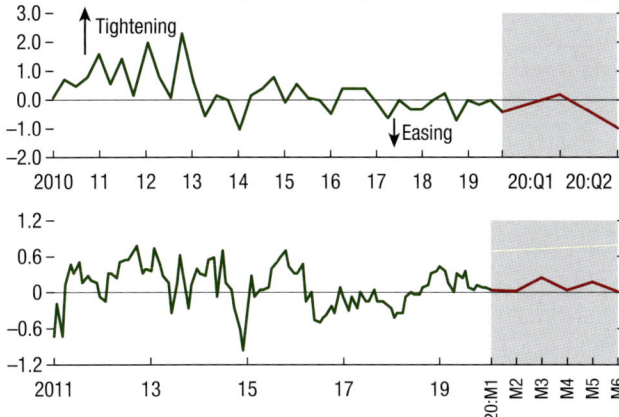

In Japan, conditions in the bond market tightened in March and remained slightly on the tight side in the second quarter.

6. Credit Supply Conditions in Japan
(Bond market, excess bond premium, percent—monthly)

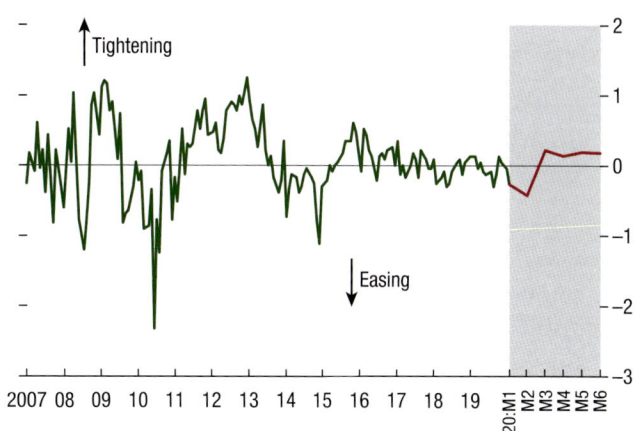

Sources: Bank of Japan; Bloomberg Finance L.P.; Dealogic; Federal Reserve Board; Haver Analytics; Moody's Analytics; Refinitiv Datastream, Eikon; S&P Market Intelligence; and IMF staff calculations.
Note: Panel 1 shows the change in the 75th percentile of the one-year end-of-period expected default frequency of nonfinancial firms rated between Baa1 and B3 (lower medium grade to highly speculative grade) at the end of 2019 in each Group of Seven country between the end of 2019 and each of the first six months of 2020. Panel 2 shows the quarter-on-quarter change in bank lending standards from the bank lending survey conducted by respective central bank; change is shown in the form of an index ranging from −100 to 100. Canada, euro area economies, and the United Kingdom report a balance of opinions weighted by asset size with a base value of 0; Japan reports a balance of opinion weighted by the level of easing or tightening; the United States reports an unweighted balance of opinion in two categories by firm size (large versus small); and the figure shows the simple average of the two. See Online Annexes 3.3 and 3.4 for methodological details on the construction of the series shown in panels 3–6. Credit conditions in Canada and in the Japanese syndicated loan market could not be computed because of insufficient data. M = month.

purchases by the Federal Reserve bringing down term premiums, investors' search for yield pushed them toward yield-providing assets, especially those within the perimeter of central bank support. Second, expectations of no rise in the policy rate for several years reduced investors' incentives to get exposure to floating rates. As syndicated loan rates are floating and bond rates are fixed, some investors may find bonds relatively more attractive in the current environment. A separate analysis for investment-grade syndicated loans and leveraged loans indicates that conditions moved from easy to tight during the second quarter in both segments.[28]

The dynamics of credit conditions in the United Kingdom's bond market mirrored those in the United States, but no tightening was observed in the syndicated loan market, on average (Figure 3.5, panel 4).

[28]Loan covenant quality in North America appears to have continued to weaken during the first quarter, reaching its all-time worst level (according to Moody's)—to the benefit of borrowers who would need that flexibility during the crisis (Moody's Investors Service 2020).

A yield curve that shifted toward zero, as in the United States, may also have contributed to making the corporate bond market attractive to investors. In the euro area, where key policy rates remained unchanged around zero, bond market conditions continued to be broadly neutral, on average, during the first half of the year, but a clear loosening of conditions took place in the loan market during the second quarter (Figure 3.5, panel 5). In Japan, the March bond market tightening persisted through the end of June, but overall risk aversion was within the normal range observed over the past decade (Figure 3.5, panel 6).

All in all, the recent evolution of the excess bond premium suggests that conditions in bond markets were generally favorable during the second quarter, especially in the United Kingdom and the United States. In the United States, however, bank lending standards were tight, and the bank loan market was a clear outlier compared with the other G7 economies, where the change in lending standards ranged from a small tightening to a large easing. These differences across economies and markets likely reflect the relative strengths of the different policy responses targeting the two markets, in particular the scope of government-sponsored loan guarantee programs as well as investors' search for yield in an environment of ultra-low interest rates and shifting expectations about future policy rates.[29]

Greater Financial Stress Initially for Some Vulnerable Firms

Beyond aggregate indicators, changes in credit conditions are also likely to be visible through their differential impact on firms with different characteristics, as some firms may be more vulnerable to aggregate funding liquidity shocks than others. First, firms that generally have more restricted access to credit markets—for example, because of their relatively smaller size—may be more exposed to a deterioration in risk appetite than the rest of the corporate sector.[30] Second, firms with a worse liquidity position because of a lower stock of cash or higher short-term debt that needs to be rolled over are more sensitive to a tightening of credit conditions. In addition, firms with higher leverage may also suffer more during episodes of financial stress.

A comparison between the stock market performance of firms most vulnerable to funding shocks and that of other, less vulnerable firms can therefore be a useful complement to the aggregate analysis presented earlier in the chapter to better understand the behavior of lenders with respect to credit to firms. In what follows, the analysis focuses on vulnerabilities to funding liquidity shocks measured at the end of 2019 along three dimensions: (1) small size (low total assets), (2) low cash and short-term financial investments relative to industry peers (as a share of total assets), and (3) high short-term debt net of cash and short-term financial investments (as a share of total assets).[31] The

analysis examines the effect of these three vulnerabilities over and above the effect of leverage-related vulnerabilities, which clearly amplified the effect of the negative cash flow shock related to COVID-19 in five of the seven economies (Figure 3.6, panels 1 and 2).[32]

Evidence of *relatively* greater financial stress measured by cumulative abnormal returns—that is, the cumulative difference between the actual returns and the returns predicted by a simple one-factor asset pricing model—is pervasive for relatively smaller firms. Their underperformance during February–March in Germany, Japan, the United Kingdom, and the United States was close to, or greater than, 10 percentage points (Figure 3.6, panel 2). Furthermore, firms that entered the COVID-19 crisis with relatively high liquidity vulnerabilities also experienced relatively greater financial stress than those with higher liquidity buffers in some economies during late February and March. Panel 3 of Figure 3.6 shows the cumulative abnormal returns of two groups of US firms: those with low and high relative cash. While the stock market performance of the two groups is indistinguishable until late February, a wedge in favor of the latter group appears at that time and becomes wider during the second half of March. A more formal econometric investigation, which controls for a number of firm characteristics (including the industrial sector) at the end of 2019, as well as the expected size of the pandemic-related revenue shock, confirms that visual impression: firms with relatively less cash suffered more financial stress in the United Kingdom and the United States, and those with a relatively higher level of short-term debt (net of cash) suffered more in France, the United Kingdom, and the United States (Figure 3.6, panel 4).[33] In these five cases, the underperformance of firms with liquidity vulnerabilities between early February and end-March was about 5 percentage points.

Policies that Helped Relieve Funding Stress

Precise measurement of the effects of policy announcements and actions in the context of the COVID-19 crisis is an extremely challenging task.

---

[29]It is plausible that, in each country, the structure of the financial sector (for example, market-based versus bank-based) played a role in the choice of policy instruments and calibration of the policy response across different markets, which in turn may explain the relative dynamics of supply conditions in the various markets.

[30]See Holmstrom and Tirole (1997) for a theoretical discussion. Duchin, Ozbas, and Sensoy (2010) and Hadlock and Pierce (2010) discuss various financial constraint indicators commonly used in the empirical corporate finance literature.

[31]A high level of short-term debt net of cash exposes a firm to rollover risk. A low level of cash reduces a firm's room to maneuver in case credit conditions tighten (see, for example, Joseph and others 2020).

[32]See Online Annex 3.5 for methodological details. For size, relative cash, and liquidity gap (leverage), a firm is deemed vulnerable if it belongs to the weakest tercile (half) of the distribution of the characteristic at the end of 2019.

[33]The finding for the United Kingdom echoes that of Joseph and others (2020).

Figure 3.6. Firm-Level Stock Market Performance

High-leverage firms suffered more financial stress during late February and March in the United States ...

1. Cumulative Abnormal Return of US Firms with Low and High Leverage during February–March 2020
(Percent)

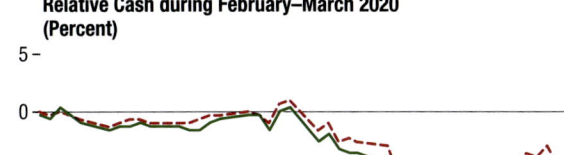
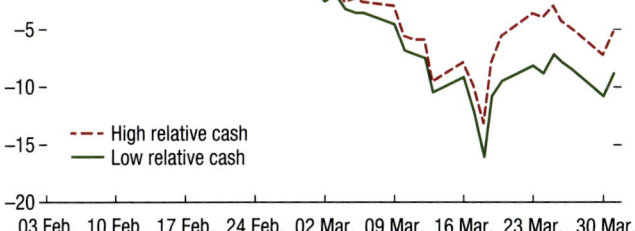

... and in four other Group of Seven economies, and small firms underperformed in four economies.

2. High-Leverage Firms' and Small Firms' Relative Equity Performance during February–March 2020
(Percentage points)

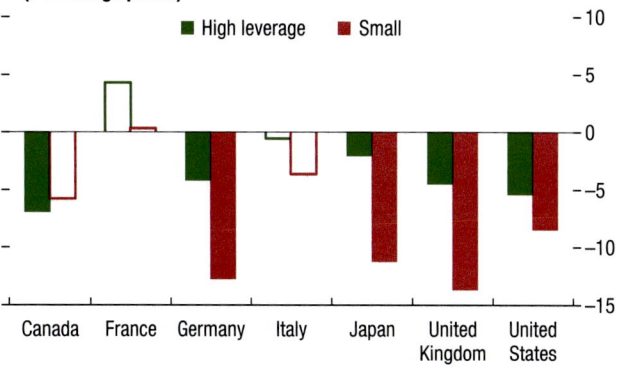

US firms with less cash than their industry peers suffered more financial stress during late February and March ...

3. Cumulative Abnormal Returns of US Firms with Low and High Relative Cash during February–March 2020
(Percent)

... as did UK firms with relatively less cash and French, UK, and US firms with a high liquidity gap.

4. Liquidity-Poor and Cash-Poor Firms' Relative Equity Performance during February–March 2020
(Percentage points)

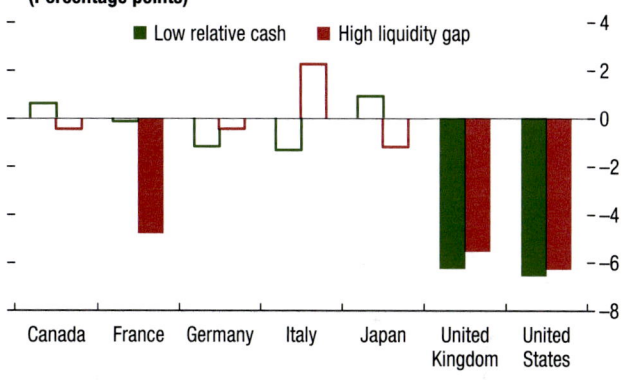

Sources: Refinitiv Datastream; S&P Capital IQ; and IMF staff calculations.
Note: Firm characteristics are as of the end of the fourth quarter of 2019. Leverage in panels 1 and 2 is defined as the debt-to-asset ratio. A high-leverage (low-leverage) firm is one in the top (bottom) half of the leverage distribution. In panels 2 and 4, equity performance is based on cumulative abnormal returns during February 3–March 31, 2020, and firm-level characteristics are controlled for. "Relative cash" is defined as in Joseph and others (2020), and a low-relative-cash (high-relative-cash) firm is one in the lowest (highest) tercile of the relative cash distribution. "Small" is defined as being in the lowest tercile of the distribution of total assets. "Liquidity gap" is defined as total short-term financing minus cash and short-term investments as a ratio of total assets. A high-liquidity-gap firm is one in the highest tercile of the distribution. Solid colored bars indicate statistical significance at the 5 percent level. Empty bars indicate lack of statistical significance at conventional levels. See Online Annex 3.5 for methodological details.

A variety of policy measures—monetary, fiscal, and financial—were announced over a short period of time, sometimes on the same day, making it difficult to isolate their effects. Important details of announced policy packages were sometimes released with a lag, and policy measures announced on different days could have had strong complementarities. Furthermore, because many of the economic policy measures announced early on in the crisis were concurrent with negative news about the progression of the pandemic and its effect on the real economy and financial markets—as

well as with the announcement of containment policy measures imposing restrictions on economic activity—assessment of their impact is extremely difficult.[34] In the face of these challenges, and with full acknowledgment of the associated limitations, this chapter follows

[34]For example, the March 12 announcement by the Federal Reserve Bank of New York of new large repo operations coincided with one of the worst declines in US stock market history. The announcement, however, was a surprise and took place in the middle of the trading day, at a time when the intraday decline was already very large.

two simple approaches to try to gauge the impact of key policy announcements on corporate funding liquidity stress. First, it examines the effect of policy announcements on the *relative* stock market performance of the most vulnerable firms over a horizon of two trading days, taking into account the negative impact of global financial market volatility during days when it was extreme.[35,36] Second, it assesses the overall impact of the policy response by extending the window of the analysis (to the end of June) of the *relative* stock market performance of the groups of vulnerable firms that have underperformed during February–March, as identified in the previous section. In both cases, several firm characteristics are controlled for.[37] As in the previous section, the relative performance of firms most vulnerable to adverse funding liquidity shocks (controlling for solvency and other firm characteristics) is interpreted as a symptom of changing credit supply conditions. The focus on those firms does not suggest that policies explicitly targeted them but that policies to support the economy (and credit provision in particular) may benefit them relatively more.

Policy announcements appear to have had a positive effect on the relative stock market performance of smaller firms (relative to larger firms) as well as on those with high leverage (relative to those with low leverage). Pooling all 85 announcement days in the sample, this effect amounts to about 0.3 percentage point of overperformance a day over two days for smaller firms and about 0.1 percentage point a day over two days for high-leverage firms. By contrast, no significant effect can be found for firms with liquidity vulnerabilities (Figure 3.7, panel 1). Given the small number of announcement days, identifying significant effects at the country level is challenging. Yet the data suggest a positive effect for small firms in Canada and for small firms and high-leverage firms in Japan.

It is plausible that some types of vulnerable firms were more affected by certain types of policy announcements than others. Some policies, such as government guarantees or purchases of corporate securities by central banks, have a *direct* impact on corporate funding and solvency, whereas others, such

as macroprudential measures or changes in financial sector regulation, have only an *indirect* impact. Comparing announcement days when at least one policy with a *direct* impact was announced with those when policies with only an *indirect* impact were announced, it appears that policies with a *direct* impact benefited firms with liquidity vulnerabilities relatively more.[38] The effect amounts to 0.2 percentage point of overperformance a day over two days for liquidity-poor firms and to 0.13 percentage point a day over two days for cash-poor firms (Figure 3.7, panel 2). No difference across types of policies is observed for high-leverage firms and small firms.[39]

The analysis of the stock market performance of vulnerable firms through the end of June confirms that stress at smaller firms had generally disappeared by then—except in the United Kingdom, where it remained significant—while strains in high-leverage firms remained in Germany and Japan (Figure 3.7, panel 3). Stress at firms with liquidity vulnerabilities, however, persisted in France, the United Kingdom, and the United States (Figure 3.7, panel 4), echoing findings from the aggregate analysis of the loan markets in the US economy.

Conclusion and Policy Considerations

The tightening of credit conditions that took place across G7 economies in March as the COVID-19 pandemic gathered momentum was quelled to a very large extent thanks to an unprecedented set of powerful

---

[35]The analysis does not try to assess whether program eligibility mattered for firms' financial performance.

[36]Global financial market volatility is defined as extreme when the Chicago Board Options Exchange Volatility Index (VIX) is above the 80th percentile of its distribution during February–June 2020.

[37]See Online Annex 3.6 for methodological details.

[38]When estimated separately, the effect of measures with an indirect impact is not statistically significant. It is plausible that such measures, including changes in financial sector regulation or macroprudential policy, take longer to have an effect on financing conditions for nonfinancial firms than measures with a direct impact. Among measures with a direct impact, the announcements of on-budget fiscal measures supporting firm solvency appear to have been the most powerful: excluding announcement days when such measures were announced, the difference between the effect of measures with a direct impact and those with an indirect impact loses significance. Among the other four types of measures with a direct impact, corporate asset purchase programs appear to have been relatively more powerful.

[39]While it is very plausible that major policy announcements in the United States had positive spillover effects on other G7 economies, spillover analysis is impeded by the occasional concurrence of major announcements in the United States with those in the other countries. Focusing on days when an announcement was made in the United States only, no evidence can be found that the announcement had a positive effect on the relative performance of vulnerable firms in other G7 economies. Spillovers to emerging markets are discussed in Chapter 2 of this report.

Figure 3.7. The Effect of Policies on Vulnerable Firms

Policy announcements helped relieve financial stress on average in small firms and high-leverage firms ...

... and policies targeting the corporate sector directly had a stronger effect on cash-poor and liquidity-poor firms than policies with an indirect impact.

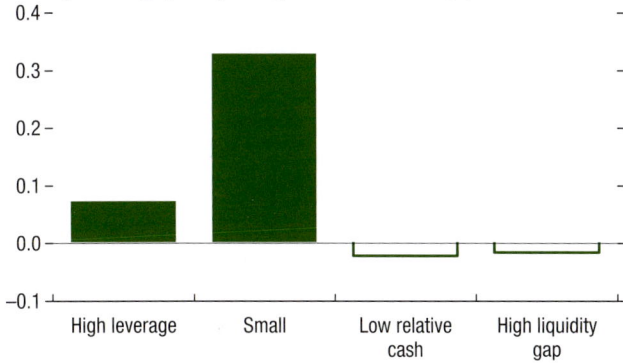

1. **Effect of Policy Announcements on the Relative Equity Performance of Vulnerable Firms**
   (Percentage points, average effect over two days)

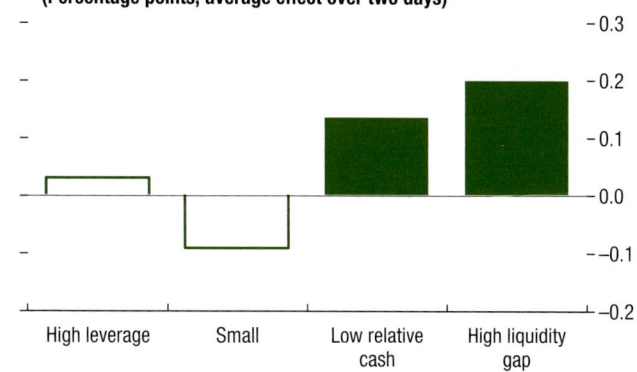

2. **Relative Effect of Announcements of Policies Targeting the Corporate Sector Directly on the Relative Equity Performance of Vulnerable Firms**
   (Percentage points, average effect over two days)

The relative performance of small firms improved during the second quarter ...

... but strains remained for liquidity-poor and cash-poor firms at the end of June.

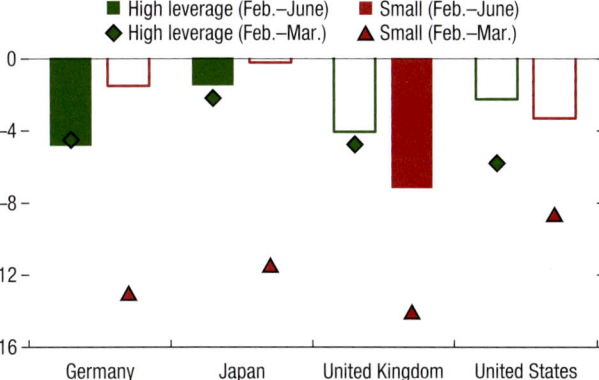

3. **High-Leverage and Small Firms' Relative Equity Performance during February–June 2020**
   (Percentage points)

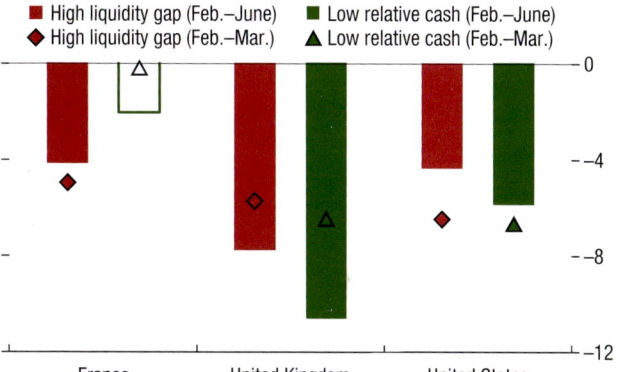

4. **Cash-Poor and Liquidity-Poor Firms' Relative Equity Performance during February–June 2020**
   (Percentage points)

Sources: IMF, COVID Policy Tracker; press releases and press reports; Refinitiv Datastream; S&P Capital IQ; Yale Program on Financial Stability; and IMF staff calculations.
Note: In panels 1 and 2, the effect of policy announcements is calculated net of the effect of extreme volatility, and equity performance is based on cumulative abnormal returns on the day of the policy announcement and the following day. Leverage is defined as the debt-to-asset ratio. A high-leverage (low-leverage) firm is one in the top (bottom) half of the leverage distribution. "Relative cash" is defined as in Joseph and others (2020), and a low-relative-cash (high-relative-cash) firm is one in the lowest (highest) tercile of the relative cash distribution. "Small" is defined as being in the lowest tercile of the distribution of total assets. "Liquidity gap" is defined as total short-term financing minus cash and short-term investments as a ratio of total assets. A high-liquidity-gap firm is one in the highest tercile of the distribution. In panels 3 and 4, equity performance is based on cumulative abnormal returns during February 3–June 30, 2020. Solid colored bars indicate statistical significance at the 5 percent level. Empty bars indicate lack of statistical significance at conventional levels. See Online Annex 3.6 for methodological details.

policy interventions. Despite the deterioration in its solvency, the nonfinancial corporate sector, as a whole, was generally able to obtain the funding it needed to continue operating during the second quarter.[40] Yet signs of tighter credit conditions also surfaced during the second quarter in some segments of the credit market or did not fully dissipate for some types of firms with a viable business model but vulnerable to adverse liquidity shocks. In particular, while US bond markets have been buoyant, bank-dependent firms, as well as those with pre–COVID-19 liquidity vulnerabilities, continue to face a more difficult environment. Firms with pre–COVID-19 liquidity vulnerabilities in the United Kingdom also appear to have been left behind, despite overall favorable credit conditions. An interesting topic for future analysis would be further exploration of the reasons for the cross-country differences in the evolution of credit supply conditions documented in the chapter.

While most G7 central banks have already signaled their intention to leave their pandemic-related facilities in place for the foreseeable future, it may be increasingly difficult for governments to maintain the same level of fiscal support because of fiscal space concerns or other political economy considerations. The latest bank lending survey of the euro area suggests that tighter bank lending standards may be around the corner, as government guarantee programs are set to end soon (European Central Bank 2020). Yet the evidence analyzed in this chapter suggests that it is the policies supporting firms directly that have had the most beneficial effect on firms with liquidity vulnerabilities. Policies also appear to have cushioned financial strains in smaller firms. It is thus critical to carefully calibrate any withdrawal of fiscal policy support to funding markets.

Beyond the calibration of funding and liquidity support by fiscal and monetary policymakers, a key issue for financial stability in the near to medium term will be the deterioration in corporate solvency as a result of the pandemic-induced decline in profitability and increased corporate indebtedness. This deterioration will have a severe impact on banks' asset quality and capital adequacy (see Chapter 4), which in turn could limit the credit supply to firms over the next several quarters.

Chapter 1 of this report provides a policy road map to navigate the gradual reopening and the recovery phases of the COVID-19 crisis (see Table 1.2 in that chapter) and discusses policy trade-offs relevant to corporate funding issues documented in this chapter, including the impact on fiscal space and sovereign contingent liabilities as well as the risk of capital misallocation. Once the recovery is well entrenched, the experience of the COVID-19 shock on corporate funding markets must also be examined to determine the reasons for the fragility they experienced in March. The regulation of nonbank financial institutions must be revisited and mechanisms to enhance their resilience to large liquidity shocks devised, as discussed in recent GFSRs.

The evidence provided in this chapter also indicates that liquidity and leverage-related vulnerabilities have amplified the impact of the COVID-19 shock. The experience of the current crisis, therefore, is a reminder to supervisory authorities to continue to monitor corporate vulnerabilities closely and offers an opportunity for them to consider the benefits of macroprudential policy tools for the nonfinancial corporate sector (IMF 2020).

---

[40]Because of lack of firm-level data for unlisted small and medium-sized enterprises in 2020, the analysis could not establish the degree to which this conclusion carries over to those firms.

References

Acharya, Viral V., and Sascha Steffen. 2020. "The Risk of Being a Fallen Angel and the Corporate Dash for Cash in the Midst of COVID." CEPR COVID Economics Vetted and Real-Time Papers 10, Centre for Economic Policy Research, London.

Adrian, Tobias, Paolo Colla, and Hyun Song Shin. 2013. "Which Financial Frictions? Parsing the Evidence from the Financial Crisis of 2007 to 2009." *NBER Macroeconomics Annual* 27 (1): 159–214.

Anderson, Julia, Francesco Papadia, and Nicolas Véron. 2020. "Government-Guaranteed Bank Lending in Europe: Beyond the Headline Numbers." Peterson Institute for International Economics. https://www.piie.com/blogs/realtime-economic -issues-watch/government-guaranteed-bank-lending-europe -beyond-headline

Banerjee, Ryan, Anamaria Illes, Enisse Kharroubi, and José-Maria Serena. 2020. "COVID-19 and Corporate Sector Liquidity." *BIS Bulletin* 10, Bank for International Settlements, Basel.

Bank of England. 2020. "Credit Conditions Survey—Quarter Two." https://www.bankofengland.co.uk/credit-conditions -survey/2020/2020-q2

Becker, Bo, and Victoria Ivashina. 2014. "Cyclicality of Credit Supply: Firm Level Evidence." *Journal of Monetary Economics* 62: 76–93.

Board of Governors of the Federal Reserve System. 2020. "The July 2020 Senior Loan Officer Opinion Survey on Bank Lending Practices." Washington, DC. https://www .federalreserve.gov/data/sloos/sloos-202007.htm

Chodorow-Reich, Gabriel. 2014. "The Employment Effects of Credit Market Disruptions: Firm-Level Evidence from the 2008–09 Financial Crisis." *Quarterly Journal of Economics* 129 (1): 1–59.

Duchin, Ran, Oguzhan Ozbas, and Berk A. Sensoy. 2010. "Costly External Finance, Corporate Investment, and the Subprime Mortgage Credit Crisis." *Journal of Financial Economics* 97 (3): 418–35.

Duval, Romain, Gee Hee Hong, and Yannick Timmer. 2020. "Financial Frictions and the Great Productivity Slowdown." *Review of Financial Studies* 33 (2): 475–503.

Eren, Egemen, Andreas Schrimpf, and Vladyslav Sushko. 2020. "US Dollar Funding Markets during the COVID-19 Crisis—The Money Market Fund Turmoil." *BIS Bulletin* 14, Bank for International Settlements, Basel.

European Central Bank. 2020. "The Euro Area Bank Lend-ing Survey—Second Quarter." https://www.ecb.europa .eu/stats/ecb_surveys/bank_lending_survey/html/ecb .blssurvey2020q2~d8de5b89f0.en.html#toc1

Gilchrist, Simon, and Egon Zakrajšek. 2012. "Credit Spreads and Business Cycle Fluctuations." *American Economic Review* 102 (4): 1692–720.

Gourinchas, Pierre-Olivier, Sebnem Kalemli-Ozcan, Veronika Penciakova, and Nick Sander. Forthcoming. "COVID-19 and Business Failures." IMF Working Paper, International Monetary Fund, Washington, DC.

Hadlock, Charles J., and Joshua R. Pierce. 2010. "New Evidence on Measuring Financial Constraints: Moving Beyond the KZ Index." *Review of Financial Studies* 23 (5): 1909–40.

Holmstrom, Bengt, and Jean Tirole. 1997. "Financial Inter-mediation, Loanable Funds, and the Real Sector." *Quarterly Journal of Economics* 112 (3): 663–91.

International Monetary Fund (IMF). 2020. "United States: Financial System Stability Assessment." IMF Country Report 20/242, International Monetary Fund, Washington, DC.

Ivashina, Victoria, and David Scharfstein. 2010. "Bank Lending during the Financial Crisis of 2008." *Journal of Financial Economics* 97 (3): 319–38.

Joseph, Andreas, Christiane Kneer, Neeltje Van Horen, and Jumana Saleheen. 2020. "All You Need Is Cash: Corporate Cash Holdings and Investment after the Financial Crisis." Bank of England Working Paper 843, London.

Kapan, Tumer, and Camelia Minoiu. 2020. "Liquidity Insurance versus Credit Provision: Evidence from the COVID-19 Crisis." Unpublished.

Li, Lei, Yi Li, Marco Macchiavelli, and Xing Alex Zhou. 2020. "Runs and Interventions in the Time of COVID-19: Evi-dence from Money Funds." Social Research Science Network. https://papers.ssrn.com/sol3/papers.cfm?abstract_id=3607593

Moody's Investors Service. 2020. "Default Report." April.

Rigobon, Roberto. 2003. "Identification through Heteroskedas-ticity." *Review of Economics and Statistics* 85 (4): 777–92.

4

BANK CAPITAL

COVID-19 CHALLENGES AND POLICY RESPONSES

Chapter 4 at a Glance

- The coronavirus disease (COVID-19) crisis may pose challenges to the capital of banks, even though they entered the crisis with higher capital ratios than before the global financial crisis and despite the large policy interventions aimed at containing the economic fallout from the current crisis.
- Forward-looking simulations based on a new global stress test tool show that in a baseline scenario consistent with the October 2020 *World Economic Outlook* (WEO) bank capital falls sharply but recovers quickly, while an adverse scenario suggests sustained damage to average capital ratios.
- In the adverse scenario, a weak tail of banks, corresponding to 8.3 percent of banking system assets, would fail to meet minimum regulatory requirements, and the capital shortfall relative to broad statutory regulatory thresholds reaches $220 billion.
- In absence of the bank-specific mitigation policies already implemented, the weak tail of banks would reach 14 percent of banking system assets, and the global capital shortfall would be $420 billion.
- Bank-specific mitigation policies would help reduce financial stability risks if the crisis recedes promptly but may pose risks to banks' capital adequacy if the crisis proves to be longer lasting.

Will Banks Remain Adequately Capitalized?

Banks entered the current COVID-19 crisis with higher levels of capital than before the global financial crisis, and policymakers have quickly deployed an array of policies to support economic activity and the ability of banks to lend. However, the sheer size of the shock and the likely increase in defaults from firms and households may pose challenges to banks' profitability and capital positions. A forward-looking simulation of the trajectory of capital ratios in a sample of about 350 banks from 29 jurisdictions, accounting for 73 percent of global banking assets, shows that such ratios would decline as a result of the COVID-19 crisis, but remain, on average, comfortably above regulatory minimums. However, there is heterogeneity across and within regions, and a weak tail of banks, accounting for 8.3 percent of banking assets in the

sample, might fail to meet minimum regulatory capital requirements in an adverse scenario. Government loan guarantees and other bank-specific policies that adjust the calculation of capital ratios help relieve the decline of reported capital ratios and reduce the incidence of bank capital shortfalls. In considering the duration of these and other measures, policymakers should pay attention to the intertemporal trade-off they pose, as policies that reduce the financial stability risks of a transitory shock may increase vulnerabilities related to banks' loss-absorbing capacity and overall indebtedness if the crisis proves to be persistent. Policies aimed at limiting capital distributions and ensuring adequate funding for deposit guarantee programs, as well as contingency plans that lay out how to respond to possible pressures, would help deal with the consequences of a potentially adverse scenario.

Prepared by staff from the Monetary and Capital Markets Department (in consultation with other departments): The authors of this chapter are John Caparusso and Claudio Raddatz (lead authors), Yingyuan Chen, Dan Cheng, Xiaodan Ding, Ibrahim Ergen, Marco Gross, Ivo Krznar, Dimitrios Laliotis, Fabian Lipinsky, Pavel Lukyantsau, Elizabeth Mahoney, Nicola Pierri, and Tomohiro Tsuruga with contributions from Hee Kyong Chon, Caio Ferreira, Alejandro Lopez, and Luc Riedweg under the guidance of Fabio Natalucci (Deputy Director). Magally Bernal was responsible for word processing and the production of this report.

Introduction

In many respects, the COVID-19 crisis presents the largest shock that banks have experienced since the Great Depression (see the October 2020 WEO). Authorities have adopted unprecedented policy measures to blunt the impact of this shock. Governments have introduced substantial fiscal support to households and businesses (see the October 2020 *Fiscal Monitor*), monetary policy rates have been cut worldwide, and many central banks have implemented large asset purchase programs to support markets and to maintain the credit flow to the real economy (see the April 2020 *Global Financial Stability Report* [GFSR]).

Importantly, policymakers have taken steps to avoid the procyclical credit crunch that was evident during the global financial crisis, encouraging banks to use the flexibility embedded in the global regulatory framework to deal with the temporary consequences of the COVID-19 shock and thus stifle negative feedback loops that could amplify the impact of the crisis. Following a decade during which banks aggressively built their capital positions, standard setting bodies have issued guidance to support national authorities in their policy response to the pandemic. Policymakers have released capital buffers to sustain the flow of credit to households and firms. Banks have also been allowed, for loans whose deterioration is attributed to the shock, to defer the recognition of bad debts and the reporting of loan loss provisions and to waive the increase in risk-asset weightings and the deduction of provision charges from capital. Banks have also been compelled (by regulation or strong administrative guidance) to cancel capital distributions.

Despite the large negative impact of the pandemic on the global economy during recent quarters, banking systems have so far been able to weather these economic difficulties, due in part to aggressive policy support. Following an initial plunge, bank equity prices have partially recovered. While banks' assessment of borrower credit quality has naturally deteriorated, bank credit expanded in March as corporate borrowers drew on committed credit lines and has since remained stable. Nonetheless, credit conditions have remained tight. Despite significantly increased loan loss provisions in virtually all systems, most banks continue to report positive earnings, and capital positions have declined only modestly over the initial quarters of the crisis.

This chapter addresses two central questions.
- How prepared are banks to withstand continued challenging economic conditions in the coming years?
- How much would bank-specific regulatory policies recently implemented help them face these scenarios?

The chapter also discusses policy options to deal with the potential challenges that banks could face in the baseline and adverse scenarios, and highlights the intertemporal trade-off that arises from targeted policies that encourage banks to use the flexibility embedded in the regulatory regime to sustain the flow of credit to borrowers facing liquidity problems in response to a transitory shock.

Initial Impact of COVID-19 on the Global Banking Industry

After spending the past decade building capital and liquidity buffers following the regulatory reforms put in place after the global financial crisis, banks came into the COVID-19 crisis in much better shape than they did before previous crises (Figure 4.1, panel 1). However, bank profitability was already challenged in many jurisdictions amid the prolonged period of low interest rates and low term spreads in recent years (Figure 4.1, panel 2). This low-interest-rate environment is likely to persist for several years, as policymakers have engaged in further expansive monetary policies to support the flow of credit to the real economy (see the April 2020 GFSR).

Despite the stronger initial position of banks and the aggressive response of policymakers, the initial stage of the COVID-19 crisis has confronted banks with significant challenges. The initial contractionary shock triggered a scramble for liquidity. In the United States, corporate borrowers aggressively drew on committed credit lines, causing a sudden increase in loans that drove down bank capital ratios.[1] Since then, bank credit in the United States and Europe has remained largely flat. Crucial elements of financial system plumbing (for example, repo and US Treasury markets) encountered liquidity challenges, as did emerging market banks in US funding markets, and financial markets were severely stressed for several weeks. Increased loan loss provisioning—particularly among US banks, for which the onset of the crisis coincided with

---

[1]Risk weights for undrawn credit lines are in the range of 20–50 percent, whereas those for drawn credit lines are 100 percent. Therefore, the large drawdown of committed credit lines has an immediate material impact on risk-weighted assets, the denominator of bank capital ratios.

Figure 4.1. Historical Context: Magnitude of the Current Crisis and the Ex Ante Position of Banks

Banks, particularly in Europe and in emerging market economies, massively improved their capital positions in the last decade ...

... despite low profitability challenging capital accretion in some regions.

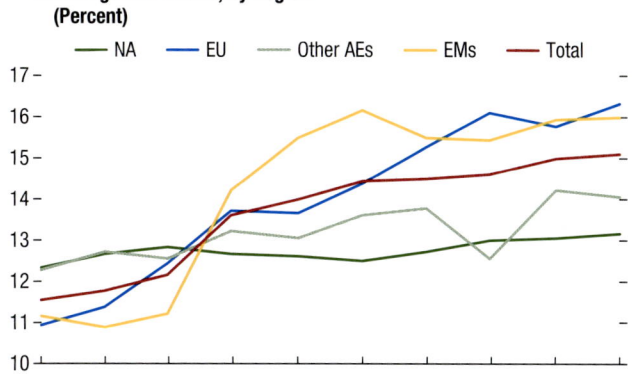

1. Average Tier 1 Ratio, by Region
(Percent)

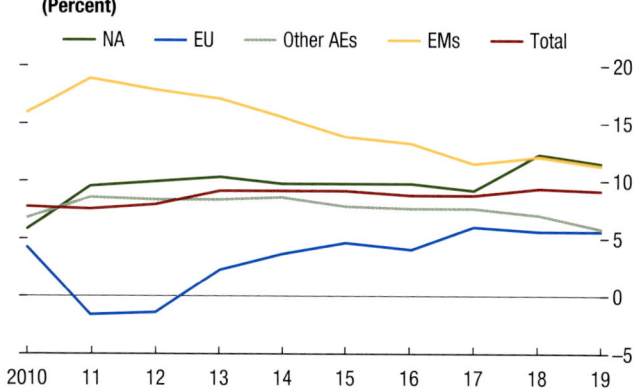

2. Average Return on Equity, by Region
(Percent)

Bank lending standards tightened sharply—to near the 2008 peak in the United States.

Banks attribute tightening to deteriorating borrower conditions, not to capital or liquidity constraints.

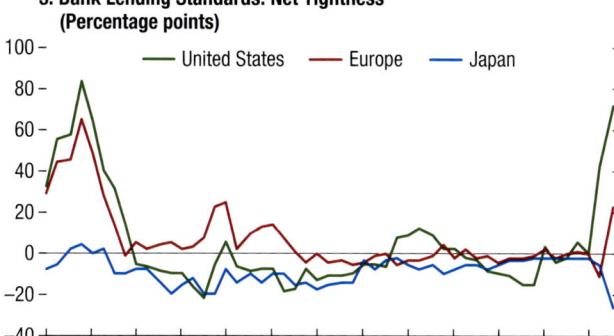

3. Bank Lending Standards: Net Tightness
(Percentage points)

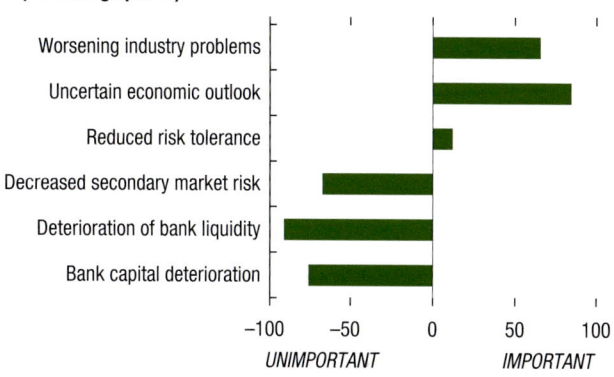

4. Causes of Bank Credit Tightening
(Percentage points)

Source: Haver Analytics.
Note: Bank lending standards for Europe are based on the European Central Bank's one-quarter forward expectations, while both the U.S. and Japan are based on the most recent quarter. Other AEs = other advanced economies, including Japan, Australia, Hong Kong SAR, and Singapore; EMs = emerging markets; EU = Europe, including the United Kingdom and continental Europe; NA = North America, including United States and Canada.

a transition to "expected credit loss" accounting standards—weighed on bank financial results in the first quarter of 2020.[2] In the second quarter,

financial market stress subsided, but most banks took sharply higher loan loss provisions and tightened lending standards as the economic outlook continued to deteriorate (Figure 4.1, panel 3), with

---

[2]The transition to expected credit losses in the United States became effective on January 1, 2020, and virtually all US banks chose to book large provisions for "transitional" increases in loan loss reserves. In one extreme example, Citi took a $4.2 billion current expected credit losses transitional charge, more than half of the $7 billion total 2020 first-quarter loan loss provision. The Federal Reserve promulgated a regulation allowing banks to defer transition-related provisions, but most large banks chose to retain the transition charges recognized on January 1. However, US

bank regulations mitigate the impact of this transition charge on bank capital. Before the COVID-19 outbreak, the Federal Reserve announced a rule allowing banks to phase in the impact of current expected credit losses transition provisions over three years. During the first quarter of 2020, the regulator lengthened the phase-in path to zero capital charges over two years, followed by a three-year phase-in path.

Figure 4.2. Mitigation Policies Announced since February 1, 2020, by Category and Jurisdiction

Among the wide range of policy responses to the COVID-19 shock and slowdown, this chapter focuses on three that relate most directly.

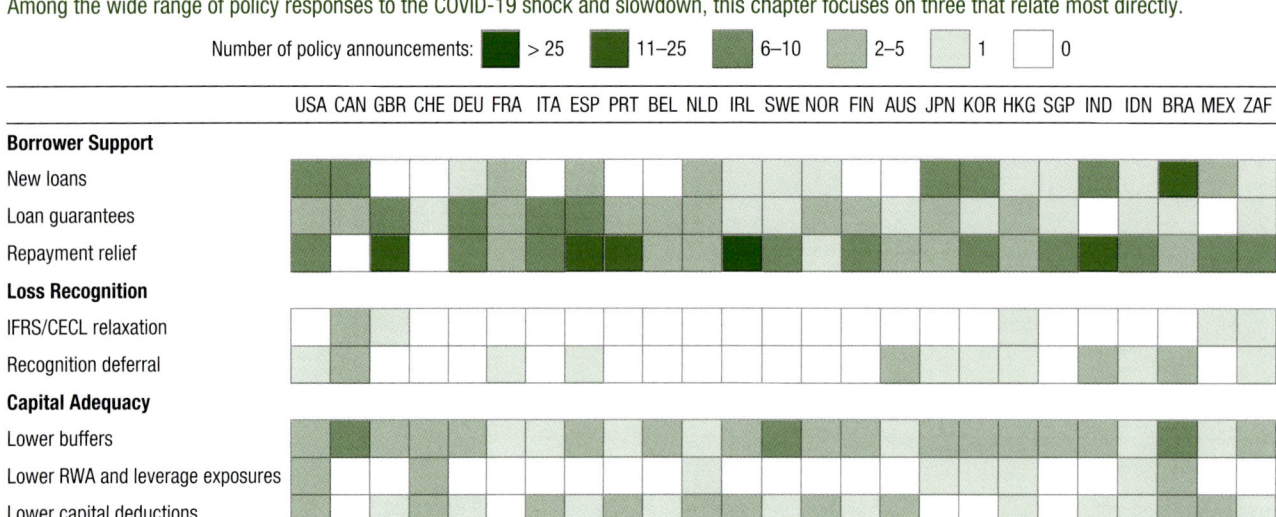

Sources: Financial Stability Board; KBW; Yale School of Management; and IMF staff estimates.
Note: The intensity of the colors in the figure denotes only the number of measures announced but has no bearing on the absolute or relative economic magnitude of those policies. For instance, a single large policy announcement in one jurisdiction could surpass in economic relevance many announcements by a different jurisdiction. The figure includes policy announcements up to July 10, 2020. Austria, Denmark, Greece, and Luxembourg are not included in the analysis due to incomplete data. See Online Annex 4.1, www.imf.org/en/Publications/GFSR, for an explanation of the data and methodology on which this policy taxonomy is based. The row labeled "Lower buffers" also includes public announcements by authorities explicitly encouraging banks to use the flexibility embedded in the regulatory framework to use the capital conservation buffer to support lending, although these statements do not entail a formal change in the rulebook. Data labels use International Organization for Standardization (ISO) country codes. CECL = current expected credit loss; IFRS = International Financial Reporting Standards; RWA = risk-weighted assets.

loan officers in the United States reporting the tightest credit standards since 2005.

As improved liquidity conditions relieved borrowers' appetite for precautionary borrowing, the first-quarter spurt of loan growth slowed or reversed for most banks. This relieved risk-weighted asset pressure on capital ratios (Figure 4.1, panel 4). During the second quarter of 2020, some major banks (particularly in the United States) also reported large capital-market-driven gains.

The Reactions of Financial Sector Authorities to the COVID-19 Crisis

Governments around the world have responded to the economic disruption of the COVID-19 crisis with policies of unprecedented scope and magnitude to support the real economy, prevent permanent damage to the balance sheets of firms and households, and maintain the flow of credit to the real economy. These policies extend from broad macroeconomic policies to specific measures that directly address bank balance sheet management (Figure 4.2).

This chapter focuses specifically on the impact of government loan guarantee programs and capital adequacy policies that can be directly quantified (henceforth, "bank-specific" policies). Other policies have an indirect effect on banks' capital adequacy. For example, fiscal stimulus and monetary policy indirectly support banks' financial results through macroeconomic channels. Policies to support bank funding could affect bank capital by lowering costs and allowing banks to sustain their level of activity. Policies intended to support borrowers' repayment ability, including repayment moratoria, may reduce banks' need to set aside provisions for loan losses—and thus bolster capital—by lowering the probability that a borrower will enter default (probability of default). Nonetheless, some of these policies may also simply postpone loss recognition.

Within the risk-based capital framework, the policies analyzed in this chapter can alter the capital space through three channels.

- **Increasing capital levels:** This has been promoted mainly through restrictions (often "voluntary" guidance) on distribution of profits through dividends and share buybacks. Most of these come with specific end dates (typically not later than the end of 2020).

Figure 4.3. Magnitude of Announced Mitigation Policies

The magnitude of loan guarantees varies widely across countries.

1. Loan Guarantees
(Percent of GDP)

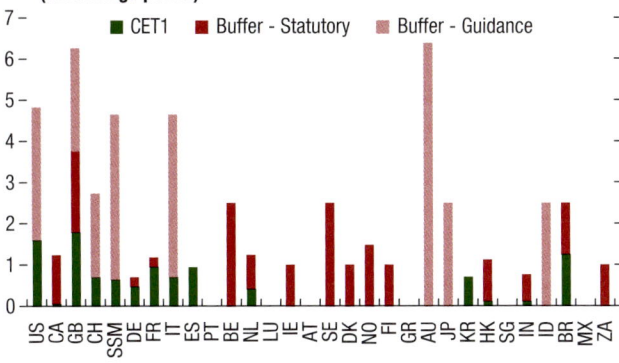

Many jurisdictions have relaxed statutory capital buffer requirements to support banks' credit underwriting.

2. Change in Statutory Bank Capital Buffers since February 1, 2020
(Percent of risk-weighted assets)

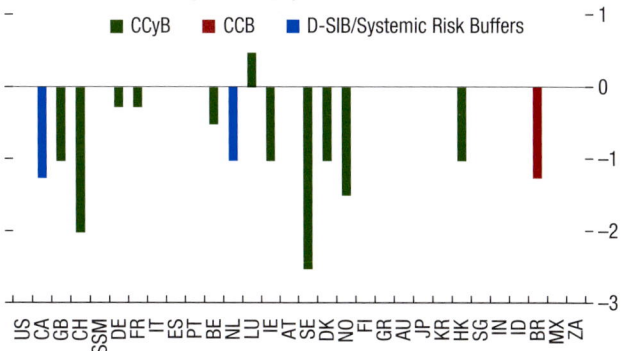

Some jurisdictions have also taken steps to improve reported capital ratios or lower required capital buffers.

3. Estimated Pro Forma Increase in CET1 Capital Ratio and Buffer from Announced Policies
(Percentage points)

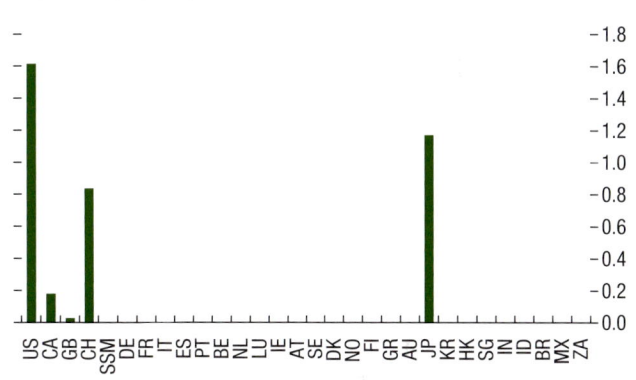

A few countries highly sensitive to capital market depth have also taken steps to improve leverage ratios.

4. Increase in Leverage Ratio from Announced Policies
(Percentage points)

Sources: Bloomberg Finance L.P.; Financial Stability Board; IMF (2020b); KBW; SNL Financial; Yale School of Management; and IMF staff estimates.
Note: Figures include the 29 countries captured in the bank stress test, plus data on the SSM as a supervisory jurisdiction. "Loan guarantees" is based on the announced programs, not actual take-up of guaranteed loans. Loan guarantee data are not captured for Austria, Finland, Greece, Hong Kong SAR, Ireland, Luxembourg, and Portugal. D-SIB surcharges are not captured as a separate buffer in several jurisdictions, mainly because D-SIB requirements are often expressed in terms of the overall CET1 ratio. Countries are identified by two-digit International Organization for Standardization (ISO) code and indicate policies pronounced by the European Central Bank and the European Banking Authority. Figures for individual European countries indicate local policies distinct from those announced by European authorities. CCB = capital conservation buffer; CET1 = common equity Tier 1; CCyB = countercyclical capital buffer; D-SIB = domestic systemically important bank; SSM = Single Supervisory Mechanism.

Policymakers have issued such guidance for the large European banks and for all banks in Brazil, Italy, Spain, Switzerland, the United Kingdom, and other countries. Government loan guarantees can also boost capital levels by reducing the loss that a bank experiences when a borrower defaults and the need to set aside loan loss provisions for this event (loss given default).

- **Lowering risk-weighted assets or "leverage exposure"—the capital ratio denominators:** National regulators have typically waived risk-asset weights for loans covered by government guarantees (Figure 4.3,

panel 1).[3] In some instances, policymakers have also reduced risk weights on banks' exposures to targeted borrowers, often small businesses, to encourage credit to this segment. A few countries—Japan, the United Kingdom, and the United States—have exempted central bank reserves, and the latter

[3]This is distinct from the effect of government guarantees on the borrowers' "point-in-time" probability of default resulting from improved access to funding—which is captured in the analysis of the corporate sector—and from their effect on the "loss given default," previously discussed and quantified in the next section.

two have exempted holdings of government bond holdings, from banks' leverage exposure measures (the denominator of the leverage ratio). These policies are intended to facilitate large asset purchase programs and to encourage banks to continue to intermediate in government bond markets.

- **Releasing some capital buffers:** In many jurisdictions, policymakers have increased banks' overall space between reported and regulatory capital levels by releasing the countercyclical capital buffer that is designed to be used during downturns (Figure 4.3, panel 2). In some instances, policymakers have formally released required capital buffers, effecting a reduction in *statutory* capital buffers. In other cases, policymakers have publicly reminded banks that some buffers—typically the capital conservation buffer of 2.5 percent of total capital aimed at preventing banks from breaching the minimum regulatory capital adequacy ratio—could be used to support lending and be gradually rebuilt through retained earnings as conditions improve. This chapter characterizes the latter as reductions in the "*guidance* buffer" that determines de facto minimum capital levels.

These policies combined are estimated to have already improved banks' reported common equity Tier 1 (CET1) ratios and, either by statute or by guidance releasing some capital buffer requirements, regulators have further expanded the capital space between banks' current positions and broad regulatory capital levels (Figure 4.3, panel 3).[4] In addition, although this section focuses on the CET1 capital position because that is the binding constraint for most banking systems where bank market-making activity is not large, policymakers in a few jurisdictions (Japan, Switzerland, United States) have also eased constraints on banks' leverage ratios, typically by excluding government bonds, central bank reserves, or other low-risk assets from the leverage exposure denominator (Figure 4.3, panel 4).

Bank Capital Ratios in the Wake of COVID-19 and the Role of Policies

This chapter assesses the consequences of the COVID-19 crisis for the future capital ratios of global

banking systems in a forward-looking manner using the latest baseline projection of the economic outlook and the adverse scenario outlined in the October 2020 WEO (Figure 4.4). These two scenarios provide a broad assessment of the potential paths of the pandemic; however, given the unprecedented nature of the shock, uncertainty remains.

These macro scenarios implicitly incorporate the effects of broad macroeconomic and monetary policy interventions, including interest rate cuts, unconventional monetary policies, fiscal measures, social safety net packages, and other policies that support the real economy. By improving the liquidity of borrowers, these policies indirectly affect the condition of banks. However, the consequences of bank-specific policies for the distribution of banks' capital may not be fully captured in macro aggregates. The chapter also assumes that the accounting impact of bank-specific policies on bank balance sheets is not fully captured in macro trajectories.

The assessment relies on a recently developed global stress test (see Online Annex 4.1) that uses publicly available data on the financial statements of about 350 banks in 29 major banking systems—accounting for 73 percent of global banking sector assets—to estimate how key components of banks' financial statements react to macroeconomic variables.[5] The future paths of these variables are embedded in the scenarios used to conduct a forward-looking simulation of the evolution of the profitability and capital position of each of the banks in the sample, which is then aggregated across different regions and across global systemically important banks.

The stress test exercise relies on publicly available data. While this allows for a global assessment of the prospective health of the banking system, it comes at the cost of lower data granularity and higher reliance on statistical methods than in supervisory stress tests. This narrows the types of policies that can be analyzed in this context and also requires several assumptions to map the impact of those policies to

---

[4]Capital requirements that include all statutory buffers (but exclude recent statutory reductions) are defined in this chapter as "statutory broad capital requirements." Capital requirements that exclude buffers released by recent informal guidance statements are defined as "guidance capital requirements."

[5]Online Annex 4.1 is available at www.imf.org/en/Publications/GFSR. The jurisdictions included are Australia, Austria, Belgium, Brazil, Canada, Denmark, Finland, France, Germany, Greece, Hong Kong SAR, India, Indonesia, Ireland, Italy, Japan, Korea, Luxembourg, Mexico, The Netherlands, Norway, Portugal, Singapore, South Africa, Spain, Sweden, Switzerland, the United Kingdom, and the United States. In each jurisdiction, the largest banks covering up to 80 percent of banking assets are included. Therefore, the simulation does not include the consequences of the scenarios for the solvency of small banks.

Figure 4.4. Scenarios for Stress Test Simulation

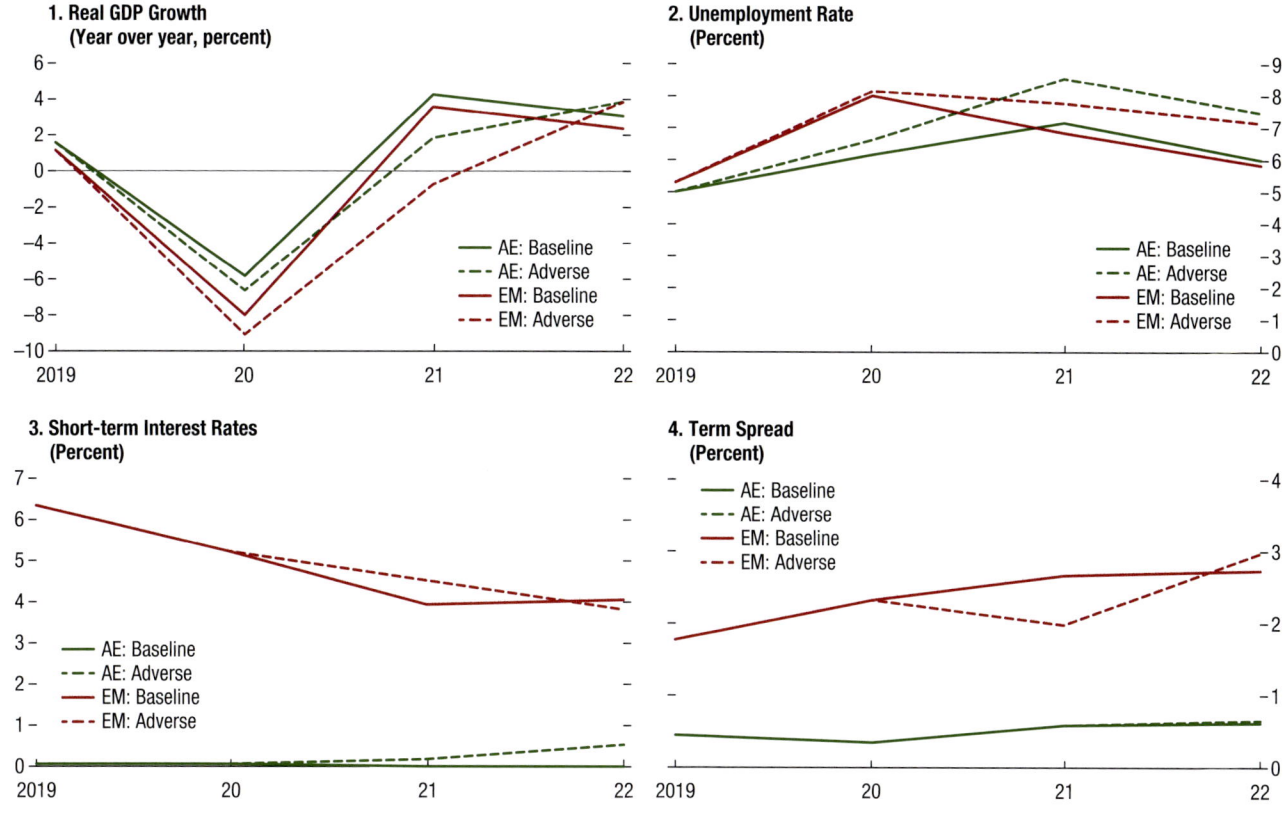

Source: IMF, October 2020 *World Economic Outlook*.
Note: Median across sample countries in each group. AE = advanced economy; EM = emerging market.

banks' financial statements.[6] The base model is augmented by a satellite model that explicitly considers the contribution of corporate and consumer risk to banks' loan loss provisions and is used to estimate the impact of government guarantees (see Box 4.1).[7]

[6]Given the lower granularity of the data, the global stress test also relies more heavily on econometric methods than standard supervisory stress tests and is simpler than models that would typically be used by authorities. It is a stand-alone solvency stress test that does not consider interaction with other risks, such as liquidity and contagion risks or macro-feedback effects, such as between the banking sector and the sovereign, which might amplify the impact of initial shocks, nor does it take into consideration spillovers across interconnected banking systems. Also, the exercise does not allow for behavioral responses by banks that may change their balance sheets. The model also assumes that bank balance sheets remain static during the simulation period, which does not allow banks to reach lower levels of capital by deleveraging (see Online Annex 4.1).

[7]The COVID-19 crisis has had a heterogenous impact across sectors beyond nonfinancial corporations and households. For instance, the transportation and entertainment industries have suffered disproportionately from the social distancing measures implemented to mitigate the spread of the disease. For this reason, it would be desirable to incorporate further sectoral disaggregation in the analysis, but more granular decompositions of banks loan portfolios are typically available only for a small subset of banks.

Consequences of COVID-19 for Bank Capital before Bank-Specific Mitigation

The consequences of each scenario for banking systems' future capital ratios are first simulated without adjusting for how the bank-specific mitigation policies discussed earlier alter the recognition of provisions, calculation of risk-weighted assets, or flexibility in using existing capital buffers.

The results of the stress test show a significant decline in CET1 of the global banking system, reaching minimum levels of 9.6 percent in the baseline scenario and 9.3 percent in the adverse scenario—a drop of 3.6 percentage points and 3.9 percentage points, respectively, below the CET1 level in 2019. The trajectory of aggregate CET1 recovery also varies importantly across scenarios. In the baseline scenario, CET1 steadily recovers after reaching a trough in 2020, but is still 0.7 percentage points below its initial level at the end of the simulation in 2022. In contrast, the capital position decline is much more persistent in the adverse scenario, with CET1 levels remaining 2.4 percentage points below their initial levels by 2022 (Figure 4.5, panel 1).

Figure 4.5. Bank Solvency under COVID-19 without Policy Mitigation

Banks' capital ratios fall significantly ...

... driven by large provision costs.

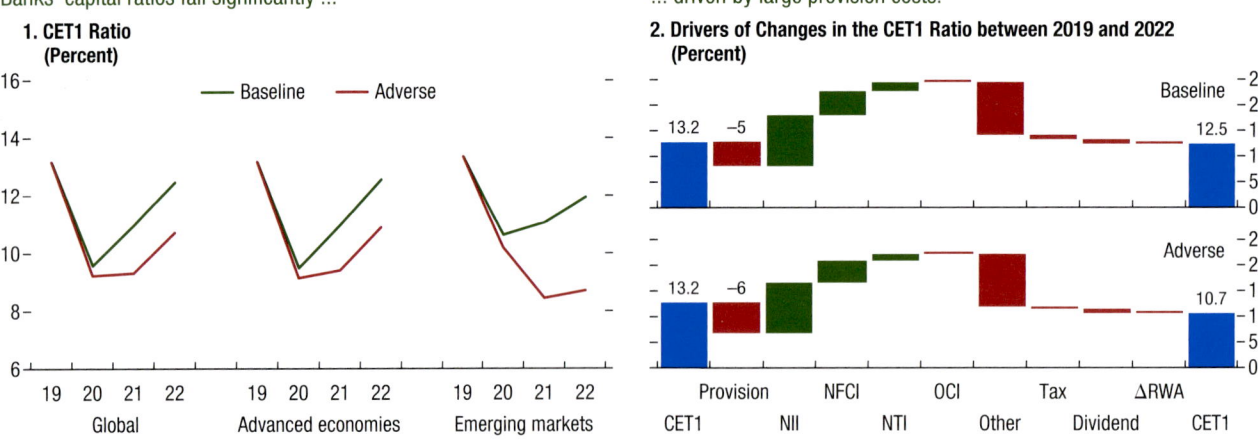

1. CET1 Ratio
(Percent)

2. Drivers of Changes in the CET1 Ratio between 2019 and 2022
(Percent)

Near fifteen percent of the global banking system will fall below 4.5% CET1 ratio.

The maximum capital shortfall against a broad statutory capital requirement could reach over $400 billion.

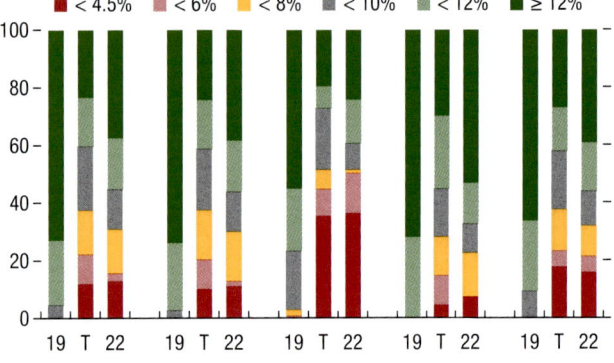

3. Distribution of Bank Assets by CET1 Ratio under Adverse Scenario
(Percent; T = trough year)

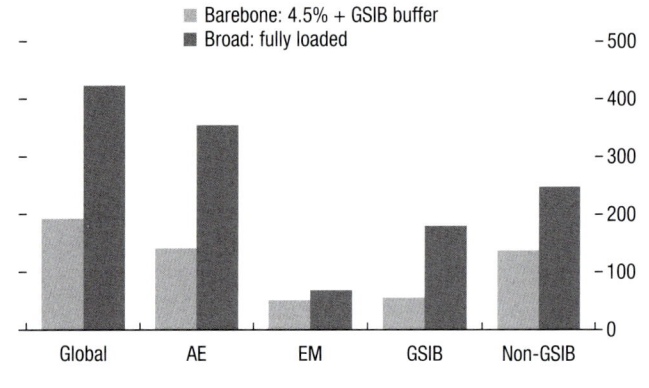

4. Maximum Broad Capital Shortfall under Adverse Scenario
(Billions of US dollars)

Sources: Haver Analytics; SNL Financial; and IMF staff estimates.
Note: In panel 2, green and red bars denote increases and decreases in capital, respectively. AE = advanced economies, which comprise euro area, low-rate AEs, North Atlantic, and other AEs; CET1 = common equity Tier 1; EM = emerging markets; GSIB = global systemically important bank; NFCI = net fee and commission income; NII = net interest income; NTI = net trading income; OCI = other comprehensive income; Other = several financial accounts, including operating expenses and non-operating items; RWA = risk-weighted assets.

The decline in the CET1 ratio over the simulation horizon stems mainly from an increase in loan loss provisions (Figure 4.5, panel 2). In the baseline scenario, higher loan loss provision expenses contribute to a 5 percentage point decline in CET1, whereas in the adverse scenario their contribution is 6 percentage points. This is directly related to the different trajectories of economic activity in the two scenarios, where the rebound projected in the baseline scenario for 2021 results in lower provisioning expenses. In contrast, the increase in risk-weighted assets plays only a minor role in driving the changes in CET1.

The sizes of the aggregate decline and the contribution of different components vary across regions. The maximum decline in CET1 in the baseline scenario is much larger in advanced economies (Figure 4.5, panel 1). The situation reverses, however, in the adverse scenario, where advanced economies see a maximum decline in CET1 of about 4.0 percentage points, compared with 4.9 percentage points for emerging markets. This difference is a result mainly of higher provision costs in emerging markets due to the relative economic underperformance of this group of countries in the adverse scenario and the varying sensitivity of banks in these economies to macro-financial conditions.

The trajectory of aggregate capital ratios masks significant heterogeneity across banks. Even at their trough, and in the adverse scenario, more than half of the banks in the sample (by assets) have CET1 ratios above 10 percent—much higher than the minimum requirement of 4.5 percent. But banks accounting for 13 percent of assets in the sample fall below 4.5 percent in the adverse scenario, with an additional 3 percent of assets below 6 percent (Figure 4.5, panel 3). The weak tail of banks—defined as those with CET1 ratio below 4.5 percent plus their GSIB buffer—amounts to 14 percent by assets. In the baseline scenario, the weak tail is 5 percent.

In the adverse scenario, there is also heterogeneity across regions and between global systemically important banks and other banks. Global systemically important banks fare better than the average bank, in part because of their stronger initial capital ratios resulting from their mandatory systemic buffers. However, 8 percent of these banks' assets end the simulation period with capital ratios below 4.5 percent. Among non–global systemically important banks, 16 percent of bank assets fail to maintain a 4.5 percent CET1 ratio. Banks from emerging markets are the most severely affected, with almost 40 percent of total banking assets ending the simulation period with CET1 ratios below 4.5 percent. Banks from advanced economies fare better, although there is still a 12 percent of banks' assets below 4.5 percent by 2022.

Across regions and types of banks, the main difference between banks that fail to meet regulatory minimums and the rest of banks is the initial level of CET1. Banks that fall below 4.5 percent CET1 ratio plus GSIB buffer during the simulation period are mainly distinguished by their lower initial capital levels—about 0.8 percentage point below those that maintain their ratios above regulatory minimum levels. Also, banks with a high propensity to fall below minimum capital standards generate meaningfully lower returns than peers that maintain adequate capital throughout adverse conditions.

The importance of the weak tail of banks can also be assessed by estimating the capital shortfall, which is the difference between simulated CET1 ratios and those set by regulation. The shortfall is measured against two benchmarks: the regulatory minimum for CET1—corresponding to a ratio of 4.5 percent plus the bank-specific capital surcharge for each global systemically important bank—and a broad regulatory threshold that also includes the current statutory levels of the capital conservation buffer and the countercyclical buffer in place as of June 2020.[8] The first threshold defines a "barebones capital shortfall" with respect to a level of capital at which supervisory action would take place. The second threshold defines a "broad capital shortfall" relative to a capital ratio that includes the statutory buffers currently in effect.[9] Banks facing a shortfall relative to this broad statutory threshold have the capital space to provide credit by using remaining statutory buffers as envisioned by the international regulatory framework, particularly where regulators have issued guidance announcements making those buffers available. However, they may feel less willing to expand lending activity for precautionary reasons or because of market pressure.

The two measures of capital shortfall in the adverse scenario show important variation across groups of banks (Figure 4.5, panel 4). At the global level, the barebones capital shortfall is about $200 billion, and the broad capital shortfall reaches about $420 billion (0.6 percent of sample banking assets). In both cases, global systemically important banks capture an important part of the shortfall, which is largely explained by the size of these institutions. The differences across regions are driven by differences in the size of their banking systems, with the level of capital shortfalls being much larger for advanced economies. When considering the broad measure, the global shortfall represents 0.8 percent of the GDP of countries where at least one bank has a capital shortfall. Across those countries, the average broad shortfall is 1.1 percent of GDP.

[8]For large US banks this includes the stressed capital ratio levels recently defined by the Federal Reserve instead of the countercyclical capital buffer and the capital conservation buffer. While many jurisdictions have recently released the countercyclical capital buffer, the buffer is above zero in a few. The calculation does not include the effect of "guidance" statements regarding banks' ability to use remaining statutory buffers.

[9]The calculation assumes that countercyclical capital buffers will remain at current levels—0 percent in almost all countries—and does not assume that this buffer will revert to a pre-pandemic or "normalized" level that is difficult to determine a priori.

Effect of Bank-Specific Policies on Capital Ratios

As discussed, authorities have implemented policies aimed at giving banks flexibility to maintain the flow of credit to the real economy. These policies, which include government loan guarantees and capital adequacy policies, affect the need to set aside provisions and the way in which capital ratios are computed and should therefore also improve measured bank capital ratios over the next three years.

The mitigating impact of some of these policies can be quantified in the stress testing exercise as follows:

- *Government guarantees:* The impact of government guarantees on banks' provisions is captured by their impact on banks' expected losses. These losses are the product of banks' exposure to firms, the probability of default of those firms, and the loss experienced by banks when firms default. Government guarantees can be understood as reducing the latter term—known as the "loss given default"—because, under these conditions, the guarantee would be executed. Because of lack of data on the extent to which banks originate guaranteed loans, all banks in a country are assumed to benefit equally from the guarantee in a proportion equal to the ratio of government guarantees to total corporate loans. Because announced guarantee programs apply mostly to new loans, this assumption likely overestimates their initial impact. It is also assumed that guarantees are used to the full extent of announced amounts (full uptake).[10] In the model, a lower uptake of government guarantees would lead to a proportional increase in provision expenses and therefore a proportionally lower impact of the policy on loan loss provision expenses.

- *Capital adequacy policies:* The three categories of capital adequacy policies are quantified from the estimated impact of each announced policy on each bank. For example, the effect of canceling dividends is quantified from stress test model forecasts. The release of capital buffers is estimated by multiplying the percentage reduction by forecast risk-weighted assets. Changes to the calculation of risk-weighted assets similarly apply to the announced change to the relevant exposure class. In a very few instances, bank-specific policies are

applied on a bank-specific basis.[11] These increments are integrated into each bank's balance sheet positions at the end of each period.

In quantifying the impact of these policies, it is assumed that they are maintained over the three-year horizon of the scenario, unless an explicit expiration date was mentioned when the policy was announced. Although this assumption avoids speculating about the timing of withdrawal of some of these policies, it may be too benign, especially in the baseline scenario, in which authorities might decide to withdraw them as the economy recovers during the latter part of the simulation window.

Bank-specific mitigation policies improve average capital ratios across countries and scenarios. In the adverse scenario, the CET1 ratio for advanced economies is about 110 basis points higher at the end of the simulation when both government loan guarantees and capital adequacy policies are considered. In the simulations, the improvement in capital ratios is a result largely of the decline in provision expenses because of government loan guarantees; capital adequacy policies explain about a third of the overall improvement in CET1 at the end of the simulation period in advanced economies (Figure 4.6, panels 1 and 2). In the sample of emerging market economies, capital adequacy policies do not play a meaningful role, as these policies are largely absent in this sample. Given the estimated impact of loan guarantees, the final uptake of these policies—the extent to which the announced guarantee programs are used—could be an important driver of the final solvency position of the banking system. As discussed, an ultimate uptake of half the announced amount would reduce the mitigating effect of the policy roughly by half.

Government loan guarantees and capital mitigation policies reduce the share of bank assets with CET1 ratios below 4.5 percent in the adverse scenario from 13 percent without mitigation policies to 8 percent when those policies are in place (Figure 4.6, panel 3, compared with Figure 4.5, panel 3). Among global systemically important banks, these policies reduce the share of assets with CET1 below 4.5 percent from 8 percent to 3 percent. This decline is also important for non–global systemically important banks, going

---

[10]Many of these programs were announced only a few months ago, so the extent to which the guarantees will be used by banks to originate loans is still unclear.

[11]Online Annex 4.1 describes the estimation of policy mitigation effects in greater detail.

Figure 4.6. Bank Solvency under COVID-19 with Policy Mitigation

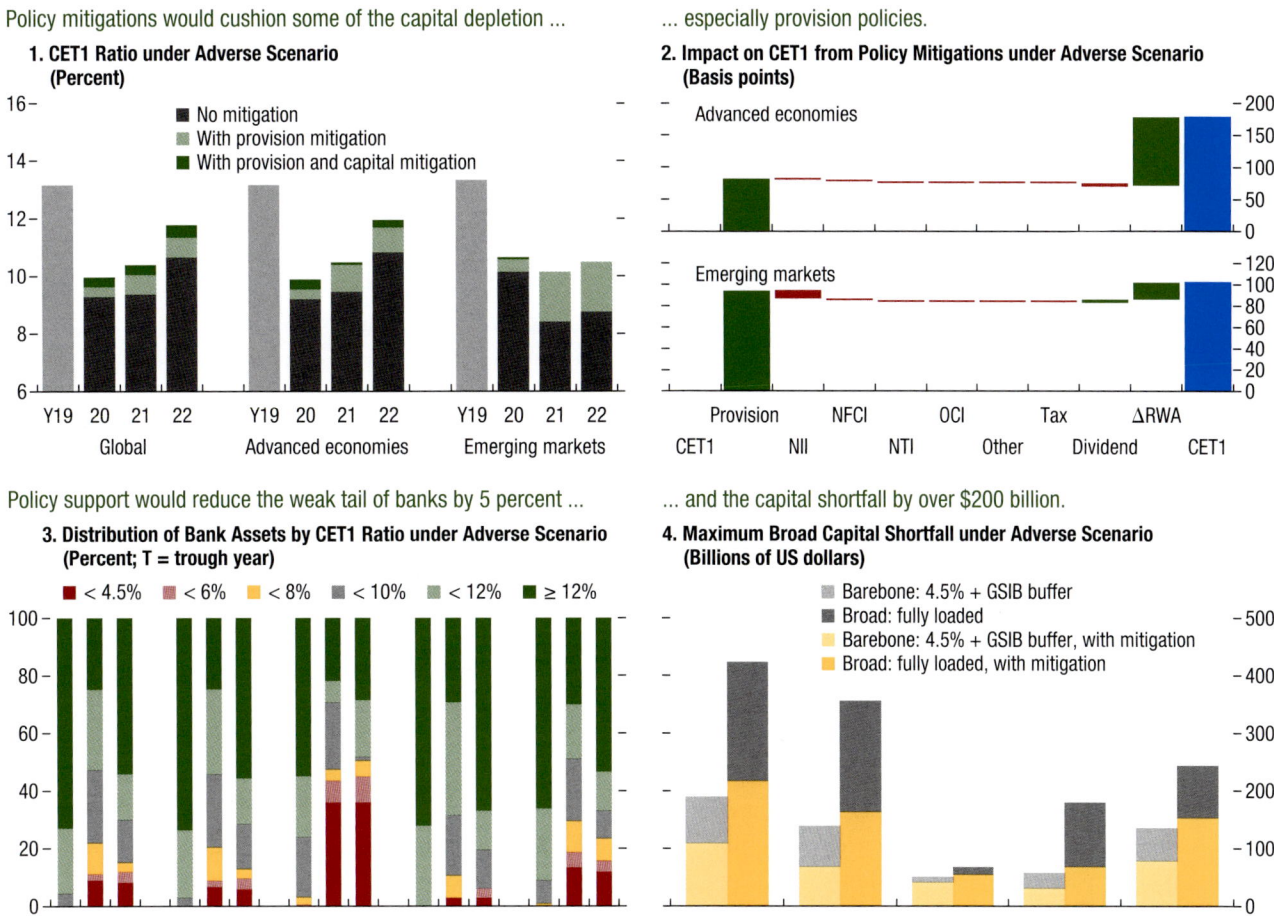

Policy mitigations would cushion some of the capital depletion ...

1. CET1 Ratio under Adverse Scenario
   (Percent)

■ No mitigation
■ With provision mitigation
■ With provision and capital mitigation

... especially provision policies.

2. Impact on CET1 from Policy Mitigations under Adverse Scenario
   (Basis points)

Advanced economies

Emerging markets

CET1   Provision   NII   NFCI   NTI   OCI   Other   Tax   Dividend   ΔRWA   CET1

Policy support would reduce the weak tail of banks by 5 percent ...

3. Distribution of Bank Assets by CET1 Ratio under Adverse Scenario
   (Percent; T = trough year)

■ < 4.5%   ■ < 6%   ■ < 8%   ■ < 10%   ■ < 12%   ■ ≥ 12%

... and the capital shortfall by over $200 billion.

4. Maximum Broad Capital Shortfall under Adverse Scenario
   (Billions of US dollars)

■ Barebone: 4.5% + GSIB buffer
■ Broad: fully loaded
■ Barebone: 4.5% + GSIB buffer, with mitigation
■ Broad: fully loaded, with mitigation

Source: Haver Analytics.
Note: Provision mitigation policies include guarantees only. Estimation of the impact of capital mitigation is explained in Online Annex 4.1. AE = advanced economies; CET1 = common equity Tier 1; EM = emerging markets; GSIB = global systemically important bank; NFCI = net fee and commission income; NII = net interest income; NTI = net trading income; OCI = other comprehensive income; Other = several financial accounts, including trading and investment income, operating expenses, and non-operating items; RWA = risk-weighted assets.

from 16 percent to 12 percent. In advanced economies, the policies analyzed shrink this segment of banks from 12 percent to 6 percent, and in emerging markets, the consideration of these policies in the simulation has only a small effect on the troubled tail of banks. Overall, the weak tail of banks, whose CET1 ratio fall below 4.5 percent plus GSIB buffers, declines from 14 percent to 8.3 percent of bank assets.

The mitigating role of bank-specific policies also maps into lower barebones and broad capital shortfalls (Figure 4.6, panel 4), with an especially remarkable decline for global systemically important banks. Across banks, the broad capital shortfall is about $220 billion, half of which corresponds to the barebones shortfall.

In economies where banks with shortfalls are headquartered, the broad shortfall represents about 0.4 percent of their combined GDP, and, across countries, the average shortfall is about 0.7 percent of GDP. In terms of the initial CET1 ratios of those banks that experience a shortfall during the simulation, in the adverse scenario the global shortfall reaches 6.5 percent and the average is 7.7 percent. All in all, the bank-specific policies quantified in this chapter mitigate the impact of the adverse scenario on bank capital ratios, but the impact is still sizable, and a share of global systemically important bank assets would still be part of the weak tail of banks, even when maximizing the impact of these policies on capital ratios. The capital shortfall relative to a minimum capital standard that treats all guidance statements as reducing capital buffers is lower—about $110 billion, or about 0.2 percent of global GDP. However, reduction of capital levels to the extent of these informal capital releases would likely be unsustainable.

Some policies that are more challenging to quantify would also lead to an improvement in bank capital ratios. Most important, several countries have provided guidance on loan classification, provisioning, and disclosure, and have revised the automatic reclassification for restructured loans. Others have gone further and changed the criteria for the reclassification of loans or frozen those classifications. The effects of these policies on loan loss provisions, in principle, are captured through GDP effects of continued credit flow. However, the changes in reclassification criteria for credit also spare it from increased risk-asset weighting. Because the quantity of loans that would have been reclassified in the absence of these measures cannot be quantified in advance and is generally not reported, the stress test model cannot capture the risk-weighted asset savings associated with these policies.

Overall, while the bank-specific policies quantified in this section help improve banks' capital ratios over the simulation period, the main contribution of the broad policy packages implemented by authorities likely comes from the support they provide to the macroeconomy. This is because the increase in loan loss provision expenses in response to the macroeconomic scenario is the main driver of the simulated decline in capital ratios, even after accounting for the bank-specific mitigation policies. A more adverse macroeconomic scenario, as would be the case in the absence of the broad support measures implemented, would have likely resulted in significantly lower capital ratios. Although counterfactual forecasts for the trajectory of the global economy in the absence of broad support policies are not available, the important difference in simulated capital ratios between the baseline and adverse scenarios suggests how broad macroeconomic support has likely helped banks' capital adequacy.

The policies discussed in this section support the solvency of banks, but they also pose intertemporal trade-offs that could become relevant in the future. Delaying provision expenses because of temporary liquidity shocks to borrowers can help prevent borrowers' liquidity challenges from immediately turning into

insolvency, thus reducing lending procyclicality and supporting banks' profitability and solvency. Similarly, the use of capital buffers creates lending space to support the real economy. Hence, these policies can help bridge the impact of the COVID-19 shock and reduce the chances that a transitory shock will have permanent consequences for financial stability and the global economy. However, if the pandemic and the containment measures last longer than initially expected, ultimately affecting the solvency of borrowers despite the mitigating role of these policies, banks will need larger future provisions and will have lower buffers against future shocks, including from a meaningful second wave of the virus. Maintenance of generous guarantee programs over an extended period of time could also jeopardize fiscal solvency if defaults eventually materialize and could lead to further bank losses related to their sovereign exposures. Furthermore, given the unusual degree of uncertainty around the depth and duration of the COVID-19 recession, a severely adverse scenario with stronger consequences for the banking sector cannot be ruled out.

Summary and Policy Discussion

COVID-19 has had important consequences for the global banking sector and will pose further challenges. Should a quick rebound in economic activity not materialize, corporate and household solvency problems will likely deteriorate further and collateral values may decline, resulting in greater credit losses and posing challenges for banks globally. These challenges could interact with other, more structural challenges, such as the low profitability observed in some regions in an environment of persistently low interest rates and term spreads, a scenario that has become increasingly likely in the wake of the pandemic.

The simulations presented in this chapter show that, on aggregate, the banking systems analyzed would remain solvent in coming years, although there is heterogeneity across and within regions. The aggregate solvency is partly due to the buffers accumulated as a result of the regulatory reforms introduced after the global financial crisis. In fact, banks analyzed in this chapter had a median CET1 ratio of 11.9 in 2007, compared with 16.2 percent in 2019. This improvement in the initial solvency conditions carries over to the minimum CET1 ratios achieved in response to the COVID-19 crisis.

Nonetheless, while aggregate capital ratios remain above regulatory minimums, at a global level and within regions there is a weak tail of banks that could see their solvency challenged. The size of this tail depends largely on the depth and persistence of the crisis, becoming sizable across almost all regions and groups of banks in an adverse scenario with a persistent decline in economic activity. Some global systemically important banks are also part of this weak tail, which could have broader repercussions for financial stability in an adverse scenario.

Policies adopted by governments, central banks, and bank regulators have helped ease banks' challenges amid the COVID-19 crisis. Direct support to borrowers (both firms and households)—and liquidity provision to key markets, banks, and other financial intermediaries—have had a marked effect on bank capital ratios through the resultant improvement in macroeconomic conditions. On top of this support, government loan guarantees and capital adequacy policies have provided a second line of defense that has eased and will likely continue to ease pressures, as shown in the quantitative forward-looking analysis of this chapter.

The majority of regulatory responses taken so far are consistent with the core standards implemented after the global financial crisis and with internationally agreed guiding principles. National authorities have taken capital and liquidity measures using the flexibility embedded in the prudential framework to help support lending to the real economy. Authorities have clarified the usability of capital and liquidity buffers, encouraged banks to use these buffers to absorb losses and sustain credit, and restricted capital distributions to preserve capital. However, in several cases, regulatory easing was achieved by lowering minimum requirements below Basel framework levels. Such deviations risk undermining the credibility of the internationally agreed standards, could contribute to market segmentation, and may increase the risks to bank safety and soundness. Standard setting bodies (like the Basel Committee) and national authorities have also encouraged banks to work constructively and prudently with borrowers and have issued guidance on how to treat restructured loans and public and private moratoria for prudential asset classification and provision. Nonetheless, some measures that run contrary to these recommendations have been observed, such as the freezing of asset classification status and provisioning requirements. These measures

affect the reliability of financial statements and capital ratios, and risk undermining the confidence in the banking system. Moreover, they may lead to lending to insolvent borrowers while not recognizing loan losses, which may not only jeopardize the financial soundness of banks but also the recovery as credit is diverted from productive uses.

Looking ahead, the benefits of these policies in easing banks' capital constraints and maintaining the flow of credit to the real economy should be carefully balanced against their potential medium-term risks to financial stability. Although using the flexibility embedded in the prudential framework in accordance with recommendations made by standard setters could help reduce procyclicality and negative feedback loops in response to temporary liquidity shocks, relaxing loan classification and provisioning rules undermines transparency and data reliability as financial statements and prudential ratios may no longer adequately reflect the true strength of banks. A decline in the quality of information could lead to a loss of confidence in the banking system, with adverse implications for stability. It is thus important that some of these measures be carefully phased out as the economy recovers, especially in the baseline scenario. It is also essential that, in any scenario, banks promptly recognize losses for borrowers that become insolvent as evidence of impairment becomes available. More broadly, phasing out government support, including government guarantees, too quickly would lead to lasting damage to the economy, but phasing it out too late could risk damaging public finances or unduly keeping insolvent borrowers afloat.

Despite the mitigating effect of government policies, in the adverse scenario simulated in this chapter, there is a weak tail of banks that fail (or nearly fail) to meet minimum regulatory requirements. This finding highlights the usefulness of forward-looking stress tests to assess the health of banking systems and to guide prospective policy responses to the current crisis. When conducted by regulators or supervisors, this type of assessment would rely on more granular data than used in this global exercise, and thus would provide additional richness.

Once the assessment is done, however, what should authorities do about banks that could become troubled? The answer to this question should take into consideration country-specific circumstances. Acting now to strengthen the financial safety net, including deposit guarantee programs, resolution regimes, and central bank liquidity facilities, is key. Capital preservation measures will help, including temporarily limiting the distribution of dividends, as some countries have already done. For countries that allowed banks to draw down capital buffers, the stress test results will help guide the timing and pace at which these exceptional measures can be unwound. Supervisors could use this information to reassess forward-looking capital plans and take measures aimed at preserving and supporting

plans to rebuild capital gradually for the most vulnerable entities to ensure confidence, avoid procyclicality, and preserve financial stability.[12] Preparing contingency plans that detail how the authorities will respond to possible future pressures is critical to support effective policy responses if the adverse scenario materializes.

---

[12]For a broader discussion of the banking regulatory and supervisory actions to deal with COVID-19, see IMF (2020a).

Box 4.1. The Role of Corporate and Consumer Risk in the Evolution of Banks' Loan Loss Provisions

The COVID-19 crisis is likely to impact the credit risk of both firms and households. Households and firms may have different effects on bank provisioning and capital, according to the severity of the shock and the composition of the lending portfolios. Disentangling the impact of these two sources of credit risk is important to evaluate the policy response to the crisis as both the magnitude and type of support measures differ across these two sectors.

A satellite model of loan loss provisions that considers the mix of bank loans across corporate (firms) and consumer (households) loans was developed to complement the core global stress test model. This model relies on the local projection method to decompose bank loan loss provisions into a component related to household risk (captured by the unemployment rate or changes in house prices) and another related to corporate loans risk (captured by a measure of the probability of default of the corporate sector). It provides a starting point for a more nuanced discussion of the implications of bank business models for future financial performance and for tackling the impact of mitigation policies that target specific sectors (see Online Annex 4.1 for additional details).

This box has been prepared by Nicola Pierri and Tomohiro Tsuruga.

A forward-looking simulation of the evolution of loan loss provisions (as a share of total loans) in the baseline scenario of the *World Economic Outlook* and the share of them explained by corporate and consumer risk shows that the crisis generates a strong but gradual response that peaks during the first half of 2021 (Figure 4.1.1). At its peak, the increase in the loan loss provision ratio is about 1 percentage point in advanced economies and about 0.4 percentage point in emerging market economies.

Most of the increase is due to heightened corporate risk, although households play a significant role in advanced economies because of their larger share on advanced economy banks' portfolios. These results show that the level and composition of total provisions depends on the mix of bank loan portfolios and on the relative size of the shocks to firms and households. The analysis highlights the importance of considering the loan mix for the assessment of the impact of the crisis and the analysis of policy responses. In the chapter, these insights are carried to the global stress testing model to assess the impact of policies that affect a specific sector, such as the government loan guarantees that tend to be focused on corporate loans. If data were available, this type of analysis could also be used to further disaggregate the impact of the crisis on different productive sectors.

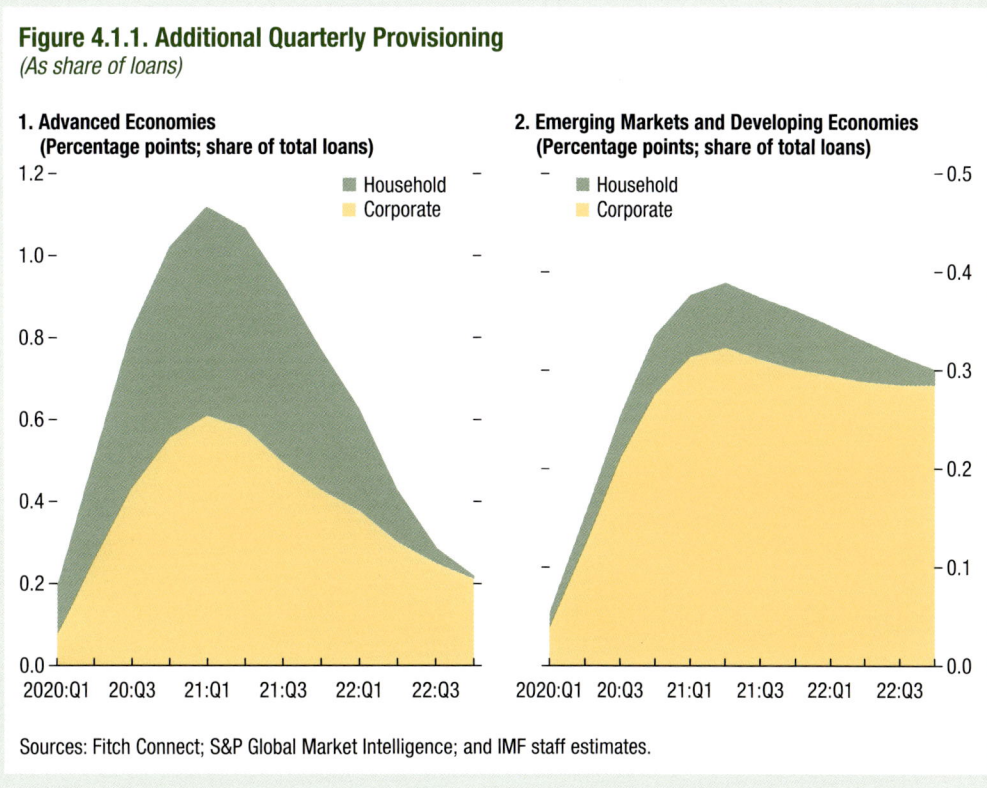

Figure 4.1.1. Additional Quarterly Provisioning
(As share of loans)

Sources: Fitch Connect; S&P Global Market Intelligence; and IMF staff estimates.

References

International Monetary Fund (IMF). 2020a. "Banking Sector Regulatory and Supervisory Response to Deal with Coronavirus Impact." Special Series on COVID-19. https://www .imf.org/~/media/Files/Publications/covid19-special-notes/ enspecial-series-on-covid19banking-sector-regulatory-and -supervisory-response-to-deal-with-coronavir.ashx

———. 2020b. "Fiscal Monitor Database of Country Fiscal Measures in Response to the COVID-19 Pandemic." https:// www.imf.org/en/Topics/imf-and-covid19/Fiscal-Policies -Database-in-Response-to-COVID-19.

CORPORATE SUSTAINABILITY

FIRMS' ENVIRONMENTAL PERFORMANCE AND THE COVID-19 CRISIS

Chapter 5 at a Glance

- Tighter financial constraints and weaker economic conditions can act as a drag on firms' environmental performance.
- The coronavirus disease (COVID-19) crisis could substantially reduce firms' green investments, reversing gains in their environmental performance made in past years.
- Climate policies and green investment packages are therefore warranted to support a green recovery and the transition to a low-carbon economy.
- Policies aimed at fostering sustainable finance such as better disclosure standards and product standardization could further help mobilize green investments and alleviate firms' financial constraints.

The shutdown in economic activity as a result of the COVID-19 crisis has resulted in a temporary decline in global carbon emissions, but the long-term impact of the pandemic on the transition to a low-carbon economy remains uncertain. While the economic fallout from the crisis may constrain firms' ability to invest in green projects, thus slowing down the transition, the COVID-19 crisis could also induce a structural shift in consumer and investor preferences toward environmentally friendly products, providing an opportunity to introduce mitigation policies that help diversify away from fossil fuel production. Looking back at previous episodes of financial and economic stress, this chapter finds that tighter financial constraints and adverse economic conditions are generally detrimental to firms' environmental performance, reducing green investments, and setting back their progress by several years. This suggests that the COVID-19 crisis could potentially slow down the transition to a low-carbon economy. In light of the urgent need to reduce global greenhouse gas emissions, it also underlines the importance of climate policies and green investment packages to support a green recovery and the energy transition. Policies aimed at fostering sustainable finance, such as improved transparency and standardization, could further help mobilize green investments and alleviate firms' financial constraints.

The authors of this chapter are Zhi Ken Gan, Pierpaolo Grippa, Pierre Guérin, Oksana Khadarina, Samuel Mann, Felix Suntheim (team lead), and Yizhi Xu, with contributions from Alan Feng, Germán Villegas Bauer, and Julia Xueliang Wang, under the guidance of Fabio Natalucci, Mahvash Qureshi, and Jérôme Vandenbussche. Harrison Hong served as an expert advisor.

Introduction

The shutdown in economic activity as a result of the COVID-19 crisis resulted in a sharp decline in global carbon emissions (Figure 5.1, panel 1).[1] Daily emissions in early April 2020 fell by about 17 percent compared with 2019 levels, though most of this decline has reversed since then as economic activity has picked up across countries. Such a reversal in emissions is in line with what turned out to be only a temporary decline in the price of carbon emission allowances in March 2020 (Figure 5.1, panel 2). Overall, recent studies forecast a temporary reduction in emissions of about 4 to 7 percent in 2020, far from the large and sustained decrease in emissions required under the Paris Agreement to limit the increase in global temperature to well below 2°C (Le Quéré and others 2020).[2]

There is also a possibility that the transition to a low-carbon economy could be delayed should the economic scarring from the pandemic crisis run deep, inducing economic agents and policymakers to sideline or postpone environmental objectives. Heightened economic uncertainty, a sharp drop in energy prices, and corporate balance sheet vulnerabilities may result in a reduction in investments and research in long-horizon, capital-intensive green

---

[1] In the short term, there is an almost one-to-one relationship between economic growth and emissions (Hale and Leduc 2020).

[2] The UN Environment Programme (2019) estimates that emissions need to decline by 2.7 percent annually in order to reach the 2°C goal by 2030.

Figure 5.1. The Energy Transition during the COVID-19 Crisis

Carbon emissions declined rapidly as COVID-19 became a global pandemic ...

... but, unlike during the global financial crisis, the decline has been short-lived, with a rebound in emissions.

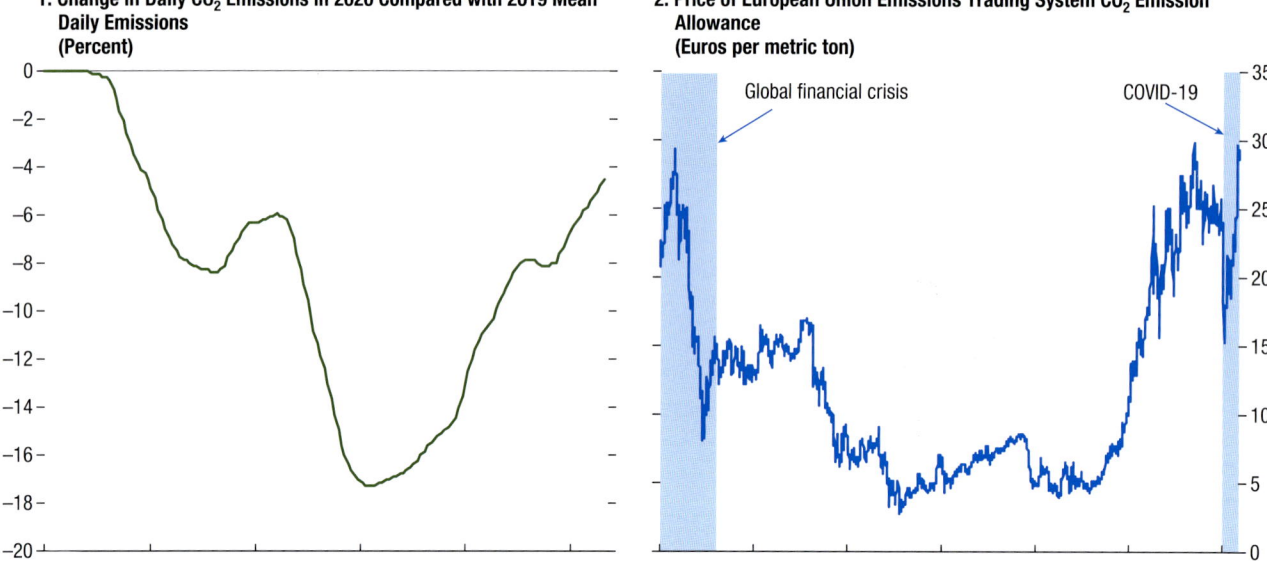

1. Change in Daily CO_2 Emissions in 2020 Compared with 2019 Mean Daily Emissions
(Percent)

2. Price of European Union Emissions Trading System CO_2 Emission Allowance
(Euros per metric ton)

Sources: Global Carbon Project; Refinitiv Datastream; and IMF staff calculations.
Note: Panel 1 shows the reduction in daily CO_2 emissions in 2020 compared with 2019 mean levels. Panel 2 shows the price of futures contracts on carbon emission allowances traded on the Intercontinental Exchange. The European Union Emissions Trading System was subject to several changes in regulation over the sample period that may have affected the price level.

projects. In addition, subsidies or economic rescue packages aimed at softening the impact of the crisis may slow the transition—for example, by supporting firms or activities not compatible with long-term climate mitigation goals.

At the same time, the current crisis could also present an opportunity to accelerate the transition to a low-carbon economy by inducing structural shifts in consumer and investor preferences toward environmentally friendly products in the event economic agents change their beliefs about the likelihood of other catastrophic events, such as those linked to climate change.[3] In the corporate sector, for example, climate change has become an increasingly important topic since the onset of the pandemic, as is evident from firms' earnings calls transcripts (see Box 5.1). More generally, an increased awareness of the benefits of long-term disaster prevention could facilitate

implementation of green policy measures such as carbon taxes.[4]

Against this backdrop, this chapter aims to address the following two key questions: (1) How has the COVID-19 crisis affected green financing so far? (2) What can be learned from past economic crises about the likely behavior of the corporate sector in the near and medium terms with respect to the greening of the economy?

The COVID-19 Crisis and Financing the Energy Transition

The COVID-19 crisis has not led to a sustained decline in green financing so far. Issuance of green corporate bonds, which has trended up over the past decade, declined in March 2020 in the midst of the financial market turmoil, but it has picked up since,

[3]Survey evidence suggests that voters have become more worried about other global threats, such as climate change, after experiencing the COVID-19 pandemic (Geman 2020).

[4]Calls for implementing "green recovery" packages in the aftermath of the COVID-19 crisis have come from different quarters, including the private sector in some cases. For example, in June 2020 more than 100 global investors called for a green European Union recovery plan. The EU coronavirus recovery package earmarks about 37 percent of the funds for climate protection.

Figure 5.2. The COVID-19 Crisis and Green Investments

Green bond issuance dropped in the first quarter of 2020 before picking up again beginning in April 2020.

1. Green Corporate Bond to Total Corporate Bond Issuance and Total Green Corporate Bond Issuance, January 2014–June 2020

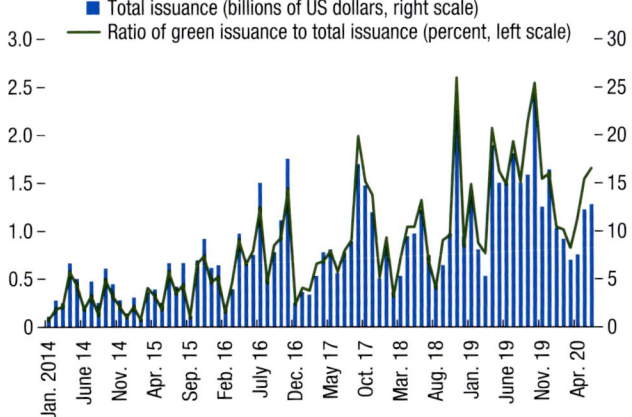

Bank lending has shifted to green firms over the past decade.

2. Total Amount of Syndicated Loans to Firms with Environmental Scores Higher than Median and Firms with Environmental Scores Lower than Median, 2009:Q1–2020:Q1
(Billions of US dollars)

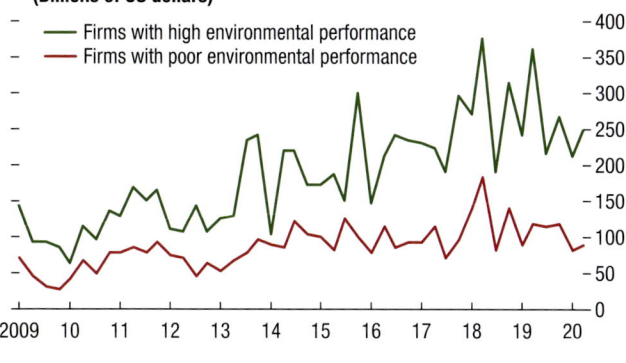

Flows into sustainable and environmental equity funds slowed in the first quarter of 2020 but remained positive.

3. Sustainable and Environmental Fund Flows as a Share of Fund Size, 2003:Q1–2020:Q1
(Moving averages; percent)

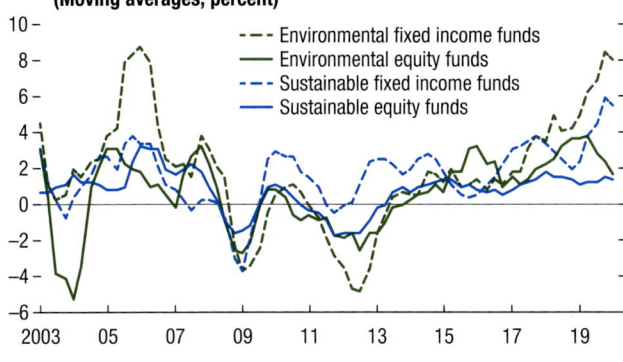

Equity indices with a focus on environmental issues performed at least as well as the overall market.

4. Cumulative Returns of Green and Conventional Equity Market Indices
(Percent)

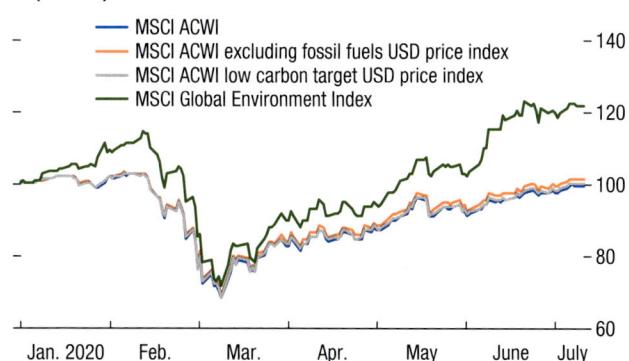

Sources: Bloomberg Finance L.P.; Dealogic; Morningstar; Refinitiv Datastream; and IMF staff calculations.
Note: Panel 1 shows global green corporate bond issues. Panel 3 shows quarterly flows into sustainable or environmental fixed-income or equity funds.
MSCI ACWI = Morgan Stanley Capital International All Country World Index.

with the share of green bonds in total corporate bond issuance returning to 2019 levels (Figure 5.2, panel 1). In the syndicated loan market, loans to firms with an above-median score in environmental performance have increased over the past decade compared with loans to firms with a below-median score.[5] Lending to both

types of firms dropped slightly in the first quarter of 2020 (Figure 5.2, panel 2).

Investment funds with a focus on sustainable or environmental investments have continued to attract investors throughout the crisis, especially fixed-income funds, with only a small drop in aggregate inflows in

[5]Firm-level environmental, social, and governance data come with several caveats. First, the data cover only publicly listed firms, so the results do not necessarily carry over to the entire economy, which includes unlisted small- and medium-sized enterprises. Second, there is a lack of standardization and transparency across data providers, so environmental scores from different providers

may capture different features of environmental performance. Third, as some scores are self-reported by firms, accuracy may vary across the sample. See Online Annex 5.1 for a description of the variables used in this chapter. All annexes are available at www.imf.org/en/Publications/GFSR.

some asset classes (Figure 5.2, panel 3).[6] A possible driver of the good performance of sustainable and environmental funds may have been the relatively high returns that green investments have experienced during this crisis in general (Figure 5.2, panel 4).

Overall, the impact of the COVID-19 crisis on the financing of green investments so far seems to have been modest and short-lived. However, given the severity and possible persistence of the shock—in terms of output decline, the extent of potential scarring, and the heightened economic uncertainty—there could be significant strains on corporate balance sheets. It is therefore challenging to forecast whether such trends will continue and ultimately what the overall impact of the crisis will be on firms' environmental performance and on their ability to contribute to global climate change mitigation efforts. In view of this concern, the analysis in the next section examines firms' environmental performance during previous episodes of financial and economic stress to draw possible implications for the current episode.

Lessons from Past Economic Crises for Firms' Environmental Performance during the COVID-19 Crisis

Existing research focusing on the United States suggests that the environmental, social, and governance (ESG) performance of financially constrained firms—that is, firms that face difficulties in raising external capital—is generally weaker relative to unconstrained firms (Hong, Kubik, and Scheinkman 2012).[7] Therefore, a deterioration in financial or economic conditions that results in a tightening of firms' financial

constraints is likely to reduce their ability to invest in green projects and cut greenhouse gas emissions.

Extending this analysis to a global sample and specifically analyzing firms' environmental performance shows that tighter financial constraints are indeed associated with worse environmental performance (Figure 5.3, panel 1). Proxying firms' financial constraints by firm size (logarithm of total assets), rating status, interest coverage ratio, ability to pay dividends, and the commonly used Kaplan-Zingales index, the environmental performance of financially constrained firms is in each case significantly weaker than that of unconstrained firms. Specifically, environmental performance falls by 10 points when firm size drops from the median to the 25th percentile of the firm size distribution. When a firm does not pay dividends or when it is not rated, its environmental score is 4 points and 3 points lower, respectively, than the score of dividend-paying and rated firms. The environmental score is 1 point lower when an aggregate measure of financial constraints (the Kaplan-Zingales index) is above the median of the sample distribution. Similar results are obtained when considering firms' carbon intensity instead of their environmental performance.

A key channel through which financial constraints can affect firms' environmental performance is a decline in investments in green technologies. Constrained firms may postpone or reduce such investments if they do not directly contribute to revenue generation. Moreover, financially constrained firms may face difficulties in borrowing against future profits to invest in research and development, consequently postponing investments in intangibles that could potentially improve their environmental performance. Regression analyses support these hypotheses and suggest that financially constrained firms are less likely to make investments that reduce future environmental risks, such as treatment of emissions or installation of cleaner technologies (Figure 5.3, panel 2). For example, the probability that a firm will make an environmental investment falls by 6 percentage points when firm size drops from the median to the 25th percentile of the firm size distribution.

These results have important implications in the current COVID-19 context. An adverse macro-financial shock that increases uncertainty and amplifies firms' financial constraints is likely to affect firms' environmental performance and has the potential to significantly impede their ability to invest in

---

[6]Sustainable funds explicitly indicate all kinds of sustainability; impact; and environmental, social, and governance (ESG) strategies in their prospectus. Environmental funds invest in environmentally oriented industries. See the October 2019 *Global Financial Stability Report* for a discussion of sustainable finance and financial stability.

[7]Because financial constraints are not directly observable, different proxies are used in the literature (see Online Annex 5.2): firm size (large firms are expected to be less financially constrained than small firms), rating status (firms with a rating may have easier access to capital markets than those without), the interest coverage ratio (defined as earnings before interest and taxes divided by interest expenses, reflecting a firm's debt repayment capacity with higher values indicating less financially constrained firms), the ability to pay dividends, and the Kaplan-Zingales index (an aggregate measure of financial constraints).

Figure 5.3. Financial Constraints, Financial Stress, and Environmental Performance

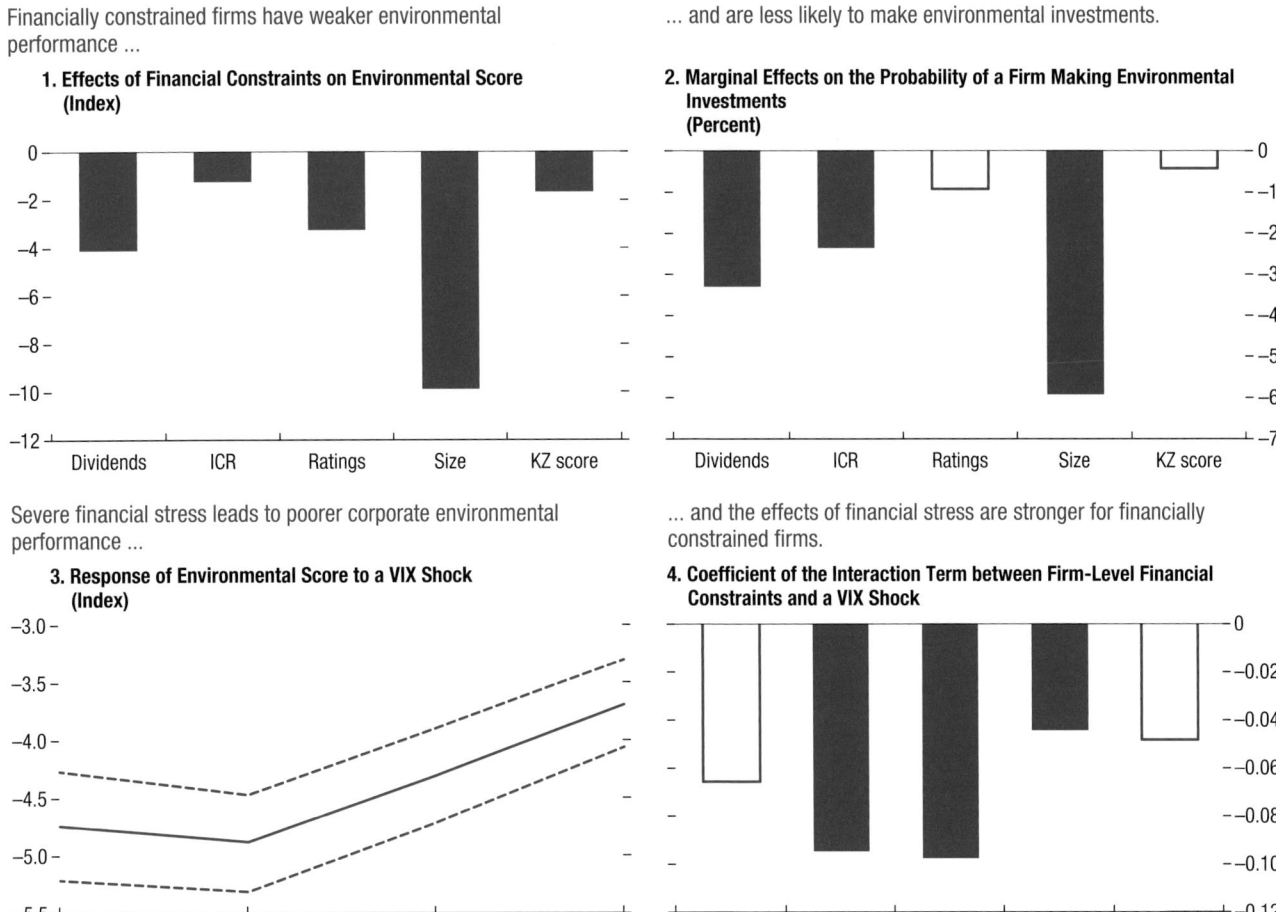

Financially constrained firms have weaker environmental performance ...

1. Effects of Financial Constraints on Environmental Score (Index)

... and are less likely to make environmental investments.

2. Marginal Effects on the Probability of a Firm Making Environmental Investments (Percent)

Severe financial stress leads to poorer corporate environmental performance ...

3. Response of Environmental Score to a VIX Shock (Index)

... and the effects of financial stress are stronger for financially constrained firms.

4. Coefficient of the Interaction Term between Firm-Level Financial Constraints and a VIX Shock

Sources: Refinitiv Datastream; Standard & Poor's; and IMF staff calculations.
Note: "Dividends" refers to firms that do not pay dividends, "ICR" to firms with earnings below interest expenses, "Ratings" to firms that do not have a rating from Standard & Poor's, "Size" to the log of total assets (the sign of this variable is reversed so that higher values indicate smaller firms), and "KZ score" to firms above the median of the Kaplan-Zingales index score distribution (more financially constrained firms have higher KZ scores). Panel 1 shows regression estimates of environmental scores on financial constraints. Regressions include firm-level controls as well as industry, country, and time fixed effects. Firm-level controls are the log of total assets and earnings, except when using "Size" as a measure of financial constraint, when only earnings are used as a firm-level control. Panel 2 shows the marginal effects of a given financial constraint measure on the probability of a firm making an environmental investment. The probit models include the same control variables and fixed effects as in panel 1. In panel 3, $t = 0$ is the year of the shock. The Chicago Board Options Exchange Volatility Index (VIX) shock is the average value of the VIX over the calendar year. The solid line denotes the response to a 16.3 point increase in the VIX (corresponding to the difference in the average value of the VIX in 2020, using data up to July 31, 2020, relative to the average value in 2019). The dashed lines denote 90 percent confidence intervals. Responses are obtained with the local projection approach from firm-level panel regressions that include firm-level controls, country-specific output gaps, the price of oil, and country and industry fixed effects. Panel 4 shows interaction terms at a one-step horizon between the VIX shocks and the lagged firm-level financial constraint variables. The same control variables as in panel 3 are used. In panels 1, 2, and 4, solid bars indicate significance at the 10 percent level. ICR = interest coverage ratio.

green projects. To quantify the extent of the impact, two types of shocks are analyzed here: (1) a global financial stress shock (proxied by the Chicago Board Options Exchange Volatility Index [VIX]) and (2) a real economic activity shock capturing a sudden drop in domestic output.[8]

[8]See Online Annex 5.3.

The analysis shows that a sudden jump in the VIX, comparable to the average level that prevailed in the first half of 2020 during the COVID-19 pandemic, would lead to a persistent drop in firms' environmental performance by up to 5 points, with the pre-shock performance level not attained for at least three years after the shock (Figure 5.3, panel 3). Absent policy actions and behavioral changes, this would imply that

Figure 5.4. Economic Shocks and Environmental Performance

Contractionary economic shocks lead to lower corporate environmental performance ...

... and carbon intensity deteriorates following contractionary economic shocks.

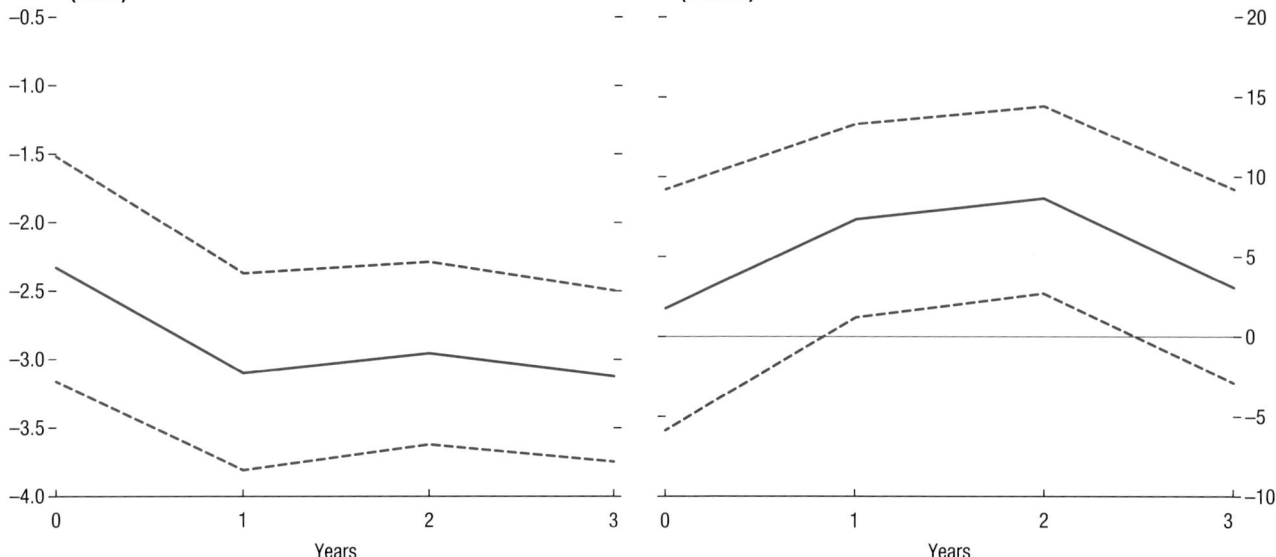

1. Response of Environmental Score (*y*-axis) over Time (*x*-axis) to a Fall in the Output Gap
   (Index)

2. Response of the Logarithm of Total CO$_2$ Emissions Relative to Revenues (*y*-axis) over Time (*x*-axis) to a Fall in the Output Gap
   (Percent)

Sources: Refinitiv Datastream; and IMF staff calculations.
Note: In panels 1 and 2, the real economic activity shock is scaled as a 10 percentage point drop in the output gap. The regression includes firm-level controls (log of total assets, earnings, and a dividend dummy variable), the price of oil (log West Texas Intermediate), the Chicago Board Options Exchange Volatility Index, and country and sector fixed effects. Dashed lines represent 90 percent confidence interval.

average corporate environmental performance would return to the levels that were last observed in 2006. Moreover, the adverse effect of global financial shocks on environmental performance is magnified when firms are financially constrained (Figure 5.3, panel 4). For example, for firms with an interest coverage ratio below 1 or for unrated firms in 2019, the global financial stress shock observed thus far in 2020 is estimated to lower environmental performance by 2 additional points, compared to firms with an interest coverage ratio above 1 or rated firms.[9]

A large decline in the output gap (10 percentage points, about 50 percent larger than that observed in the Group of Seven [G7] economies during the global financial crisis), would lead to a 3 point

decline in firms' environmental performance in the medium term (Figure 5.4, panel 1).[10] Similarly, firms' carbon intensity—captured by their total carbon emissions relative to revenue—could increase by up to 8.5 percent in the medium term after such a decline in the output gap (Figure 5.4, panel 2), even though the initial response of carbon intensity to economic shocks may be small because of the cyclical dynamics of carbon dioxide emissions observed during recessions (Figure 5.1, panel 1; Hale and Leduc 2020).

In addition to direct global financial and economic shocks, changes in oil prices could also impact corporate environmental performance by affecting

[9]These economic effects are calculated by multiplying the interaction term by a 16.3 point increase in the VIX (corresponding to the difference in the average value of the VIX in 2020, using data up to July 31, 2020, relative to the average value in 2019).

[10]Other more global measures of economic activity shocks such as the forecast error for the current-year global GDP growth relative to the *World Economic Outlook* projection, or the global economic activity shock from Baumeister and Hamilton (2019) also lead to a fall in corporate environmental performance in the medium term.

firms' incentives and their financial constraints. The onset of the COVID-19 crisis was accompanied by a steep decline in the international price of oil.[11] The effect of such a decline in oil prices on firms' environmental performance is, however, ambiguous. On the one hand, it may relax firms' financial constraints and reduce the incentives for businesses to improve their energy efficiency and shift away from fossil fuels, including by hindering the development of clean energy sources by making investments in new projects less profitable.[12] On the other hand, low oil prices could benefit the energy transition by hurting the profitability of the oil sector and leading to lower investments in the fossil fuel sector and a decline in production, thereby making it easier for clean energy firms to compete.

In principle, the effect of an oil price shock on environmental performance is likely to depend on the underlying source of the shock—that is, whether it is a demand- or supply-driven shock. A negative global demand shock associated with a decline in economic activity that reduces the demand for oil could be associated with lower corporate environmental performance as investments into cleaner energy sources are delayed because of already tight financial conditions for firms. Conversely, a drop in oil prices due to an oil supply shock could trigger an increase in global economic activity (Baumeister and Hamilton 2019), easing firms' financial constraints and allowing them to improve their environmental performance.

Econometric analysis suggests that the source of the oil price fluctuation is indeed key to understanding firms' environmental response to a shock. Historically, when oil prices have fallen due to demand-side factors, environmental corporate performance has been weaker. By contrast, when oil prices have declined due to an oil supply shock, environmental performance of firms has improved (Figure 5.5). To the extent that the COVID-19-induced oil price shock is largely a

Figure 5.5. Oil Market Shocks and Environmental Performance

Lower oil prices due to demand factors are associated with lower corporate environmental performance.

Response of Environmental Scores to Oil Market Shocks that Lower the Real Price of Oil across all Industries
(Index)

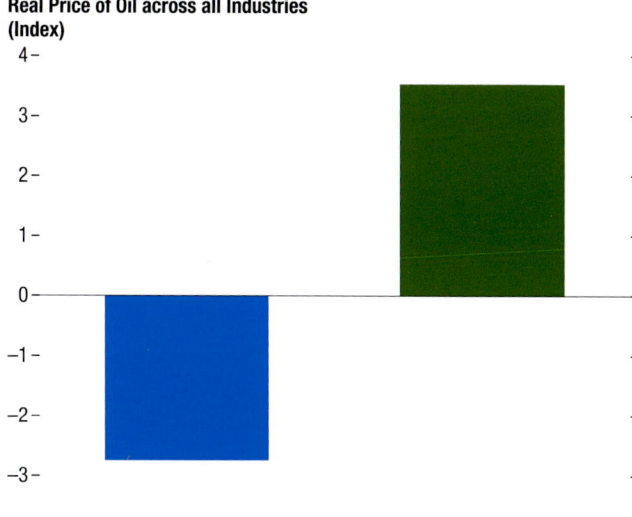

Sources: Refinitiv Datastream; and IMF staff calculations.
Note: The oil market shocks are obtained from Baumeister and Hamilton (2019). All shocks are unit shocks that lead to a fall in the real price of oil. Responses at a two-year horizon are represented. Controls in the regression are the log of total assets, earnings, a dividend dummy variable, country-specific output gaps, the Chicago Board Options Exchange Volatility Index, and the price of oil (log West Texas Intermediate). The regressions include country and sector fixed effects. Solid bars indicate significance at the 10 percent level.

demand-driven shock, firms' environmental performance is thus likely to suffer.[13]

Overall, these results indicate that tighter financial constraints are associated with weaker corporate environmental performance. Adverse global financial and output shocks that increase uncertainty and amplify firms' financial constraints weigh significantly on their environmental performance. Furthermore, a reduction in oil prices against the backdrop of a decline in global economic activity is unlikely in itself to lift corporate environmental performance. Thus, absent strong supportive policy actions, tighter financial constraints and weaker economic activity related to the COVID-19 crisis are likely to act as a drag on firms' environmental performance in the future.

[11]Global energy demand declined by 3.8 percent in the first quarter of 2020. The demand for oil, coal, and to a lesser extent gas and nuclear energy is projected to decline substantially by the end of 2020 (IEA 2020).

[12]Acemoglu and others (2019) discuss the long-term effects of the shale gas boom, which reduces carbon dioxide emissions from coal in the short term, while increasing aggregate production and directing energy innovation to shift away from clean energy to fossil fuels.

[13]Difficulties to reach an agreement among the OPEC+ coalition also contributed to the collapse in oil prices in early 2020, but a decomposition of the oil price shock in March and April 2020 suggests that it was largely driven by demand-side factors. See Online Annex 5.3.

Conclusions and Policy Recommendations

The COVID-19 crisis has resulted in a temporary decline in global carbon emissions, but its long-term impact is uncertain. On the one hand, the crisis may increase awareness of catastrophic risks and bring about a major shift in consumer preferences, corporate actions, and investor behavior. On the other hand, the historical evidence presented in this chapter suggests that there is a real possibility that, barring public interventions, investment by firms to improve their environmental performance may decline in this time of macro-financial stress.

To achieve the reduction in emissions needed to keep global warming below 2°C, an increase in green investments, in combination with steadily rising carbon prices, is critical (October 2020 *World Economic Outlook*; October 2019 *Fiscal Monitor*). Public policies and green recovery packages are important to offset the potential deterioration in firms' environmental performance resulting from the crisis (see the October 2020 *Fiscal Monitor*).

In addition, to alleviate firms' financial constraints and to aid green investment, it will be key to put in place policies that support the sustainable finance sector, such as better disclosure standards, development of green taxonomies, and product standardization (see the October 2019 *Global Financial Stability Report*).

Box 5.1. Climate Index Based on Firms' Earnings Calls

To measure how firms' exposure to and awareness of climate change have evolved over time, a firm-level climate index was constructed for this chapter based on quarterly earnings call transcripts using a climate change dictionary built from four climate change glossaries.[1] To construct the index, earnings call transcripts from 4,109 firms located in 46 countries are used.

Panel 1 of Figure 5.1.1 shows the share of earnings call transcripts that mention specific phrases related to climate change, such as "climate change," "CO_2,"

or "emissions." A sharp increase in discussions involving climate change topics is observed in 2020, coinciding with the COVID-19 pandemic. This could, for example, be the result of the COVID-19 crisis increasing firms' focus on catastrophic events and long-term risks.

The *climate change discussion index* is then constructed for each firm by assigning a value of 1 to each earnings call transcripts that contains a phrase included in the dictionary. Panel 2 shows the average of the index over time. It is noteworthy that in the earnings calls of energy sector firms, mentions of climate-change-related terms spiked after the Paris Agreement in 2016, highlighting the importance of policy risk for this sector. The increase in discussions involving climate change over the past few years is consistent across countries (Online Annex 5.4).

This box was prepared by Alan Feng and Germán Villegas Bauer.
[1]Following a similar approach as Engle and others (2020), the glossaries are obtained from the British Broadcasting Corporation, the Intergovernmental Panel on Climate Change, the United Nations, and the US Environmental Protection Agency. See Online Annex 5.4 for a list of all terms. All annexes are available at www.imf.org/en/Publications/GFSR.

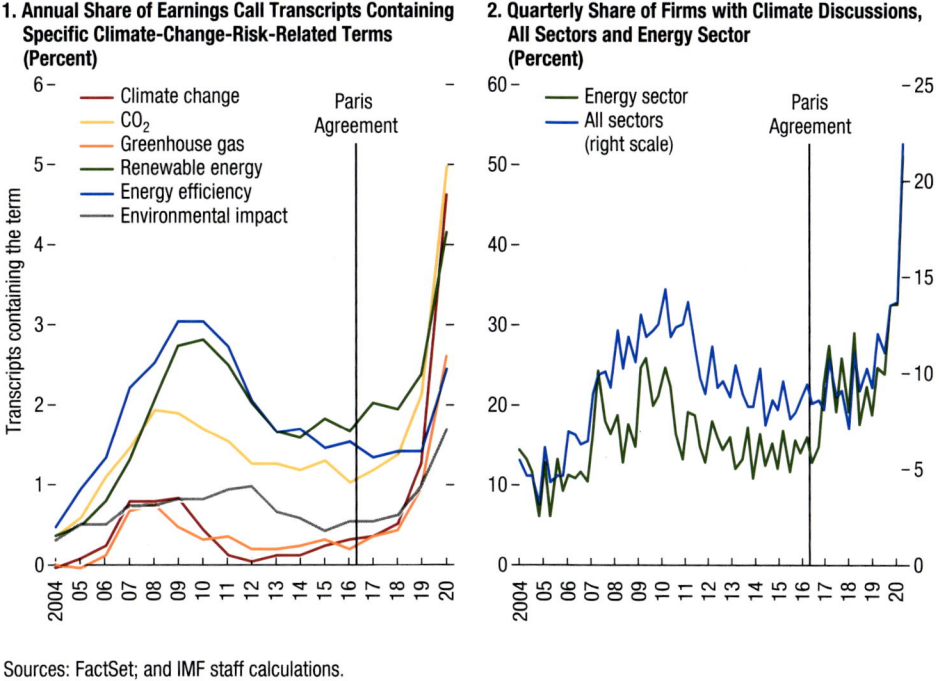

Figure 5.1.1. Climate Index

Climate change discussions have increased during the COVID-19 crisis.

1. Annual Share of Earnings Call Transcripts Containing Specific Climate-Change-Risk-Related Terms
(Percent)

After the Paris Agreement, firms in sectors exposed to transition risk became more aware of climate risks—or opportunities.

2. Quarterly Share of Firms with Climate Discussions, All Sectors and Energy Sector
(Percent)

Sources: FactSet; and IMF staff calculations.

References

Acemoglu, Daron, David Hemous, Lint Barrage, and Philippe Aghion. 2019. "Climate Change, Directed Innovation, and Energy Transition: The Long-Run Consequences of the Shale Gas Revolution." 2019 Meeting Papers 1302, Society for Economic Dynamics.

Baumeister, Christiane, and James D. Hamilton. 2019. "Structural Interpretation of Vector Autoregressions with Incomplete Identification: Revisiting the Role of Oil Supply and Demand Shocks." *American Economic Review* 109 (5): 1873–910.

Engle, Robert F., Stefano Giglio, Bryan Kelly, Heebum Lee, and Johannes Stroebel. 2020. "Hedging Climate Change News." *Review of Financial Studies* 33 (3): 1184–216.

Geman, Ben. 2020. "Survey: Florida Voters Link Climate and COVID-19." Axios (June 30). https://www.axios.com/florida -voters-climate-change-coronavirus-0e7182d8-81ae-45bf-a7d1 -a910a094725f.html

Hale, Galina, and Sylvain Leduc. 2020. "COVID-19 and CO_2." *FRBSF Economic Letter*, July 6, Federal Reserve Bank of San Francisco.

Hong, Harrison, Jeffrey D. Kubik, and José A. Scheinkman. 2012. "Financial Constraints on Corporate Goodness." NBER Working Paper 18476, National Bureau of Economic Research, Cambridge, MA.

International Energy Agency. 2020. "Global Energy Review 2020." https://www.iea.org/reports/global-energy-review-2020

Le Quéré, Corinne, Robert B. Jackson, Matthew W. Jones, Adam J. P. Smith, Sam Abernethy, Robbie M. Andrew, Anthony J. De-Gol, David R. Willis, Yuli Shan, Josep G. Canadell, Pierre Friedlingstein, Felix Creutzig, and Glen P. Peters. 2020. "Temporary Reduction in Daily Global CO_2 Emissions during the COVID-19 Forced Confinement." *Nature Climate Change* 10: 647–53.

UN Environment Programme. 2019. *Emissions Gap Report*. Nairobi.

IMF Special Series on COVID-19

The IMF has responded to the COVID-19 crisis by quickly deploying financial assistance, developing policy advice, and creating special tools to assist member countries. The Special Notes Series (**IMF.org/COVID19notes**) features the latest analysis and research from IMF staff in response to the pandemic. Below are four recent Notes from the dozens published to date.

Banking Sector Regulatory and Supervisory Response to Deal with Coronavirus Impact (with Q and A)

Rachid Awad, Caio Ferreira, Ellen Gaston, and Luc Riedweg

This note discusses the challenges that the COVID-19 pandemic poses for the banking sector and possible regulatory and supervisory responses that can maintain the balance between preserving financial stability, maintaining banking system soundness, and sustaining economic activity.

Unconventional Monetary Policy in Emerging Market and Developing Economies

David Hofman and Gunes Kamber

This note discusses the use of unconventional monetary policies in emerging market and developing economies with a focus on two objectives: (i) increasing monetary policy space to help central banks meet their output and inflation goals; and (ii) mitigating limitations to monetary transmission that may hamper the provision of credit where it is most needed.

Considerations for Designing Temporary Liquidity Support to Businesses

Phakawa Jeasakul

This note discusses key considerations for designing temporary liquidity support to otherwise viable businesses to allow them to continue operations during the COVID-19 pandemic.

Monetary and Financial Policy Responses for Emerging Market and Developing Economies

Thomas Harjes, David Hofman, Erlend Nier, and Thorvardur Olafsson

This note provides an overview of appropriate central bank policy responses to the severe economic and financial impact of the COVID-19 pandemic in emerging market and developing economies. It covers monetary, exchange rate, and macroprudential policies, as well as capital flow measures.

The views expressed in these notes are those of the author(s) and do not necessarily represent the views of the IMF, its Executive Board, or IMF management.

COVID-19 Policy Tracker

This periodically updated policy tracker summarizes the key economic responses 196 governments are taking to limit the human and economic impact of the pandemic. **IMF.org/COVID19policytracker**